SHELDON'S GIFT

Sheldon's Gift

Music, Movies, and Melodrama in the Desirable City

Thomas L. Olson

North Star Press of St. Cloud, Inc.
St. Cloud, Minnesota

Copyright © 2009 Thomas Olson

Cover photo courtesy Goodhue County Historical Society.

ISBN: 0-87839-318-8
ISBN-13: 978-0-87839-318-3

First Edition: September 2009

All rights reserved.

Printed in the United States of America

Published by
North Star Press of St. Cloud, Inc.
P.O. Box 451
St. Cloud, Minnesota 56302
www.northstarpress.com

Dedication

For Frances and Lyle
Who lived, loved, and rest in Red Wing

Acknowledgements

This book was possible only because of the Minnesota Historical Society's library, collections, and excellent facilities. The society's staff, from parking attendants to librarians, to the society's many volunteers was helpful and enthusiastic. To a person they live the society's motto: History Matters. I am also grateful to the Goodhue County Historical Society and especially librarian Diane Buganski who provided many photographs. Barbara Larsen of the National Archives, Central Plains Region in Kansas City, Missouri, gave invaluable assistance in making available the extensive transcripts of John Wright's federal lawsuit.

I appreciate especially the help of the Hennepin County Library for their prompt responses to my interlibrary loan requests and for making WESTLAW freely available. The extensive periodicals collection of the Minneapolis Public Library was also useful.

The late Larry Bentson was kind enough to share with me helpful and delightful insights about small town and city film exhibition in the 1940s and 1950s, about his father-in-law, E.R. "Eddie" Ruben, and about the workings of Minneapolis film distributors along "film row" on Currie Avenue. Steve Schmidt and Sean Dowse gave generous amounts of their time for conversations about the Sheldon Auditorium restoration, its history since, and its plans for the future.

This book would not have been written except for a chance conversation with our friend, writer, and librettist Marisha Chamberlain. Along the journey Marisha has continued to share her insights and wisdom about how to tell a good story with an old

Sheldon's Gift

historian who hears but cannot always effect change. I am also grateful to my friend Douglas Hedin, a lawyer and scholar who edits *The Minnesota Legal History Project*. Doug has been generous with his encouragement and criticism, set me right countless times as I wandered the legal labyrinth, and has read and commented critically and helpfully on several chapters. I appreciate as well the encouragement and gentle criticism of my friend and historian Donald Sofchalk and his late wife, Helen. Both have been friends, mentors, and opera seatmates for decades. New friends have also helped. Corinne and Seal Dwyer, editors and publishers at North Star Press have offered invaluable guidance and support.

My children, Erika Olson-Gross and Alison Olson-Cox have endured patiently my stories about old Red Wing, its show houses and their characters. As an attorney, Alison especially has listened to more than enough about Red Wing's courtroom dramas and city hall intrigues. Above all, my wife, Elizabeth Lewis, has tolerated four years of this retiree's project. She has taken time from her own work to listen, read, and always to offer encouragement along with questions and criticism. She has suffered through my streams of verbal and written consciousness, worries and anxiety, and research and writing blocs large and small. Although all responsibility for errors of fact or judgment is mine alone, this work is infinitely better for her thoughtful commentary and caring forbearance.

CONTENTS

Preface		xi
Chapter 1	The Desirable City	1
Chapter 2	Sheldon's Gift	16
Chapter 3	Celluloid	38
Chapter 4	The Set-Up	63
Chapter 5	Boom Boosters and Bust-Up	79
Chapter 6	Gentleman's Agreement	95
Chapter 7	Chief	116
Chapter 8	Longcor's Complaint	129
Chapter 9	The Best Years of Our Lives	143
Chapter 10	The Lost Audience	165
Chapter 11	Wright Made Wrong	179
Chapter 12	Conspiracy	200
Chapter 13	Ruin and Restoration	214
Epilogue		233
Bibliography		245
Index		255

PREFACE

In a chance sidewalk conversation I related the outlines of an event—a true tale of supposed good versus supposed evil—from my teenage 1950s in Red Wing, Minnesota. In it, theater owner John Wright sued the city and its municipal auditorium—a playhouse that once hosted top Broadway touring companies but for years had operated almost exclusively a city-run movie house. As the motion picture exhibition business sagged everywhere, Wright's claim, not surprisingly, challenged the city's tax-free, no-fee competition to his struggling private business.

Wright's suit was neither surprising nor unusual. Private vs. public ownership cases involving public utilities, liquor sales, and more recently sports stadiums have been fought for decades. Still, *John Wright & Associates v. City of Red Wing* was out of the ordinary. When Wright won a significant Minnesota Supreme Court victory, the citizens of a city whose merchants and manufacturers lauded small businesses demonized him unmercifully. Wright, in the public's imagination, became a conflated Simon Legree, Ebenezer Scrooge, and Lex Luthor.

Some weeks later I concluded that revisiting Wright after so many years—an article on his years-long state and federal cases--would be a rewarding undertaking. Could anyone have been so incorrigibly evil? Undeniably, I fancied that in a way I was embarking on the journey that Josephine Tey's Inspector Grant sets upon in *Daughter of Time* to exonerate malevolent Henry III. Of

Sheldon's Gift

course there was nothing as rip-roaring as slain princes in the tower. Still, the verbal horsewhippings of Wright and "Bad Dicky," the last Plantagenet, bore similarities!

As research progressed I realized that I couldn't tell Wright's story without looking back, first to 1930's flim-flam, politics, and machinations, and then still further to a 1918 back room connivance. Reluctantly at first and then enthusiastically I embraced a far larger story of Midwest small city entertainments spanning a century and a half. Well beyond a modest article, it became a account of highbrow and lowbrow entertainments, Broadway productions, vaudeville, stock companies, community theater, multiple lawsuits, suspect conflagration, and of America's ubiquitous diversion—the movies.

In narrative and analysis, Sheldon's Gift offers historical perspective on subjects relevant today not only for the role of the performing arts in preserving and enhancing community but also on the role of government and philanthropy in a nation that reveres free enterprise. In Red Wing, the latter value ran headlong against a progressive-era realization that competition was frequently ruinous and in this instance, if unchecked, might cost taxpayers plenty. Importantly, because of politically charged municipal ownership and high profile problems, Red Wing's experience offers extraordinary insights into the operation, finances, and unique problems of performance arts and motion picture exhibition in small cities. Red Wing's T.B. Sheldon Memorial Auditorium, now known simply as the Sheldon, is one of a handful of Midwest opera house survivors. No other, standing or bulldozed, owns such a rich, controversy-laden, complex, and compelling story.

                                              T.L.O.
                                              Las Cruces, NM
                                              May 2009

Chapter One

The Desirable City

"Better yet, its people . . . believe with all their hearts that Red Wing is what it is widely called—'The Desirable City.'"
~Franklyn Curtiss-Wedge *History of Goodhue County Minnesota* (1909)

"Opera houses were considered an essential cultural attribute. Their value as a place, where all could meet and share experiences, was as important as the experiences themselves."
~Glenn and Poole, *Opera Houses of Iowa* (1993)

"The company can rest assured of a full house should they revisit Red Wing."
~*Red Wing Argus* (November 1884)

In *Life on the Mississippi*, Mark Twain wrote that Saint Paul's whiskey-selling "Pigs Eye" Parrant was a "van-leader" of civilization. Missionaries, immigrants, gamblers, desperados, land speculators, lawyers, and undertakers, he argued, followed the whiskey trade. "All these interests bring the newspaper; the newspaper starts up politics and a railroad; all hands turn to and build a church and a jail—and behold, civilization is established for ever in the land." "Look history over," he wrote. "You will see."[1]

Omitted from Twain's chronology of civilization's relentless march was the apprearance of theater, music, and oratory, which, in Minnesota, pre-dated even Parrant's 1837 arrival. As early as the 1820s at Fort Snelling, at the confluence of the St. Peter's [Minnesota] and Mississippi rivers, the library held many plays. Soldiers often put on dramas for their comrades, with one noting very early on that he had acted almost every part of *Othello*.[2]

SHELDON'S GIFT

By the early 1850s, when St. Paul's population was less than 10,000, traveling or "road" stock companies landed regularly from steamboats to present *Hamlet, Othello, Macbeth, The Merchant of Venice,* and others to packed audiences.[3] In the summer of 1857, the year Henry Van Liew constructed a temporary theater building, the city entertained three visiting companies.

Fifty miles down river, at the head of the unglaciated high bluff "driftless" country, is Red Wing. There, "van leaders" operating from havens in Wisconsin, sold whiskey illegally to the Mdewakanton band and were condemned by the next to arrive—missionaries.[4] There, although the new community's population was under 1,000, its first "theater," opened on the second floor of F.F. Philleo's Main Street commercial building in 1856. Used for "conventions, lectures, [and] social entertainments,"[5] Philleo Hall became home, in 1857, to the Red Wing Lyceum, organized to sponsor lectures and concerts.[6] Although steamboat traveling entertainments and theater companies arrived in Red Wing regularly, lectures delivered by local physicians and clergy[7] were early mainstays. There was also local theatrical talent. In 1857, enterprising settlers constructed a showboat, *The Theater*, upon which they traveled the Mississippi as a repertoire company.[8]

Although river towns St. Paul, Stillwater, Red Wing, and Winona and then St. Peter, Mankato, and New Ulm first drew visiting entertainments, the same general pattern subsequently repeated itself in community after community. Immigrants moving west brought books, plays, and musical instruments. Before long, literary and musical societies were organized, and family gatherings were transformed into community events. Soon professional actors, musicians, and orators began to call. Although theatrical troupes often performed in tent shows and did so into the early twentieth century, communities soon built permanent cultural venues.[9] These private facilities, often located on a commercial building's second or third floor, were multi-purpose centers. Chairs were moved aside to host dances. There was a formal stage for musical and theatrical events. Community and religious groups met in them. Politicians, orators, authors, and poets lectured and read.

Red Wingites anticipated a grand future. Although all small cities became hotbeds of boosterism, Red Wing had much to recommend it. It was a port on America's largest interstate expressway, the Mississippi River. It was an early com-

The Desirable City

mercial and banking center for a vast plain of some of the best agricultural land in America. Following the Civil War, it became for a time the world's largest primary wheat market. It was a lumber and millwork center. There was a tannery and flour mills. The Chicago, Milwaukee and St. Paul railway's main line served it.[10] As the city grew and prospered, its institutions and architecture, sectarian and secular, began to reflect its confidence, optimism, and worldly success.

Although Philleo's Hall survived for many years, in 1867 a larger, more elegant entertainment center was built when T.B. Sheldon and J.M. Hodgman constructed the Music Hall building at the northeast corner of Main and Plumb Streets.[11] Sheldon and Hodgman's First National Banking Association occupied the ground floor and professional offices the second.[12] The Music Hall, which occupied the third floor and seated 600, was an active venue. In one single week, early in its history, it hosted a lecture, a concert, and a theater stock company.[13] That pace and variety continued. In the winter of 1875, the Music Hall presented, among other events, police and masquerade balls, lectures, the Mendelssohn Quintet, and an adult spelling bee.

Music Hall builidng at northeast corner of Plum and Main. Built in 1862 and demolished in the 1980s (c. 1900). (Courtesy of the Goodhue County Historical Society)

Music Hall interior shortly before demolition. (Courtesy of the Goodhue County Historical Society)

Minstrel shows and Uncle Tom's Cabin companies were ubiquitous then and for decades to come. When the Georgia Minstrels appeared in 1875, a reviewer noted that the performers were "genuine darkies" whose quality was "hardly up to a first class imitation troupe."[14] African Americans, in other words, were more entertaining when they were whites in black face.

  One group that hired the Music Hall was the Turnerverein, a German cultural society that appeared in at least twenty-five Minnesota communities, most famously at New Ulm. These multi-purpose orders promoted music and theater, which were "deeply embedded" in German traditions, and physical culture.[15] In 1875 the society completed, at the northeast corner of East Avenue and Third Street, its impressive Turner Opera Hall. On its ground floor was a dining room, bar and living quarters for the manager or "wirt." On the main floor was exercise space and a theater accommodating up to 900. Although the Music Hall continued in business for a time, the larger Turner Hall soon became the city's primary entertainment center. "Blind Tom," an African-American boy pianist, dedicated the new opera house in July 1875. Minstrels and Uncle Tom companies not surprisingly drew good-sized crowds. Orchestra concerts frequently concluded with a dance. The Turners presented a wide variety of amateur and professional drama with Shakespeare, Shiller, Goethe, and

Moliere being well accepted.[16] Opera was also heard as when the Carreno-Donaldi company, sponsored by local grocers Bixby and Webster, appeared in 1882.[17]

That Red Wing, prosperous as it was, could, with a population of just 5,000[18] support pastime venues accommodating nearly 1,000 patrons is a remarkable testimony to the importance of music, theater, singing, dancing, and oratory.[19] It is worth noting, however, that nineteenth-century opera houses were sized primarily to accommodate fireman and other balls and community events requiring large spaces. Although concerts and dramas sometimes filled the seats, full houses weren't necessarily a reliable measure of an entertainment's success.

Turner Hall at northeast corner of East Avenue and Third Street. Completed in 1875 and destroyed by fire in 1882. (Courtesy of the Goodhue County Historical Society)

It is also important that none of Red Wing's nineteenth-century venues depended entirely on entertainment admissions for financial survival. The Turner Opera House, as a part of the Turnerverein Society, operated as (to borrow today's language) a not-for-profit institution that had memberships, banquets, and other sources of income. Elsewhere, Masonic lodges and other fraternal societies doubled as opera houses. The ubiquitous private for-profit enterprises that occupied upper floors of commercial blocks were also multifunction arenas that hosted community events as well as professional performances. What is more, building owners typically relied upon retail and office rents as well as opera house income. In truth, theater and music were subsidized. There were commercial successes to be sure. But when entertainments drew poor audiences, other income mitigated the loss.

SHELDON'S GIFT

As railroads crisscrossed the Midwest and even small communities became accessible to traveling entertainers, the number of opera houses exploded.[20] Why the name "opera house" rather than "theater" is a matter of minor dispute. A common view is that "opera" had a positive image while "theater" carried negative religious connotations connected with frivolous or impure subject matter and with actors who led debauched lives.[21] That conflict existed in Red Wing. When local clergymen attacked the theater in 1882, the *Advance*, which derided sanctimonious religion, defended it. Although the newspaper admitted that some theater was "low and debased," the answer, it said, was not to abandon it but to "understand and conquer the degeneracy" and "judge for yourself."[22] Other accounts suggest "opera house" had an elegant sound befitting the grand aspirations of young communities. In either case, it is held, opera was seldom staged and unsuccessful financially.[22] That view suggests that opera was unpopular and that tastes were unsophisticated.

It is true that staged grand opera appeared infrequently in small cities and was often unsuccessful financially. Opera, then and now, with its demand for outstanding voices and elaborate costumes and sets has always been expensive to mount. It is untrue, however, that opera houses flourished when tastes were less sophisticated than today.[24] Indeed, nineteenth-century Americans of all income levels were familiar with a wide variety of music and theater. This meant, for example, that they enjoyed, understood, and routinely quoted Shakespeare. In Saint Paul, touring and repertory companies performed Hamlet nine times between 1884 and 1889.[25] Shakespeare was also popular in Red Wing. It also meant a general understanding of opera, which was frequently presented in concert or unstaged performances, and of serious drama.[26] In the Midwest, with thousands of German immigrants, Wagnerian opera was well attended and understood. Ordinary citizens, moreover, were well acquainted with English and Italian opera and symphonic music. Bach, Mendelssohn, Grieg, and Beethoven were especially well liked.[27]

At the same time, nineteenth-century Americans across a wide spectrum of income and educational levels had knowledge of and enjoyed "highbrow" culture, they embraced broad interests. Without differentiation, orchestra programs, a ready example, commonly mixed military marches, symphonies, and folk tunes.

The Desirable City

Consequently, nineteenth-century Minnesotans, although there grew to be urban and rural differences, were more omnivorous culturally than at any time in the next century.

Unfortunately, the Turner Opera Hall was short-lived. On Easter Sunday evening 1882 the local Knights Templar, holding services at the Episcopal Church, were alerted by noises outside. They emerged to find horses cut loose and running in the streets and the opera house and other buildings ablaze. Streets muddied by an all-day rain delayed positioning the fire engines. Too many hoses on the water main made it impossible to throw water high enough to be effective. For a time it was feared that strong winds would cause a wholesale conflagration. When it was over, the horrific fire that began in the Webster and Perkins livery consumed the Turner Hall and a dozen commercial and residential buildings.[28] The fire proved to be too much for the Turnerverein. Their opera house, built at a cost of $24,000 but grossly underinsured for only $6,000[29] and already in foreclosure, wasn't rebuilt, and the Red Wing association disbanded.[30]

The 1882 fire created a business opportunity for George A. Wilkinson. Born in England, Wilkinson came to the United States in 1851 at age thirty-three. Settling first in Dubuque, Iowa, where he worked as a carpenter and contractor, Wilkinson came to Red Wing in 1854 to help construct Hamline University. Ownership of a brickyard followed.[31] Success enabled Wilkinson to purchase land and become one of the Midwest's first, although the term was coined later, "bonanza" farmers. At the height of the post Civil War wheat boom, Wilkinson owned one thousand acres, eight hundred planted in wheat.[32]

When wheat farming declined due to stem rust and production shifted northwest,[33] Wilkinson turned his attention elsewhere. By 1879 he had built a large commercial block on the south side of Third Street from the corner of Bush Street westward. In addition to receiving tenant rents, Wilkinson himself entered the retail shoe business. Following the Turner Opera House fire, Wilkinson visited Winona, Albert Lea, and St Paul to garner ideas and in the spring of 1884 set about construction of a new multi-purpose opera hall south of his commercial block on the west side of Bush Street.[34] The building, completed with amazing speed, opened in late August.[35]

Named the Casino,[26] Wilkinson's brick-veneered entertainment "complex" was an impressive structure. The fifty-three-by-ninety-foot main room, with a twenty-two-foot ceiling and mezzanine, seated a thousand and, for some occasions, as many as twelve hundred. The stage boasted a generous twenty-four-foot opening and twenty-seven-foot depth. The canvas-covered walls were painted with kalsomine and trompe-d'oiel frescoes of theater boxes.[37] So they could move aside easily, chairs were fastened together in groups from three to six. Two large gas reflector fixtures of forty burners each provided ceiling light. For theatrical events there were gas illumination footlights.[38] Dressing rooms and a restaurant were located in the basement. In winter, two furnaces and heavy-duty heating stoves kept patrons comfortable.[39]

The outstanding feature of the Casino, however, was not its theatrical trappings but its roller rink. In the early 1880s, a roller-skating phenomena swept America due to skate improvements (steel ball bearings) and mass production by the Henley Company.[40] By the mid-1880s, Minneapolis already had eleven rinks.[41]

When the Casino opened, Red Wing found itself with a state-of-the-art roller rink that boasted a white-birch, double-layered floor set on a layer of sand. The result was a relatively quiet and comfortable room. Spectators watched from the mezzanine that doubled as a theatrical balcony.[42] Although the Casino presented outstanding theatrical events, roller-skating, a relatively expensive pastime, produced steady income. With skates, a session cost twenty-five cents in the afternoon and fifty cents in the evening. Still, on a typical mid-week evening the Casino welcomed seventy-five skaters. Skating exhibitions were also well attended as when "Little Nell" appeared. Her skating, the *Red Wing Argus* reported, "was highly appreciated by lovers of the rollers."[43]

Musical and theatrical entertainments as well as dances, lectures, and political rallies occurred regularly. In addition to touring stock theater companies, community groups including the Catholic Dramatic Society and the Grand Army of the Republic put on plays as charitable fundraisers. In the Casino's first season, a highlight was the appearance of the Abbie Carrington Opera Company. Rather than present a full opera, the costumed company sang, in French, the second act of Ambroise Thomas's *Mignon*. Following a piano interlude and costume change, the company then sang the third act from Flotow's *Martha*.[44] Although both operas are rarely performed today, they were exceedingly popular with nineteenth- and early twentieth-century American audiences. In 1876, a new Red Wing musical study club chose *Martha* as its first subject because there were already several copies in the city, it was unobjectionable, and because the music had all of the components of opera—solos, duets, a trio and quartet, and a chorus.[45]

Although there is much unknown about the Casino, we know that it was so important to the community that the city council on at least one occasion waived its license fee.[46] We also know that George Wilkinson, contractor, farmer, and entrepreneur, likely regarded the Casino, and the small rental shops that were a part his building, as simply another business opportunity. Within a year, with the opera house managed by Colonel J.C. Hawes, who had owned a piano store,[47] Wilkinson, age sixty-six, sold his shoe emporium and began wintering in the South. Subsequently, under the ownership of Wilkinson and then his family, the Casino, a building that survives to this day, provided Red Wing with the lion's share of its entertainment and indoor recreational opportunities for the next twenty years.

By all accounts—and its longevity is itself ample proof—George Wilkinson's opera house was a success. At the same time, the Casino was caught up in a cultural change that had important implications for small cities and their opera houses. In the last quarter of the nineteenth century, a cultural shift initiated by music and theatrical leaders in Boston, New York, and Chicago spread to lesser metropolises and then small cities. It's impetus, quite probably, was in a social elite perception that mass behaviors including talking, hissing the villains, and cheering the great performers wildly was rowdyish and crude. The new ideal separated secular "highbrow" from "lowbrow" culture. This construct defined the finest art, drama, and music, always European, as so exceptional, so near Godliness, that only those of high breeding, education, and cultural exposure could understand and appreciate it. It was not for the ordinary and unrefined. "High" culture, furthermore, was dishonored when offered on programs that combined the high (Beethoven) with the low (John Phillip Sousa). "Sacred cows" were born. The late Lawrence W. Levine, who wrote extensively about this hierarchical phenomenon, dubbed it "sacralization." As a result of redefining the audience for serious theater, opera, and symphony as an elite, snobbish arbiters came close to killing cultural omnivorousness altogether.[48]

At the Casino, "highbrow" musicians and performers, or those who aspired to such status, began to shun the diverse program styles that audiences were accustomed to and enjoyed. On the Casino's opening night, Seibert's Orchestra presented an all-classical performance that included Rossini's "Bel Raggio," from *Semiramide*, sung by the orchestra's soloist; Offenbach's *Orpheus and Eurydice* overture; and a clarinet solo, "*Scena and Aria*," by Bergson.[49] Although the audience received the orchestra enthusiastically, a local reviewer commented that the program was "severely" classical.[50]

As "ordinary" audiences internalized "highbrow" fare as inaccessible, incomprehensible, and high-priced, they increasingly kept their distance. On the other side, "highbrow" patrons avoided diverse programs that they now defined as "lowbrow." In Red Wing, given its size, the audience for purely "highbrow" performances narrowed early on. When the Abbie Carrington Opera Company appeared at the Casino, for instance, the reviewer reported that it drew only a "fair sized" audience but promised that the "company can rest assured of a full house should they revisit Red Wing."[51] That promise couldn't be kept.

In metropolises, purely "highbrow" culture survived because of large populations and philanthropic subsidy. On the other hand, audience bifurcation into "highbrow" and "lowbrow" was disastrous for small cities that depended financially upon good-sized audiences garnered from across vocational and educational lines and cultural sensibilities.

By the 1890s, Red Wing's opera halls had passed through a typical progression. The first two were of the upper story, flat floor and multi-use type. A third, the Turner Opera House, was part of a lodge hall. The Casino, while retaining flat floor and multi-purpose features, had taken on, with its more comfortable seating, dressing rooms, lighting, and elaborate staging possibilities, the attributes of a true theater. From its beginnings, it became home to various entertainments

THE DESIRABLE CITY

ranging from police balls to "road companies of every type from the Boston Ideal Opera Company to the comic Ole Olson and Peter Peterson."[52]

Whatever the configuration, Red Wing's opera houses were as George Glenn and Richard Poole wrote in *The Opera Houses of Iowa*:

> . . . a meeting ground for all classes of people. The rural opera house was the *hub* [emphasis in original] of community activity and many entertainment activities occurred there. . . . Without a doubt they were the aesthetic, entertainment, frequently educational, and sometimes athletic focus of the community. Opera houses were considered an essential cultural attribute. Their value as a place, where all could meet and share experiences, was as important as the experiences themselves.[53]

Though the Casino was adequate it was not the epitome of the late nineteenth-century opera house—a freestanding structure dedicated to entertainment. In those buildings the floor was sloped. Seating was in fixed, immovable rows. There was a true balcony or two. There were actual boxes rather than faux paintings and an orchestra pit. Gold leaf and sculpted embellishments abounded. By the end of the nineteenth century such opulent opera halls existed not only in Minneapolis and St. Paul but in smaller cities as well. Where they didn't exist, they were planned or desired. A first-rate example of such a community was Fairmont, Minnesota. There, in 1899, local businessmen formed a new company and over the next three years constructed a magnificent theater that is today among a handful of that era's survivors.[54]

Red Wing had no symbolic institution to prove that it was an important center of commerce and culture. Although the wheat boom was bust and colleges had pulled up stakes, there was yet a strong sense that Red Wing, with its growing base of manufactures, had a glorious future. Indeed, by the close of the nineteenth century, Red Wing and its citizens regularly self-identified and advertised their community as, "The Desirable City."[55] No place so celebrated could hold its collective head high while it lacked a proper, free-standing, possibly splendiferous venue devoted to refined performance. The frontier days were gone. Cities were out to prove their status and opera houses represented boosterism on a grand scale.

It was, of course, more than a matter of architectural symbolism. It was also a matter of programming. Without citizens willing to purchase tickets to "high class" events, a town was doomed to accept mediocre, unpredictable and disappointing shows. Shows that played the Casino commonly came from or went to engagements in towns as small as nearby Mazeppa (population 500).[56] Indeed, in 1900 the Casino played such fare as Charles Yale's *Devil's Auction*, a vaudeville and specialty act show that had been traveling then for eighteen years. Although the show advertised that it included new acts such as "the Deltorellis, famous European musical grotesques," and "others of repute," Yale's program didn't enhance a fine city's reputation.[57]

Then, as the nineteenth century closed, a confluence of events transformed Red Wing's cultural and entertainment scene. When George Wilkinson died in 1896, his family talked of remaking the opera house as entirely commercial space. As a result, a group of unidentified businessmen considered building a new opera house on James Lawther's property at East Avenue and Third Street where the Turner Opera Hall once stood.

Lawther, a devoted Presbyterian, was born in Ireland and as a young man of twenty-three came to Red Wing in 1855. Like his contemporaries, C.E. Betcher, T.B. Sheldon, and George Wilkinson, Lawther amassed a considerable fortune. As a landlord, he once owned nineteen stores, twenty homes, and ninety farms.[58] Lawther also established a glowing philanthropic reputation. No doubt the businessmen interested in constructing a new opera house on Lawther's property sought a favorable price or outright gift of it for some element of generosity often helped make opera houses possible. When the Wilkinson interests decided not to revamp their property, however, the Casino survived, and plans for a new opera house were put on hold.

The community also desired a new library.[59] That opportunity came in 1901 when the Andrew Carnegie interests agreed to donate $17,000 toward construction provided the city contribute $1,700 annually for support. When James Lawther agreed to give his property at the former Turnerverein site, a deal was struck.[60] W.J. Longcor began construction almost immediately and the Carnegie-Lawther Library opened in October 1903.[61]

The Desirable City

Notes

[1] Mark Twain, *Life on the Mississippi* (Boston: James R. Osgood & Company, 1883), 586.
[2] Frank M. Whiting, *Minnesota Theatre: From Old Fort Snelling to the Guthrie* (Minneapolis: Pogo Press, 1988), 4-6.
[3] Ibid., 6-11.
[4] Frederick L. Johnson, *Goodhue County Minnesota: A Narrative History* (Red Wing: Goodhue County Historical Society Press, 2000), 24-25.
[5] Christian A. Rasmussen, *A History of the City of Red Wing Minnesota*, (Red Wing: n.p., 1933), 50.
[6] Madeline Angell, *Red Wing, Minnesota: Saga of a River Town*, 2nd ed. (Minneapolis: Dillon Press, 1978), 96. Midwest lyceums were modeled after the movement begun by Josiah Holbrook in Millbury, Massachusetts in 1826.
[7] Christian A. Rasmussen, *A History of the City of Red Wing Minnesota* (Red Wing: n.p., 1933), 80.
[8] Laurence E. Schmeckebier, *Art in Red Wing*, Vol. 6, Community Basis for Postwar Planning (Minneapolis: University of Minnesota Press, 1946), 40.
[9] See Jere C. Mickel, *Footlights on the Prairie* (St. Cloud, Minnesota: North Star Press, 1974), passim. Tent shows, often erected in the commercial downtown, played in Red Wing well into the twentieth century.
[10] Frederick L. Johnson, *Goodhue County Minnesota: A Narrative History* (Red Wing: Goodhue County Historical Society Press, 2000), 83-84.
[11] Known now as "Plum" Street, it was originally "Plumb."
[12] Madeline Angell, *Red Wing, Minnesota: Saga of a River Town*, 2nd ed. (Minneapolis: Dillon Press, 1978), 140.
[13] Christian A. Rasmussen, *A History of the City of Red Wing Minnesota*, (Red Wing: n.p., 1933), 86.
[14] "Local News and Brevities," *Red Wing Argus*, October 21, 1875.
[15] Frank M. Whiting, *Minnesota Theatre: From Old Fort Snelling to the Guthrie* (Minneapolis: Pogo Press, 1988), 20-27.
[16] On the Turner Opera Hall, see Madeline Angell, *Red Wing, Minnesota: Saga of a River Town*, 2nd ed. (Minneapolis: Dillon Press, 1978), 140, 149. Also see Laurence E. Schmeckebier, *Art in Red Wing*, Vol. 6, Community Basis for Postwar Planning (Minneapolis: University of Minnesota Press, 1946), 35. Both sources relied heavily on Franklyn Curtiss-Wedge, *History of Goodhue County Minnesota* (Chicago, Illinois, H.C. Cooper, Jr., and Company, 1909), passim.
[17] Advertisement, *The Advance*, February 1, 1882.
[18] Red Wing's population in 1870 was 4,260.
[19] Laurence E. Schmeckebier, *Art in Red Wing*, Vol. 6, Community Basis for Postwar Planning (Minneapolis: University of Minnesota Press, 1946), 40. In 1876 a new hall opened on the third floor of the Centennial Building on the north side of Third Street between

Sheldon's Gift

Bush Street and East Avenue. The businesses of the builders, J.S. Hoard, S.P. Jennison, and F.W. Hoyt occupied the ground floor. It seated 600 people and appears to have been used largely for church and other community gatherings.

[20]George D. Glenn and Richard L.Poole, *The Opera Houses of Iowa* (Ames: Iowa State University Press, 1993), passim.

[21]Ibid., 5-6.

[22]"This is Our Say:On the Dance, Theatre and Saloons," *The Advance*, March 22, 1882.

[23]"The Name Opera House" *Dramatic Mirror* (March 7, 1885) cited and quoted inGeorge D. Glenn and Richard L.Poole, *The Opera Houses of Iowa* (Ames: Iowa State University Press, 1993), 5-6.

[24]Susan Roth, quoted in "Opera House: Will Final Curtain Fall?" *Minneapolis Star Tribune*, November 28, 2006.

[25]Frank M. Whiting, *Minnesota Theatre: From Old Fort Snelling to the Guthrie* (Minneapolis: Pogo Press, 1988), 84.

[26]In 1900 well-known French actress Madame Elsie de Tourney presented a solo, unstaged performance of Mary Queen of Scots. See "Dramatie," *Red Wing Argus*, January 26, 1900.

[27]Lawrence W. Levine, *Highbrow/Lowbrow: The Emergence of Cultural Hierarchy in America* (Cambridge: Harvard University Press, 1988), 100-105.

[28]"Sunday's Holocaust," *The Advance*, April 12, 1882.

[29]Franklyn Curtiss-Wedge, *History of Goodhue County Minnesota* (Chicago: H.C. Cooper Jr. and Company, 1909), 601.

[30]Madeline Angell, *Red Wing, Minnesota: Saga of a River Town*, 2nd ed. (Minneapolis: Dillon Press, 1978), 172; Christian A. Rasmussen, *A History of the City of Red Wing Minnesota*, (Red Wing: n.p., 1933), 125.

[31]Franklyn Curtiss-Wedge, *History of Goodhue County Minnesota* (Chicago: H.C. Cooper Jr. and Company, 1909), 540.

[32]Madeline Angell, *Red Wing, Minnesota: Saga of a River Town*, 2nd ed. (Minneapolis: Dillon Press, 1978), 166.

[33]Frederick L. Johnson, *Goodhue County Minnesota: A Narrative History*, (Red Wing: Goodhue County Historical Society Press, 2000), 98-99.

[34]"Local News, *Red Wing Argus*, February 28, 1884.

[35]"Opening of the Casino," *Red Wing Argus*, August 28, 1884.

[36]"Casino" was a not-uncommon nineteenth-century name for a theater and derives from the primary dictionary definition of "casino" as a large room for meetings or amusements.Its definition as a place for gambling was an English use of the word.

[37]Madeline Angell, *Red Wing, Minnesota: Saga of a River Town*, 2nd ed. (Minneapolis: Dillon Press, 1978), 174; Kalsomine is a whitewash sometimes tinted for interior use.

[38]"The New Opera House," *Red Wing Argus*, August 14, 1884.

[39]"Local News," *Red Wing Argus*, October 30, 1884.

[40]James Turner, *The History of Roller Skating*, (Lincoln, Neb.: The National Museum of Roller Skating, 1997), passim.

THE DESIRABLE CITY

[41] When the Casino opened, there was another small roller rink above Johnson and Glardon's livery. See "Local News," *Red Wing Argus*, May 22, 1884.
[42] "The New Opera House," *Red Wing Argus*, August 14, 1884.
[43] "Local News," *Red Wing Argus*, October 16, 1884.
[44] "Abbie Carrington," *Red Wing Argus*, November 27, 1884
[45] "Musical," *Red Wing Argus*, March 30, 1876.
[46] "Local News," *Red Wing Argus*, August 7, 1884.
[47] "Local Brevities and Personals," *Red Wing Argus*, March 22, 1876.
[48] Lawrence W. Levine, *Highbrow/Lowbrow: The Emergence of Cultural Hierarchy in America* (Cambridge: Harvard University Press, 1988), 166-168.
[49] "Opening of the Casino," *Red Wing Argus*, August 28, 1884.
[50] Ibid. .
[51] "Abbie Carrington," *Red Wing Argus*, November 27, 1884.
[52] Laurence E. Schmeckebier, *Art in Red Wing*, Vol. 6, Community Basis for Postwar Planning (Minneapolis: University of Minnesota Press, 1946), 40.
[53] George D. Glenn and Richard L.Poole, *The Opera Houses of Iowa* (Ames: Iowa State University Press, 1993), 65.
[54] Thomas Arneson, *And the Curtain Rises:The Story of the Fairmont Opera House* (Fairmont, Minnesota: Fairmont Photo Press, 1988); passim.; also www.fairmont-operahouse.com.
[55] Franklyn Curtiss-Wedge, *History of Goodhue County Minnesota* (Chicago: H.C. Cooper Jr. and Company, 1909), 646.
[56] "Foretelling Shows," *Red Wing Daily Republican*, April 24, 1900.
[57] "Amusements," *Red Wing Daily Republican*, April 24, 1900.
[58] Philip S. Duff (column), *Red Wing Republican Eagle*, September 2, 1986.
[59] At that time, the library occupied cramped quarters in the Boxrud mercantile on Main Street.
[60] "James Lawther Donates Site for New Library," *Red Wing Republican* (Weekly), January 1, 1902.
[61] Ruth Nerhaugen, "Library Celebrating 100th Year of Service," *Red Wing Republican Eagle*, February 16, 1994.

CHAPTER TWO

SHELDON'S GIFT

"Everything sordid and base is shut out and only the plays wanted by the best element are allowed to come to the city." ~Dr. Marion Burton (March 1909)

"It is only a matter of sincere regret that Red Wing could not have greeted these artists of international renown and unquestioned merit with an audience commensurate with their fame and excellence. Why people will be content with the ordinary or even the good when the BEST is at their command at no higher price is an enigma... Not new but always strange and surprising in an intelligent and progressive community."
~Red Wing Daily Republican (March, 1909)

"If Home Sweet Home had come out of that violin the grizzly bearded grandfather yawning between numbers would have grasped the little urchin across the aisle and covered him with kisses...." ~Red Wing Daily Republican (March, 1909)

In April 1900, with talk of a new library and opera house "in the air," pioneer businessman Theodore Barnard Sheldon, age eighty, died. Sheldon, reputedly a "self-made" man, and his wife, Mary, arrived in Red Wing from Massachusetts in 1856. Like Lawther and Wilkinson, Sheldon's business interests ranged widely and included grain warehousing and trading, merchandising, banking, railroad promotion, and real estate. He and his partners built the Music Hall at Plum and Main streets. By 1891, when Sheldon was seventy, his wife, Mary, and all five of their children had predeceased him.[1] One, Nellie McLean, and Sheldon's only grandchild, died in childbirth. In 1893, Sheldon married thirty-nine-year-old

Sheldon's Gift

T.B. Sheldon, c. 1880. (Courtesy of the Goodhue County Historical Society)

Annie Langton of Milwaukee. At his death, Annie and a few distant relatives were his only survivors. His estate, considerable for the time, was valued at $160,000.[2]

Although there is no record that Sheldon was especially philanthropic during his lifetime, he was a member, as were most of Red Wing's wealthier transplanted Easterners, of Christ Church, Episcopal, where it may be supposed he was generous. In his will, how-

T.B. Sheldon home, 805 Fourth Street, Red Wing. (Photo: Eugene Debs Becker. Courtesy the Minnesota Historical Society)

ever, Sheldon bequeathed half his estate to his wife and liberally directed the other half used "for some public but not for any sectarian purpose," in Red Wing. Sheldon named his wife and two business associates, forty-year friend and partner Elijah Haskell Blodgett and Frederick Busch, then president of the Goodhue County Bank, trustees of his estate. They were directed to determine a purpose for his gift within fifteen years.[3]

Sheldon's trustees wasted no time. Although some in Red Wing favored a community endowment,[4] city officials and local newspapers anticipated a brick-and-mortar memorial. With a library being planned, informed guessers focused on a combination city hall and opera house.[5] When the trustees polled residents, some, including feminist and prohibitionist Julia B. Nelson, urged that the bequest not be divided so that the tribute to Sheldon was fitting and lasting.[6] Most, however, favored using forty to fifty thousand dollars to build a city hall/opera house with the remainder used for a school endowment, library furnishings, and parks.[7]

In December 1902, the trustees told the city council that $80,000 would not be sufficient for both a city hall and opera house and asked if the city would contribute the remaining costs of a city hall.[8] When the council took no action, the trustees settled on an opera house, purchased property at Third Street and East Avenue that was home to the Baptist Church, a monument company, and a photography studio,[9] and solicited competitive designs. Within weeks, because municipalities don't have powers not expressly granted them, local representatives introduced, and the state legislature authorized, cities to accept real property gifts.[10]

When Red Wing's city council met on March 6, 1903, Sheldon's gift was front and center. Attorney Charles P. Hall, whose father was former congressman Ossee Matson Hall, presented the trustees' terms: conditions that became the focus of disputes that raged for sixty years.[11] "Care, custody and management" of the T.B. Sheldon Memorial Auditorium would rest with a five-member board empowered to "let or lease [it] for musical and theatrical entertainments, public meetings, lectures and such other purposes as in their judgment may contribute to the education, enjoyment, improvement or amusement of the people of Red Wing." Free or reduced rate use could be granted for local entertainment of an "unusually high character" or for other local organizations' uses.[12] A governing board, with each member serving a five-year term, was to be appointed by the

Sheldon's Gift

mayor and approved by the city council. Reappointment wasn't prohibited. The trustees named Horace Rich (one year), Charles A. Betcher (two years), Ben Gerlach (three years), Charles E. Sheldon (four years) and Ossee Matson Hall (five years) as the first board.[13]

All revenues were to be paid to the city treasurer and kept in an "Auditorium Fund" to be used solely for the "care, maintenance, and conduct of said Auditorium . . ." and dispersed upon order of the board. The city could not charge the Auditorium a licensing fee, was required to provide free water,[14] and, if funds were insufficient, supply janitorial service. Finally, the board was required to carry fire insurance. Should insurance proceeds prove insufficient to cover a loss, the city was obliged to pay the remainder. If the building were "wholly destroyed" and insurance was insufficient, and if two-thirds of the city council and four-fifths of the board agreed not to rebuild, then the insurance proceeds and sale price or both were to memorialize T.B. Sheldon in a manner consistent with his wishes.[15] Councilmen, not wanting to look a gift horse in the mouth, readily accepted the terms.[16]

Alternative Plan No. 5 for the T.B. Sheldon Memorial Auditorium. (Photo: *Red Wing Daily Republican*. Courtesy *Red Wing Republican Eagle*)

Sheldon's Gift

In March 1903, five building designs were reduced to two. Both were glorious grand opera houses. One was a massive, dark stone Richardsonian structure (plan no. 5) suggestive of Adler and Sullivan's Auditorium Building (Chicago 1889). The other (plan no. 2) was a light-grey brick Renaissance edifice with city beautiful elements.[17] Although the trustees had sole power to accept a plan, they wisely appointed a citizens' advisory board[18] and put plans on public view.[19] Within weeks, the trustees chose the Renaissance design, by prominent Twin Cities architect Lowell A. Lamoreau.[20] Bids were let in April; foundation work began in May; and over the next eighteen months the J. and W.A. Elliot Company built the T.B. Sheldon Memorial Auditorium.

On the exterior were three front entry doors. High above are niches that housed busts of Shakespeare, Wagner, Goethe, and Beethoven. To the east and west are porticos or porte-cocheres. The west portico covered a circular carriage driveway (unused now for decades). Inside, the theater seated 864. Of these, 363 seats were on the main floor, thirty-two in eight side boxes, and the remaining 469 in three separate (first, second, and rear) balconies. On the balcony side walls were gigantic paintings, copies of classical works owned by T.B. Walker of Minneapolis, that were executed by Minneapolis artist Peter Claussen who also painted a drop curtain portraying an ancient Roman scene.[21] Above the stage hung an impressive crystal chandelier said to have cost $350. The cast plasterwork was of masterful quality as was the local Betcher Company's millwork.[22] An oil portrait of Sheldon hung in the lobby.[23] For performers the new theater was truly impressive. With five backstage dressing rooms, another over the stage and two under it, the largest traveling companies were accommodated.[24] A basement turbine generator that ran on city water pressure provided electric lighting. Gaslights provided backup. When the Iroquois Theater fire in Chicago that killed 600 patrons raised local fears about safety, Sheldon's trustees pointed to the new theater's asbestos stage curtain, many exits, and fire hoses.[25]

Although the Auditorium's size, a mark of community status and ability to attract better shows, might seem excessive for a city of just 8,000,[26] its capacity was similar to the Casino's and to opera houses in comparable cities.[27] Criticism of the size, mild at best, came from the *Daily Republican*, which suggested that it be larger, not smaller. Conceding that 800 seats were more than needed, the newspaper said that Red Wing would experience "certain growth" and recommended seating for 1,200. Included in that number, the paper said, should be accommodation for poor citizens who couldn't afford the theater. That, it said, would truly honor the benefactor.[28]

When the trustees offered the city a property deed in October 1904, Alderman Hiram Howe asked for reconsideration of the acceptance terms because they gave too much direct power to the board. It was too late. Howe's objection garnered no support.[29] A few years later, the council, now with second thoughts, tried to gain control by appointing elected councilmen to the board. But Charles P. Hall, then city attorney, said the gift agreement kept the board and council separate and forbade it.[30] In 1911, when the Auditorium faced a financial crisis, Mayor A.P. Pierce, who was mayor in 1903 as well, complained that events that year happened so quickly that terms weren't considered carefully.[31] Although Pierce was ducking responsibility, his point was well taken.

Although residents soon claimed Red Wing as the site of America's first municipal show house, that wasn't true.[32] The first was likely the Academy of Music Theater built in Northampton, Massachusetts, in 1890. That theater, still in existence, resulted from a gift from local businessman H.R. Lyman who was impressed by state support for theaters in Europe.[33] In 1889 Philo D. Beckwith of Dowagiac, Michigan, owner of the Round Oak Company, died and bequeathed his city the Beckwith Memorial Theater. When dedicated in 1893, boosters in the town of 7,000 described it as a "temple of the performing arts."[34] Still, public theater ownership was rare in America.

As the theater neared completion, the board hired as manager, from a long list of applicants, Ralph Graham Taber. A Red Wing man by birth, Taber had not lived in Red Wing since 1888 when he completed his legal education in the office of F.M. Wilson. Taber was hired, it was reported, because he had European and American theater experience and contacts.[35] Although that claim may have been exaggerated, if worldliness mattered, Taber had it. A later *Who's Who in America* listed him thus:

> Ralph Graham Taber, traveler and author; telegraph and train dispatcher, Mexico and Central America, 1879-1885; practiced law in Grand Forks, N.D, 1888-1889; member Alonzo M. Murphy & Co., private bankers, Spokane,

Wash., 1889-1892; also attorney for Citizen's National Bank; in charge of expedition to Hudson straits to procure exhibits for Columbia exposition in Chicago,1892; mining near Cape Cudleigh, Labrador; 1893-1898; associate editor and art manager of "Truth," New York magazine, 1895-1898; in charge of expedition to procure exhibits for Paris exposition, 1899; traveled to Africa, 1890; in charge of exhibit at Buffalo exposition, 1901; manager of T.B. Sheldon Memorial Auditorium, Red Wing, 1904-1909; mining in Rocky mountains, 1910-1913; with legal department, Great Northern Railroad, 1913-1917.[36]

Opening night, October 9, 1904, was a grand occasion. Although the play scheduled originally, *Joseph Entangled*, was cancelled because of poor reviews elsewhere, its substitute, *The Royal Chef*, a light opera touring as one of Shubert's fifteen road companies,[37] was well-received by the near-to-full house. The play's sixty performers arrived by special train—three baggage cars and two coaches—"direct" from Chicago's Garrick Theater.[38] The city's upper crust, including Annie Sheldon, held splendid parties to mark the great event.[39] In opening remarks, O.M. Hall praised Sheldon as a philanthropist and as one of a group of young men from the East who came "to subdue, master and develop the then almost unknown regions beyond the Mississippi."[40]

The variety and quality of touring companies that subsequently played the Auditorium were an entertainment triumph for a small city. Because Red Wing was located on two railway mainlines and its opera house was splendid, traveling companies became one-night mainstays en route to or from

T.B. Sheldon Memorial Auditorium interior (c. 1904). (Courtesy of the Goodhue County Historical Society)

Sheldon's Gift

Minneapolis, St. Paul, Dubuque, Cedar Rapids, Des Moines, Sioux City, or Omaha.[41] Whatever the quality of the company or the play, the presence of these shows and famous actors caused local excitement. According to Oscar Wintervold, who worked lights and curtains at the Auditorium for over fifty years:

> The traveling shows would carry every piece of equipment in large crates, scenery drops were rolled up on 40 foot batons. All lighting equipment and switchboards were moved in. Stage crews of 25 to 30 local men were required to set up the shows, change scenery, tear down sets and ship out after the shows. It was an operation like a circus.[43]

Musical comedies and romantic dramas, whose audiences in the Auditorium's first years often numbered 600 patrons or more, were popular. Melodramas less so. When *A Blot on the Scutcheon* played early in 1909, a harsh review noted that Red Wing people didn't "revel in darkness and death." The reviewer, however, thought that the company was good and hoped that on their next visit

T.B Sheldon Memorial Auditorium Grand Opening, October 1904. (Courtesy of the Goodhue County Historical Society)

Sheldon's Gift

they would present something "cheerful and inspiring." Happily, the reviewer noted, George M. Cohan's musical comedy *Little Johnny Jones* was soon to appear.[43]

Although manager Ralph Taber promoted "cheerful and inspiring" New York and Chicago road shows because they were popular, recognized stage "stars" also boosted attendance. An early booking was *Polly Primrose*, a play featuring acclaimed actress Adelaide Thurston, a Red Wing native.[44] Charles Frohman's *Clarice* (1907) and *Father of the Boys* (1908), which enjoyed respectable New York runs, starred celebrated actor William H. Crane. When Taber thought he had booked a likely hit, he bally-

Top: Three Twins advertisement, 1909. Bottom: Yama Yama Girls from the Three Twins, 1909 (Both photos: *Red Wing Daily Republican*. Courtesy the *Red Wing Republican Eagle*)

hooed relentlessly. Gigantic advertisements, frequently of a half page or more, appeared in the local newspapers as did Taber's *Auditorium News* ad copy. Posters were plastered on every available spot. What is more, Taber, aware that it was difficult, if not impossible, to fill 800 seats with locals only, promoted railway excursions from Wabasha, Lake City, Cannon Falls, Zumbrota, and other communities.[45] When the Auditorium presented *The Three Twins*, a musical comedy that ran for ten months in New York and featured the "Yama Yama Dance," special trains arrived from Lake City (220 patrons) and from Cannon Falls, Welch, Zumbrota, and Goodhue (106 patrons). The house that evening was packed and standing-room only.[46]

In addition to road shows, the playhouse in its early years offered repertoire and serious drama. Repertoire companies, although less popular than New York and Chicago road shows, became mainstays. Such companies planted themselves for several days and their offerings of two of three plays, with crowds averaging 400 to 450, boosted overall attendance. There was also serious drama. Although the Auditorium opened with a comic opera, it followed three days later with Shakespeare's *As You Like It*.[47] *Othello, Macbeth,* and others were performed. Not surprisingly, Norwegian Henrik Ibsen's plays, notably *A Doll's House* and *Peer Gynt*, also appeared. With their troubling themes, however, those works drew modest audiences as was typical throughout Minnesota including the Twin Cities.[48] When George Bernard Shaw's "serious" comedy *Candida* (1898)[49] drew poorly, the *Daily Republican*, upholding artistic values,[50] chided locals:

> It will not take many such evidences of inappreciation of first class attractions to seriously impair the prestige Red Wing has gained in the theatrical field and render impossible the securing for Red Wing anything better than the mediocre shows with which other Minnesota cities have been flooded this winter.[51]

Although there was provocative material, the emphasis, as theater historian Howard Taubman wrote, was on "flashy, empty, rodomontade that would sell."[52]

The new Auditorium also briefly buoyed enthusiasm for community theater. A major production, by a group calling itself the Red Wing Opera Company, was *The Dalai Lama or Connubial Complications in the Back Yard*. Written by Will N.S. Ivins and theater manager Ralph Taber, it was, "the story of the scrapes and escapes of a young crew of Tibetans as they dodge the matrimonial intentions of their polygamous venerable elders." It starred Ivins as Ding Dong Dak and local notables. The production previewed at the Keokuck, Iowa, opera house and played to predictably rave reviews in Red Wing on Valentine's Day 1905, just four months after the Auditorium opened. Although locals thought the show had possibilities for a New York run, that opportunity never materialized. More importantly, community theater didn't revive until the 1920s.[53]

In addition to theatrical works, the Auditorium regularly presented symphonies, lectures, and political speeches. The variety was astounding. Among others, William Jennings Bryan, "Fighting Bob" La Follette, Arctic explorer Roald Amundsen,[54] Denver Judge Ben Lindsay (juvenile delinquency), and social critic and reformer Jacob Riis[55] lectured. Concerts were numerous. In February 1905, the Auditorium presented famous Belgian violinist Ovide Musin. Musin, whose concert received a mediocre review and was attended by only a "fair-sized" audience, was accompanied by a pianist and contralto in a variety program that included Handel, Chopin, Tuscan folk songs, hymns, and an Aria from Saint-Saens' *Sampson and Delilah*.[56] Minnesota-based musicians also appeared with regularity. In 1908 the St. Olaf College band presented a wide-ranging program that included selections from Donizetti's *Lucia di Lammermoor*, *Merry Widow* waltzes, Wagner selections from *Lohengrin* and *Tannhauser*, Norwegian folk music, and closed with a rousing rendition of Sousa's *Semper Fidelius* march.[57] Although opera was occasionally staged, it was most commonly heard as arias and overtures in the programs of soloists and orchestras.

Within five years, the Auditorium became a model for respectable culture. In a speech at Grand Rapids, Michigan, in 1909, University of Minnesota professor, and later president of the University of Minnesota and then the University of Michigan, Marion L. Burton, spoke on "The Play and the Playhouse Today." In it, Burton, expressing views held by arbiters of high culture, said that serious theater, one of the great influences on modern civilization, was under assault by vaudeville and "so-called comic opera."[58] In the face of this battering, it was necessary, Burton said, to bring "culture and conscience to the playhouse." The greatest hope, he believed, was for the "best people interested in the theater," to run them for public benefit. That was the advantage of municipal theaters:

SHELDON'S GIFT

> I prophesy that ten years from now no city in the United States the size of Grand Rapids will be without its municipal theater, controlled by a committee, selected from your best cultured people, who shall protect the public against their low desires. Some one will come along and endow these theaters, as Carnegie has endowed libraries all over the country.[59]

Referring to Red Wing, Burton said that there, "Everything sordid and base is shut out and only the plays wanted by the best element are allowed to come to the city."[60] Burton's assertion was more than the quintessence of progressive elitism and "sucralization." It was downright wrong given the success, in Red Wing and elsewhere, of the lightweight entertainments Burton eschewed.[61] Burton's optimism ignored persistent and uncomfortable realities. As historian William O'Neill wrote thirty-five years ago, "In America, hope not only springs eternal, it becomes retroactive."[62]

Indeed, despite the Auditorium's décor and embellishments, purely highbrow fare drew mediocre attendance. In contrast, mixed fare, when available, drew well. In 1905 and 1906 there were a dozen or more combined "highbrow" and "lowbrow" concerts. When Swedish Songstress Anna Hellstrom appeared in 1906 on her third successful American tour, for example, her repertoire included a Donizetti (a bel canto opportunity for the Swede), selections from Verdi's *La Traviata*, and a plateful of Swedish folk songs.[63] These mixed concerts enjoyed an excellent average attendance of 566 persons.[64] On the other hand, concerts by the Minneapolis Symphony Quartet that included only Beethoven, Schubert, Tchaikovsky, Mendelssohn, and other "highbrow" composers and the Lindquist Ladies Orchestra drew small crowds.[65] In March 1909, the Maud Powell Trio (violin, piano, cello) appeared. Ticket prices, at fifty cents to one dollar, were moderate. In its review, the *Daily Republican*, noting the poor turnout, said:

> It is only a matter of sincere regret that Red Wing could not have greeted these artists of international renown and unquestioned merit with an audience commensurate with their fame and excellence. Why people will be content with the ordinary or even the good when the BEST [emphasis original] is at their command at no higher price, is an enigma.... Not new but always strange and surprising in an intelligent and progressive community.[66]

At the same time, the newspaper seemed also to understand how the culture schism affected a small city such as Red Wing. Following the Maud Powell concert, the newspaper published a second satirical review that spoke to accessibility. In it, "Sporting Editor" wrote that Powell's program, . . . had everything a commoner couldn't grasp except *Peer Gynt Suite*." There were plenty of names on the "card" the reviewer wrote, but few that could be "pronounced by any civilized man." Powell was a first rate violinist,

> but why not something nearer home, something that one craves without getting rather than getting what one does not crave? If "Home Sweet Home" had come out of that violin, the grizzly bearded grandfather yawning between numbers would have grasped the little urchin across the aisle and covered him with kisses. . . . If Maud had played "The Battle Hymn of the Republic," the audience would have gotten up on their seats and yelled and smelled smoke."[67]

The Auditorium was a source of community pride and townspeople believed they had a "stakeholder" interest in it. Progressive-era enthusiasm for municipal ownership of public interest enterprises undoubtedly fueled that belief.[68] Financially, the board's goal, to make the Auditorium self-supporting, was not at odds with municipal ownership. That aim, explicitly stated from 1904 on, was, moreover, entirely consistent with the goals of commercial theater owners who believed that a "good theater could be measured in terms of dollars brought in."[69] At first, it seemed that self-sufficiency was attainable. In 1908, Charles A. Betcher, reporting on behalf of O.M. Hall, who was attending his class reunion at Massachusetts' prestigious Williams College, said that the Auditorium "proved" it could be self-sustaining in a city of only 10,000. That, he said, was something that "many doubted four years ago." Betcher's assertion, however, came when the cash balance was just $808 and furnishings and scenery required new expenditures of $1,500.[70]

Despite its newness, tax and license benefits, and lack of debt, it isn't surprising that the Auditorium struggled financially. To begin, there was a diminishing yet persistent objection to theater. As the Auditorium's opening night approached, decency guardians who "feared the demoralizing effect that a theater might have upon the community" were staying away. With fewer than half the "parquet" seats sold, board members worried that the city would be humiliated by a thin house. Although the opening night crowd was respectable, the issue was serious enough for city council president F.M. Wilson, in his opening remarks, to refer to such people by quoting the proverb, "Evil to those who evil think."[71]

Although nineteenth-century small city venues could turn a profit due to mixed use and culturally omnivorous programs, circumstances had changed. The Auditorium could not host the Fireman's Ball. What was more, purely "highbrow" attractions, programs that satisfied "high class" citizens, drew modestly in small cities. Variety programs that combined a Beethoven and Puccini with folk songs or marches remained popular but were increasingly less available. Although the community prided itself on the Auditorium's ability to present nationally acclaimed lecturers, they too were unsuccessful financially.[72] Public programs, local talent contests, small conventions, school and religious uses, and various free events and meetings were necessary and contributed to the community but failed to cover expenses.[73]

Competition from the opera house also persisted. As the Auditorium was built, lessees Walter A. Giffin and E.P. Neill girded themselves by adding a "health club" that included basketball, physical culture classes for men and women, showers, and a three-lane bowling alley.[74] The opera house also presented entertainments that included the ubiquitous *Uncle Tom's Cabin*, a Swedish Quintet, a German theater troupe, and the University of Minnesota drama club.[75] Occasionally it enjoyed sell-outs for legitimate drama as it did with *Quincy Adams Sawyer*, a theatrical adaptation of Charles Felton Pidgin's popular novel about New England family life.[76] Even serious opera, when it was a favorite, as was *Martha*, and tickets were priced at just fifty cents, did well.[77] Most often, however, serious works also drew modestly at the Opera House. A dramatization of Dumas' *Camille*, for example, received a glowing review but also the comment that unfortunately, "the performance did not draw a very large audience—it takes McCarthy's *Mishaps* and *The Irish Pawnbroker* to do that."[78] Although the opening of the Auditorium meant, as manager Walter Giffin said, ". . . the opera house's play days are over,"[79] it struggled on for a few months, closed briefly, and then reopened. In the Auditorium's 1905-1906 annual report President O.M. Hall, noting that the year was not good, remarked that the "re-opening of the old opera house without license," had "caused a serious impairment to the revenue of the Auditorium."[80]

The opera house closed again in the spring of 1906 but was renovated and re-opened that September as the Majestic Family Theater. Manager W.J. Wells

Sheldon's Gift

promised a weekly program change, daily matinees, and ten- and twenty-cent admissions.[81] The *Daily Republican* reported that opening night was "packed" and that the redecorated theater offered a "clever" vaudeville bill along with motion pictures, good music, illustrated songs and clean humor.[82]

Surprisingly, comedic performers John and Jennifer Leslie, who arrived in Red Wing from Cleveland, Ohio, purchased the Majestic just weeks later.[83] The Majestic now promised fresh vaudeville, songs, and ladies' Wednesday and children's Saturday matinees.[84] Circuit vaudevillians, including vocalist Winifred Green and the "black-face" comedy duo, Baker and Williams, were typical headliners.[85] In addition to vaudeville, motion pictures, rentals to community organizations, and operating a bowling alley, the Leslies held amateur nights, and on election eve 1906 read poll results between acts.[86]

Unfortunately, the Leslies' business hopes evaporated when a fire that building owner Anna Wilkinson said caused $8,000 damage broke out later that month. Although the building's outer shell remained intact, the interior was ruined.[87] In his Auditorium annual report for 1906-1907, O.M. Hall noted that the Auditorium's reasonably good financial year was due partly to the Majestic fire.[88] Hall also noted that the fire enabled "the board to secure several low-priced entertainments by the better class of repertoire companies."[89] Indeed, booking more performances at lower admission prices helped. In its first full year, the Auditorium was open just sixty-two times.[90] Over the next four years, the number of events increased, to 100 in 1906-1907 and 115 by July 1909.[91]

If low-priced repertoire and stock companies aided finances, the New York and Chicago touring companies were another matter. Even with aggressive promotions Taber had his troubles. Although O.M. Hall once said that higher-priced attractions drew the largest audiences, it was far from certain that the town could support more of them or, with their high costs, that they were profitable even when well attended. What was more, the best shows insisted, because they received a percent of gross receipts, that ticket prices approximated those in large cities. That meant a top price of $1.50 or $2.00 and balcony admissions of fifty or seventy-five cents. Although Taber and others argued that top-drawer entertainment was a bargain, citizens howled about sky-high prices.[92] Increasingly, moreover, good road shows were difficult to acquire at any price. Within the theater business there was widespread disagreement as to the cause. Most blamed the lingering effects of the Panic of 1907, a financial liquidity crisis that made it difficult for producers to secure financing and kept ticket buyers away. Others, including the *Dramatic Mirror*, claimed that the "automobile craze" was responsible for a twenty-five percent fall off in trade and an even greater drop in small markets. "In a way," one theater historian noted, "it seemed as if any excuse could be offered. . . ."[93]

In Red Wing, Norman Peel, a theatrical advance man, told a local reporter that the Auditorium's mounting difficulties were in some respects peculiar to small cities. In such places, he said, it was only possible to "secure a small portion of the higher class plays and if one of these gets a 'frost' [poor review] it is difficult indeed to book another. These larger attractions do not care to play one-night stands and when they do they want the cream of the receipts—and generally get it."[94] As a result, Red Wingites who demanded the best shows and could afford the better seats began to travel to the Twin Cities to see them. Although Mayor A.P. Pierce accused those citizens of disloyalty because they would pay $2.00 for a show in St. Paul but not in Red Wing, loyalty wasn't the issue. The best shows were increasingly rare in Red Wing at any price, and the endless parade of inane melodrama and musical comedy that appeared had become tiresome to high-toned ticket buyers. As theater historian Dorothy Chansky notes:

> A major objection to these shows, which were produced and sent on the road by a cartel of New York producers, was that, besides being intellectually thin or downright frivolous—which not everyone resented—they were, in their touring incarnations, shoddily produced and sometimes falsely advertised as being original New York productions, which irritated even non idealists.[95]

As financial uncertainty grew, neither a reservoir of invested funds, an endowment, nor public subsidy, were available to help. When Sheldon's gift married Red Wing, the bride's father (Sheldon's trustees) failed to provide a dowry (endowment). Without it, there was nothing to fall back on when extraordinary costs arose or to cover losses. The concept wasn't unknown. Although considered by the trustees initially, as construction costs rose an anticipated reserve vanished. What was more, although city council president F.M. Wilson noted the need for an endowment such as existed at Paris's Comedia Francaise in his opening night remarks,[96] no action was taken.

Nor could the board, by way of the city council, ask taxpayers for help. Public support for entertainment or the arts was virtually unknown in the United States. And even though the Auditorium was touted as belonging to the people, that assertion was weakened by its goal of self-reliance based on high-quality entertainments that were priced out of most residents' reach. Because road shows insisted on a suitable (for them) price scale, ticket prices wouldn't have fallen even with a subsidy. Consequently, taxpayer underwriting would have meant a subsidy by all on behalf of a theater-going elite. Nor was Red Wing "growing" into its new theater. Despite pretensions to growth that resulted in overstating its size to as much as 12,000 before 1910, Red Wing, a city of 7,525 in 1900, grew to just 9,048 in 1910, an annual rate of less than two percent.[97]

Competition, problems attendant upon the decline of the theater business following the 1907 Panic, lack of endowment or subsidy, the bifurcation of audiences and performers into highbrow and lowbrow, and the slow growth of the area's population all contributed to financial uncertainty. Still, the Auditorium ended its first five years in the black—if just barely. Pure luck played a role for the Majestic's fire was surely that. It was also fortuitous that the spanking new structure didn't require costly repairs.[98] Most importantly, had it not been for Taber's sale of program advertising to local businesses (coerced philanthropy) and the generosity of upstanding citizens who subsidized appearances by the Apollo Club, a Minneapolis chorale,[99] the Auditorium would have experienced a sizeable deficit. The internalized realization, however, that sought-after entertainments required subsidy, coerced or genuine, was decades away.

After five years, Ralph Taber had had enough, the board had had enough of him, or, consistent with his earlier careers, he simply decided to chase new adventures. As the 1908-1909 season progressed, Taber's last, a number of attractions were cancelled due to poor advance sales, the economic problems that befell traveling companies, or both. Taber's resignation, which received little notice, was effective July 1, 1909.[100] When next heard from, in 1912, Taber was living in Oregon where he trumpeted timber interests and the Green Mountain Copper Mine. Always a promoter, to Red Wingites he touted Oregon's virtues.[101]

SHELDON'S GIFT

Notes

[1] Lizzie, Mary, Nellie, Rosa and Theodore, Jr.

[2] Franklyn Curtiss-Wedge, *History of Goodhue County Minnesota* (Chicago: H.C. Cooper Jr. & Co., 1909), 31; Madeline Angell, *Red Wing, Minnesota: Saga of a River Town*, 2nd ed. (Minneapolis, Minnesota, Dillon Press, 1978), 117-119.

[3] "Mr. Sheldon's Munificence," *Red Wing Daily Republican*, April 7, 1900.

[4] An endowment might have created one of America's first community foundations. The pioneering Cleveland Foundation dates from 1914.

[5] "City Hall and Auditorium," *Red Wing Daily Republican*, April 5, 1902.

[6] "That Sheldon Fund," *Red Wing Republican* (Weekly), April 30, 1902.

[7] "Fund of $75,000," *Red Wing Republican* (Weekly), April 23, 1902.

[8] "Ask City to Aid," *Red Wing Republican* (Weekly), December 17, 1902.

[9] "Red Wing's Present," *Red Wing Republican* (Weekly), December 24, 1902.

[10] State of Minnesota, General Laws for 1903, Chapter 22: An act authorizing cities to accept, acquire and hold property by gift, grant or devise, and to manage and control the same, March 3, 1903, 28-29.

[11] "Very Important Council Meeting," *Red Wing Daily Republican*, March 7, 1903.

[12] "The T.B. Sheldon Auditorium; Proposed Deed Trust Terms," *Red Wing Daily Republican*, March 9, 1903.

[13] Ibid.

[14] Free water was important because an on-site turbine powered by the force of city water supplied electric lighting.

[15] "The T.B. Sheldon Auditorium; Proposed Deed Trust Terms," *Red Wing Daily Republican*, March 9, 1903; "The T.B. Sheldon Auditorium: Suggestions Embodied in Communication of Trustees to the Mayor and City Council Regarding the Proposed Structure Reproduced in Full," *Red Wing Republican* (Weekly), March 11, 1903.

[16] "Local News," *Red Wing Daily Republican*, March 16, 1903.

[17] "Reproduction of the New Auditorium Cuts," *Red Wing Daily Republican*, March 18, 1903.

[18] "Local News," *Red Wing Daily Republican*, March 3, 1903.

[19] "Reproduction of the New Auditorium Cuts," *Red Wing Daily Republican*, March 18, 1903.

[20] "Selection of Plan No. 2 by Sheldon Trustees!" *Red Wing Daily Republican*, March 23, 1903.

[21] Barbara Tittle, "Beginnings," in Barbara Tittle and others, "The T.B. Sheldon Memorial Auditorium" *Goodhue County Historical Society Newsletter* 19, No. 1 (1985), n.p.

[22] "Stucco Work for New Auditorium Arrives," *Red Wing Republican* (Weekly) June 1, 1904,

[23] Annie Sheldon gifted the portrait to the Auditorium in her will. "Bulk of Estate to Relatives," *Red Wing Republican* (Weekly), July 7, 1909.
[24] Madeline Angell, *Red Wing, Minnesota: Saga of a River Town*, 2nd ed. (Minneapolis, Minnesota, Dillon Press, 1978), 225.
[25] "Auditorium to be Perfectly Safe," *Red Wing Republican* (Weekly), January 6, 1904.
[26] Red Wing census in 1900 was 7,525. *Twelfth Census of the United States, Taken in the Year 1900*, Vol. I, (Washington, U.S. Census Office, 1901).
[27] George D. Glenn and Richard L. Poole, *The Opera Houses of Iowa* (Ames: Iowa State University Press, 1993), 76-183.
[28] Editorial, "Auditorium Suggestions," *Red Wing Daily Republican*, March 18, 1903. The anticipated population growth didn't materialize. Red Wing grew from 7,525 in 1900 to 9,048 in 1910, but there, approximately, it stayed. A 1909 city directory boosted the population to a wishful 12,000. See "New Directory Gives Red Wing Nearly 12,000," *Red Wing Republican* (Weekly), June 30, 1909.
[29] "Neill Gets a Franchise," *Red Wing Republican* (Weekly), October 12, 1904; "Resolution Adopting the Auditorium," Red Wing City Council, October 7, 1904.
[30] "Aldermen Cannot Serve," *Red Wing Republican* (Weekly), September 7, 1910.
[31] "Picture Shows Cause of Play House Deficit," *Red Wing Daily Republican*, August 16, 1911.
[32] The origins of this claim are not known. Within a few years, however, it was repeated frequently and for the next seventy-five years. See "Only Municipal Theater in the United States," *Red Wing Republican* (Weekly), April 29, 1908. That article quoted Roby Danebaum in *Scrapbook* magazine who wrote a glowing but wildly inaccurate story about Sheldon and the Auditorium. In it, Danebaum noted that there were several municipally owned theaters in the United States but that Red Wing's was the only one operated "directly by a local government." That claim seemed to be a distinction without meaning. What is more, the Auditorium wasn't operated "directly" by the city. It was operated by a board appointed by the mayor but with independent decision-making and finances.
[33] Arthur Hornblow, *A History of Theatre in America from Its Beginnings to the Present Time*, Vol. 2, (Philadelphia: J.B. Lippincott Co, 1919), 325-26; http://www.academyofmusictheatre.com/history.html.
[34] Susan Jacoby, *Freethinkers: A History of American Secularism* (New York, Owl Books, 2004), 149-151.
[35] "Manager of the Auditorium Chosen," *Red Wing Republican* (Weekly), August 3, 1904.
[36] Quoted in "First Theater Manager Brought Big Shows Here," *Red Wing Daily Republican*, July 23, 1936.
[37] "The Opening Date Changed," *Red Wing Republican* (Weekly), October 5, 1904.
[38] Ibid.
[39] Madeline Angell, *Red Wing, Minnesota: Saga of a River Town*, 2nd ed. (Minneapolis, Minnesota, Dillon Press, 1978), 225.

[40]"Red Wing's New Playhouse Is Opened to the Public," *Red Wing Republican* (Weekly), October 12, 1904.

[41]Roger Bee, Gary Browne, and John Luecke, *The Chicago Great Western in Minnesota*, 2nd ed. (Anoka, Minnesota, Blue River Publications, 1984), passim.

[42]Quoted in Madeline Angell, *Red Wing, Minnesota: Saga of a River Town*, 2nd ed. (Minneapolis: Dillon Press, 1978), 226.

[43]"Robertson at Auditorium," *Red Wing Daily Republican*, January 5, 1909; "Robertson in Tragedy," *Red Wing Daily Republican*, January 9, 1909.

[44]"The First Booking for the Auditorium," *Red Wing Republican* (Weekly), August 10, 1904.

[45]Roger Bee, Gary Browne, and John Luecke, *The Chicago Great Western in Minnesota*, 2nd ed. (Anoka, Minnesota, Blue River Publications, 1984), passim.

[46]"Packed House Sees Three Twins," *Red Wing Daily Republican* (February 2, 1909),

[47]"Red Wing's New Playhouse Is Opened to the Public," *Red Wing Republican* (Weekly), October 12, 1904.

[48]"Great Play, Small House," *Red Wing Daily Republican*, January 14, 1908; "Repeated by Request," *Red Wing Daily Republican*, June 9, 1909; "Peer Gynt Presented," *Red Wing Republican* (Weekly), February 17, 1909.

[49]"Local News," and "*Candida* was a Clever Comedy," *Red Wing Daily Republican*, January 18, 1908.

[50]*The Daily Republican* not only published occasional reviews of Twin City concerts but also national reviews of the likes of Puccini's new opera, *Madame Butterfly*.

[51]"*Candida* was a Clever Comedy," *Red Wing Daily Republican*, January 18, 1908

[52]Ibid.

[53]"A Gala Night for Red Wing," *Red Wing Daily Republican*, February 15, 1905. A good brief discussion of the Red Wing Opera Company and community theater in Red Wing was written by Caroline M. Vogel for, "Souvenir Program, *Pygmalion*," (Red Wing: n.p., n.d. [April, 1971]).

[54]Amundsen's appearance was a major event. See "Honors for Amundsen," *Red Wing Daily Republican*, January 15, 1908; "Special Trains Both Ways for Amundsen Lecture Tomorrow Evening," *Red Wing Daily Republican*, February 6, 1908; "Was Pleased with Reception" *Red Wing Daily Republican*, February 8, 1908.

[55]"The Battle for Sunlight," *Red Wing Daily Republican*, February 25, 1909.

[56]"Red Wing Favored by Great Violinist Tonight," *Red Wing Daily Republican*, February 9, 1905 and "Ovide Musin Concert Given Last Evening," *Red Wing Daily Republican*, February 10, 1905.

[57]"Fine Concerts by St. Olaf's Band," *Red Wing Daily Republican*, January 11, 1908.

[58]So lowly were films that Burton did not think to add nickelodeons to his list of threats.

[59]"Red Wing Is an Example," *Red Wing Daily Republican*, March 13, 1909.

[60]Ibid.

[61]"Dream City at Auditorium," *Red Wing Daily Republican*, January 27, 1908

[62]William L. O'Neill, *Coming Apart: An Informal History of America in the 1960s* (Chicago: Quadrangle Books, 1971), 50.

SHELDON'S GIFT

[63]"An Evening of Swedish Song," *Red Wing Daily Republican*, November 13, 1906; "Mme Hellstrom at Auditorium," *Red Wing Daily Republican*, November 6, 1906. Importantly, when Hellstrom appeared in Minneapolis her program was exclusively "highbrow." See "Swedish Singer Wins Minneapolis," *Red Wing Daily Republican*, November 12, 1906.

[64]"Annual Report of the Auditorium Board," *Red Wing Daily Republican*, July 24, 1906.

[65]"Symphony at Auditorium," *Red Wing Daily Republican*, October 9, 1907; "Local News," *Red Wing Daily Republican*, May 11, 1909.

[66]"Great Artists at Red Wing," *Red Wing Daily Republican*, March 27, 1909.

[67]"Sporting Editor," *Red Wing Daily Republican*, March 27, 1909.

[68]Though municipal ownership of local electrical and gas plants never materialized, voters overwhelmingly approved bonding of $350,000 to pay for it in 1919. See: "Commercial Club Starts Action for Municipal Lighting Plant," *Red Wing Daily Eagle*, February 5, 1919; "A Study in Electric Rates" *Red Wing Daily Eagle*, February 6, 1919; "A Corporate Suicide," editorial, *Red Wing Daily Eagle*, February 19, 1919.

[69]Frank M. Whiting, *Minnesota Theatre: From Old Fort Snelling to the Guthrie*, (Minneapolis: Pogo Press, 1988), 63.

[70]"Annual Report of the Auditorium Board," *Red Wing Daily Republican*, July 8, 1908.

[71]Quoted in Madeline Angell, *Red Wing, Minnesota: Saga of a River Town*, 2nd ed. (Minneapolis: Dillon Press, 1978), 225; also "Red Wing's New Playhouse Is Opened to the Public," *Red Wing Republican* (Weekly), October 12, 1904.

[72]See *Red Wing Daily Republican* during period from September to the end of October 1906. Lecture series is discussed.

[73]"Annual Report of the Auditorium Board," *Red Wing Daily Republican*, July 24, 1906. Programming was here listed by type.

[74]"Red Wing Will Have Public Gymnasium," *Red Wing Republican* (Weekly), July 1, 1903; "The Building of Bowling Alleys," *Red Wing Republican* (Weekly), July 22, 1903.

[75]"Coming Attractions at Red Wing Opera House," *Red Wing Daily Republican*, March 31, 1903; "Local News," *Red Wing Daily Republican*, January 6, 1904.

[76]"Local News," *Red Wing Republican* (Weekly), November 18, 1903.

[77]"Local News," *Red Wing Daily Republican*, March 4, 1903.

[78]"The Play of Camille Was Well Presented," *Red Wing Republican* (Weekly), November 4, 1903.

[79]"The Last Opera House Attraction," *Red Wing Republican* (Weekly), August 24, 1904; "Advertisement," *Red Wing Daily Republican*, March 4, 1903.

[80]"Annual Report of the Auditorium Board," *Red Wing Daily Republican*, July 24, 1906.

[81]"Advertisement," *Red Wing Daily Republican*, September 10, 1906.

[82]"Vaudeville House Opened to Public," *Red Wing Daily Republican*, September 4, 1906.

[83]"Majestic Will Reopen," *Red Wing Daily Republican*, October 26, 1906.

[84]"New Bill at the Majestic," *Red Wing Daily Republican*, November 13, 1906.

Sheldon's Gift

[85]"Advertisement," *Red Wing Daily Republican*, November 1, 1906.
[86]"The Majestic Well Attended," *Red Wing Daily Republican*, November 6, 1906.
[87]"Most Stubborn Fire in Years," *Red Wing Daily Republican*, November 27, 1906.
[88]"Annual Report of the Auditorium Board," *Red Wing Daily Republican*, July 17, 1907.
[89]Ibid.
[90]"Annual Report of the Auditorium Board," *Red Wing Daily Republican*, July 24, 1906.
[91]"Annual Report of the Auditorium Board," *Red Wing Daily Republican*, August 13, 1909.
[92]"Red Wing Citizens Lucky to have Auditorium" *Red Wing Daily Republican*, December 14, 1906. Using a conservative comparison, the consumer price index, the best Auditorium seats ranged between twenty-five dollars and thirty-five dollars in today's currency and the lower priced from twelve to fifteen dollars. Other comparisons, using an index of unskilled worker wages, however, suggest that even balcony tickets in those years had a relative value of as much as forty dollars today. All indices should be used cautiously because peoples' wants and needs have changed over time. In addition, today's behaviors demonstrate that people of modest income do purchase seemingly expensive sporting and entertainment tickets, See http://www.EH Net.
[93]Gerald Bordman, et. al., *American Theatre: A Chronicle of Comedy and Drama, 1869-1914* (New York, Oxford University Press, 1994), 673
[94]"Management Not Blamed for Deficit," *Red Wing Daily Eagle*, August 18, 1911.
[95]Dorothy Chansky, *Composing Ourselves: The Little Theatre Movement and the American Audience* (Carbondale: Southern Illinois University Press, 2004), 3.
[96]"Red Wing's New Playhouse Is Opened to the Public," *Red Wing Republican* (Weekly), October 12, 1904.
[97]"New Directory Gives Red Wing Nearly 12,000," *Red Wing Republican* (Weekly), June 30, 1909.
[98]"The Business of the Auditorium," *Red Wing Daily Republican*, August 13, 1909. Although the board under O.M. Hall was more forthcoming publicly than later boards, official records and minutes are lost. Had the board budgeted depreciation it would have reported a substantial loss.
[99]"Annual Report of the Auditorium Board," *Red Wing Daily Republican*, July 17, 1907.
[100]"Local News," *Red Wing Daily Republican*, June 17, 1909.
[101]"Local News," *Red Wing Daily Republican*, August 12, 1912.

Chapter Three

Celluloid

"Red Wing will support one moving picture show and no more."
~The Gem (August 1908)
"We are simply up against it." ~Charles E. Sheldon (August 1911)

When the Majestic burned, the Auditorium stood briefly as the town's only theater. Then, in the summer of 1907, new competition arose, if not from a silver screen, then from little more than a bed sheet tacked to a wall. Motion pictures were not entirely new to Red Wing. As early as 1897, traveling shows projected movies in a "black" tent.[1] The first theatrical showing most likely occurred at the opera house about 1900 as a novelty addition to an otherwise live performance of "refined" vaudeville.[2] When the opera house reopened as the Majestic in 1906, motion pictures were already an important part of a mixed live and film program.[3] A *Daily Republican* reviewer noted about reopening night that the moving pictures were "clear and new" and that he especially enjoyed *The Bicycle Robber*.[4] When the Majestic went up in smoke that autumn, listed among the losses was the theater's new $500 Edison Majesticscope projector.[5]

In 1905-1906, the Auditorium also presented, although attendance averaged fewer than 250 patrons, two evenings of "educational and uplifting" motion pictures. In following years, the Lyman Howe show made regular appearances. Howe was a Pennsylvania entrepreneur whose several motion picture traveling units were in high demand. Although motion picture houses soon put most traveling exhibitors out of business, Howe survived, thanks to high-quality travelogues and military coverage, until the 1920s.[6]

Although movies were not new to Red Wing, motion picture theaters were. Their generic name, "nickelodeon,"[7] was seldom used in Minnesota, which preferred "electric theater" or "motion picture house."[8] In Minneapolis, the first film theater, the Wonderland, opened in 1906.[9] Just a year later, when Red Wing's first venture began, one estimate claimed that there were already 3,000 theaters nationwide.[10] Within five years that number exploded to between 8,000 and 15,000.[11] In Red Wing, between 1907 and 1911, there were three—the White Vaudette, the Grand Electric, and the Gem. Although photograph reference is scant, from their names, advertising, and what is known of such businesses, we can surmise a great deal.

The White Vaudette opened in the summer of 1907 in a single storefront at 305 Main Street and was likely a low-cost design[12] seating just 200 to 250 patrons.[13] The proprietors, Roberts and Pearson, who paid a thirty-five-dollar license fee, may have gotten into business for as little as five or six hundred dollars.[14] The interior floor remained flat. The carbon-arc projector was hand-cranked and battery-powered. There was a piano. Although many early theaters used wooden kitchen chairs, the White Vaudette was praised for its "pleasing and neat appearance from the outside and comfortable opera chairs on the inside."[15] The exterior was surely painted white, a favored color,[16] because it was clean and wholesome just as the pictures inside. For ten cents,[17] patrons saw four or more films lasting up to an hour. There was a daily matinee and continuous evening shows from 7:00 to 11:00 P.M. Programs never advertised the names of the stars but titles, such as the *Girl from Montana*, were sometimes stated. Most often advertisements simply identified "a riotous comedy" or "beautiful travelogue."[18]

The White Vaudette promised new pictures each day along with repeat showings of previous films. That there were sufficient films to make daily changes possible seems incredible. Yet as early as 1902 a catalog of the American Mutoscope & Biograph Company offered 2,500 pictures.[19] Although early theaters first acquired films through traveling salesmen and catalogs, by 1908 Minneapolis was home to multiple regional film rental exchanges.[20]

While the projectionist readied a new film, each running fifteen minutes or less, the audience was entertained by an "illustrated song." To piano accompaniment, the song, of the *Bicycle Built for Two* variety, was typically sung by a local talent as about twenty hand-colored lantern slides purporting to represent the song's storyline were projected.[21] On at least one occasion the White Vaudette presented an extraordinary talent. When operatic soprano Bessie Abott[22] appeared in concert at the Auditorium in October 1907, the little White Vaudette also featured Bessie singing "L'air De Buoux" from Faust.[23] What the Auditorium thought of Bessie's moonlighting we'll never know!

Guidebooks helped film exhibitors manage their theaters. These manuals suggested that, in cities such as Red Wing, weekly expenses were commonly eighty-five dollars and gross revenues between $110 and $150. If those estimates are correct and admission was ten cents, then 200 or more goers per day typical-

Grand Electric Theater in the Charles Betcher "block" at 310 Main Street. (c. 1908) (Courtesy of the Goodhue County Historical Society)

Celluloid

ly patronized the White Vaudette.[24] Nevertheless, as happened frequently, the White Vaudette was short-lived. Its disappearance could have been due to a lost lease, undercapitalization, a squabble between partners, or simply a desire to open a larger theater elsewhere. Whatever the reason, the White Vaudette quit advertising in January 1908 and disappeared.

As the White Vaudette departed, a new theater, the Grand Electric, under proprietor Sam Roberg, opened across the street at 310 Main.[25] Roberg was reported to have spent just $500 for building remodeling,[26] a rock-bottom cost. His wife, Emma, either played piano, sang, or both. With a format almost identical to the White Vaudette's, the Grand survived for almost two years. At first it advertised regularly but then infrequently. Perhaps Roberg was of the opinion that advertising "A Hilarious Comedy" wasn't worthwhile.[27] He did, however, advertise special attractions. As early as August 1908, for example, his Grand featured prizefight films.[28]

The Grand was in business only a few months when a new challenger, the Gem, opened at 210 Bush Street, just a block from the Auditorium. In business as the Red Wing Amusement Company,[29] its proprietors were Robert Davenport, a Red Wing merchant whose dry goods emporium, the Fair, was nearby, and his brother, William.[30]

Like the White Vaudette and the Grand Electric, the Gem occupied a single storefront and seated about 250 patrons. It was said that $2,000 and probably more was spent on remodeling. For that amount the proprietors may have, as the *Cyclopedia of Motion Picture Work* reported in 1911, removed ". . . the glass front and framing for the door and window," and replaced it "with a closed front a few feet back from the sidewalk line and into which are built the ticket seller's booth and the entrance and exit doors. . . ."[31] The sidewalk setback was desirable, the *Cyclopedia* claimed, because then "when the prospective patron steps off the sidewalk, he feels he is already within the theatre, even before he has purchased his admission ticket."[32] It is also possible that the Gem purchased an elaborate metal theater front such as those produced by the Kanneberg Roofing and Ceiling Company of Canton, Ohio.[33] It is certain that an electric sign emblazoned its façade.[34] Whatever its trimmings, and for $2,000 it most assuredly did not include all possible features, it was self-described as "The Prettiest Electric Theater West of Chicago."[35]

Sheldon's Gift

The Gem's owners touted it as completely safe. The floor sloped toward the street so that the audience entered from the street but then faced it while watching the show, a design that the proprietors said facilitated egress in case of fire. The Gem also boasted a fireproof concrete-and-steel projection booth erected outside the building's rear wall. Although there were few theater fires, patrons were acutely aware of the dangers posed by highly flammable celluloid film. The Gem took full advertising advantage of its safety. At its opening, building owner H.L. Olson, a pioneering Red Wing business and real estate owner, said that although he was reluctant to rent to a theater he was won over by the low insurance rates it was given. Contractor W.J. Longcor, pointing to the inclined floor and lack of obstructions pronounced the Gem "certainly safe."[36] When Rochester's Majestic Theater experienced a projection booth fire several months later but suffered no injuries, the Gem crowed that the Majestic modeled its safety features on its own.[37]

Meanwhile, the Auditorium, lacking projection equipment, occasionally presented "refined" traveling company films. In 1907 Ralph Taber wrote in his "Auditorium Notes" that D.W. Robertson's Famous Moving Pictures Company of New York would appear in a program of colored movies, a Chautauqua speaker, and illustrated songs. Admission ranged from fifteen to fifty cents—high for motion pictures.[38] The next day Taber explained that although Robertson had visited Red Wing previously (he probably played the Majestic), he, Taber, had no first-hand knowledge of the program.[39] Taber needed the cover. When Robertson's show played to a "good-sized" audience a few days later, the *Daily Republican* panned it. Its only positive comments regarded Mr. Baker, a basso, who portrayed an "old Negro Mammy doing a Pickaninny Lullaby" in what the paper deemed a "fine characterization."[40]

The following summer, the Auditorium again presented "high class" pictures with all seats "popularly" priced at ten cents. That program included "a wonderful new invention, the Cameraphone," a device that made "moving pictures that talk, sing, act and dance." For some time, Taber reported, inventors had tried to make pictures talk. The problem, he wrote awkwardly, was to make a mechanical talking machine "so regulated and adjusted so as to actually make the pictured figure open its lips and say words—its own words from its own lips—the motion of the lips actually producing the word as in the case of a living being." Taber went on to describe the Cameraphone as an elaborate and expensive device whereby "the voice is reproduced by compressed air being forced through delicately regulated valves, operating on the principle of the human throat." It was explained further that a "delicate electrical device controls the synchronization."[41] The Cameraphone is so good, he claimed, that it is "The Eighth Wonder of the World."[42]

"Eighth Wonder of the World" it wasn't. Instead, Cameraphone was one of many sound experiments that tried, unsuccessfully, to synchronize film with a disk recording. One difficulty was starting the film and the disk at precisely the right spot and then, in an age of hand-cranked projectors, keeping the synchronization close. When film broke, as it did frequently, splicing resulted in loss of a short length of film—and synchronization. Those problems remained unsolved for almost another twenty years.

At its best, early sound was difficult to hear because electric amplification was yet unborn. An additional problem was that disk recordings were of no more than a few minutes in length.[43] As a result, early films consisted entirely of short speeches and songs. Despite shortcomings, the Auditorium's audience seemed pleased.[44] After relinquishing the Cameraphone to Rochester's Metropolitan Theater for two weeks,[45] Taber secured its return for several more days.[46]

The Gem, meanwhile, described itself with doggerel:

> The Little Auditorium
> Union Made and Made Well
> Supplied with Fresh Air
> Coolest Place in Town
> Absolutely Safe and Sanitary[47]

In a laborers' town a union mention mattered. Reference to cleanliness and wholesomeness were typical as were lantern slides instructing the audience not to shout, spit, curse, talk, or throw things.[48] In January 1909, theater manager William Davenport attended a New York meeting of motion picture executives whose goal was to lift movies to an even higher "plane."[49] Indeed, by 1909 film versions of "highbrow" theater came to motion pictures. Along with short films, the Gem showed multi-reel, although not yet "feature-length" versions of *Macbeth*, *Damon and Pythias*, and *The Dreyfuss Affair*.[50] All of these were important steps in luring middle-class audiences to the movies but demonstrated a lower class familiarity with "highbrow" content.

Although the Gem referred to itself as the "Little Auditorium" and offered "highbrow" pictures for just ten cents, it differentiated itself by pointing out that the Auditorium played a high-class community role that the Gem couldn't emulate. In at least one instance, it advertised that theatergoers could attend a full film program and yet make the Auditorium's 8:00 P.M. curtain. In part, the Gem's deference to the Auditorium was an attempt to placate fears that the Gem threatened to steal Auditorium business. At the same time, however, the Gem warned, prophetically, that the Auditorium would do itself a disservice by entering the motion picture business:

> Red Wing will support one moving picture show and no more. That one show should be of Red Wing quality—so good that the people could get nothing better. Red Wing people are entitled to and will have this new form of cheap entertainment. Rather than let some low-grade show come from outside, let the people get a show owned by people who have the best of Red Wing always at heart. The Auditorium furnishes high-class attractions. The Auditorium would never run moving pictures. *Five- and ten-cent shows would impair its dignity, wear out the Auditorium faster than the nickels and dimes could come in, would add a big sum to the insurance cost and would endanger the property* [emphasis added]. For the Auditorium to take the precautions necessary would cost much money and would require construction which would spoil the looks of the magnificent interior and obstruct the view from a section of the house at all times. The Auditorium has its province, the Gem, whose owners admire the Auditorium as much as anybody, has its province. They will not conflict. In a small way the Gem should and will be something to be proud of, as the Auditorium is in a large way. Thus reasoned the Gem people before the Gem was built, and because of that reasoning they built THE GEM.[51]

In the summer of 1909, with the Auditorium already facing financial uncertainty, Wilbur Scott replaced Ralph Taber. Scott, whose father was a Red Wing paint and wallpaper retailer, was thirty-three years old, had served as Taber's assistant, and was described by the board as "experienced." He wasn't, however, a miracle worker. Attendance continued to decline. Although the board blamed, "the numerous five and ten cent shows operating in the city,"[52] there were, as the national economy strug-

Celluloid

gled and the quality and quantity of road shows declined, many reasons for Auditorium problems.

For 1909-1910 Scott booked the best touring companies he could get. These included *The Red Mill*, a musical comedy that played 479 performances in New York, and Victor Herbert's *Babes in Toyland*, a production "without a vulgarism."[53] But as attendance fell, Scott cancelled shows. There were no more special trains. A number of "unusual" expenses, including boiler repair, contributed to a year-end operating loss of $242.93. Looking to the future, the board's "plan" was to hope that citizens purchased more tickets.[54]

As the 1910-1911 season began, the economy improved, and one competitor, Sam Roberg's Grand Electric Theater, quit business. In August, Roberg leased the Gem. An advertisement said that Mr. Roberg would be pleased to "meet his old friends" and that he promised the "best possible show for the money."[55]

Although Roberg tried to expand his audience by introducing vaudeville acts, the Gem was already a minor combatant in an emerging theatrical "war" that began when Robert Davenport built an entirely new theater at 316 Third Street. No slap-dash remodeling, the new concrete-and-brick structure was reported to have cost $3,500 and probably considerably more. The ornate theater seated over four hundred and had, in addition to up-to-date motion picture capability, a stage, theatrical lighting, and dressing rooms. When it opened in early December 1910, Davenport asked customers to "help name the new picture theater—lucky one will receive $5.00 gold and a season ticket." The winning entry, not surprisingly, was "The Davenport."[56]

While the Davenport was built, a second new theater opened directly across Third Street in a building that had housed Red Wing's post office.[57] Although small, with fewer than 300 seats,[58] the Family, whose proprietor was John Walsh, included a stage, backstage, and motion picture equipment. With the opening of the Davenport and the Family, true vaudeville, several variety acts presented by a traveling "troupe" and accompanied by films, arrived in earnest—and, at a price lower than the Auditorium's rear balcony.

The Family billed its program as vaudeville and "refined" pictures. Although most films were typical one and two reel travelogues and simple stories, Walsh also screened sports and newsreels regularly. In November 1910 he showed pictures of the prizefight held that July 4 between Gentleman Jim Jeffries "The Great White Hope" and African-American Jack Johnson, a fight that enraged white America. Johnson, a great athlete who led a carousing, flamboyant, and extravagant life that included "consorting" with white women was notorious among whites. Not surprisingly, Johnson pummeled the older, out-of-shape Jeffries.[59] Around the country, there were efforts to stop the showing of the film for fear of white rioting. In Minneapolis, County Attorney A.J. Smith banned the film. "The spectacle of a Negro beating down a white man is disgusting and can appeal only to the lowest intelligence," he said.[60] In Red Wing, however, a town with few African-American residents, the Family presented the film, said to be "genuine," without opposition or incident.[61]

Locally and nationally the Mexican Revolution presented an opportunity to bring real "action" to the screen within days of an incident.[62] With its Mexican revolt news, regular offering of Pathes' Weekly Events, and even a showing of an amateur film of a Chicago, Milwaukee, and St. Paul train wreck a few miles east of Red Wing, the Family became the town's newsreel leader.[63] Newsreels, especially of war "action," soon became popular at the Davenport as well and were one aspect of competition at which the Auditorium lagged.[64] Lacking projection equipment, the Auditorium relied on visits from Lyman Howe whose "action" was the likes of *Our Navy*, a humdrum, travelogue-like parade of naval firepower.[65]

What with films, including the "highbrow" variety, newsreels, vaudeville, and the Auditorium's stage productions, a theatrical war for patrons existed between the Family, Davenport, Auditorium, and Gem. Years later, a Red Wing "theater man" recalled how the theaters "bucked" one another. At one time, George W. Johnson said, "ten vaudeville acts and a complete showing of motion picture features were offered for the ten-cent admission price."[66]

Throughout the fall of 1910, the Davenport and Family battled for vaudeville patrons with a procession of outlandish acts. The Davenport offered Mr. and Mrs. Ruthe in their "Spectacular Novelty Act,"[67] the "Funny Dutchman and His Frau," "Swede" Rolf (stories and dialect), and Dolline Cole (a female "baritone" who performed "coon singing"). Across the street, the Family headlined Sam Carlton, the "funny Hebrew Comedian," and a ventriloquist, "The

Celluloid

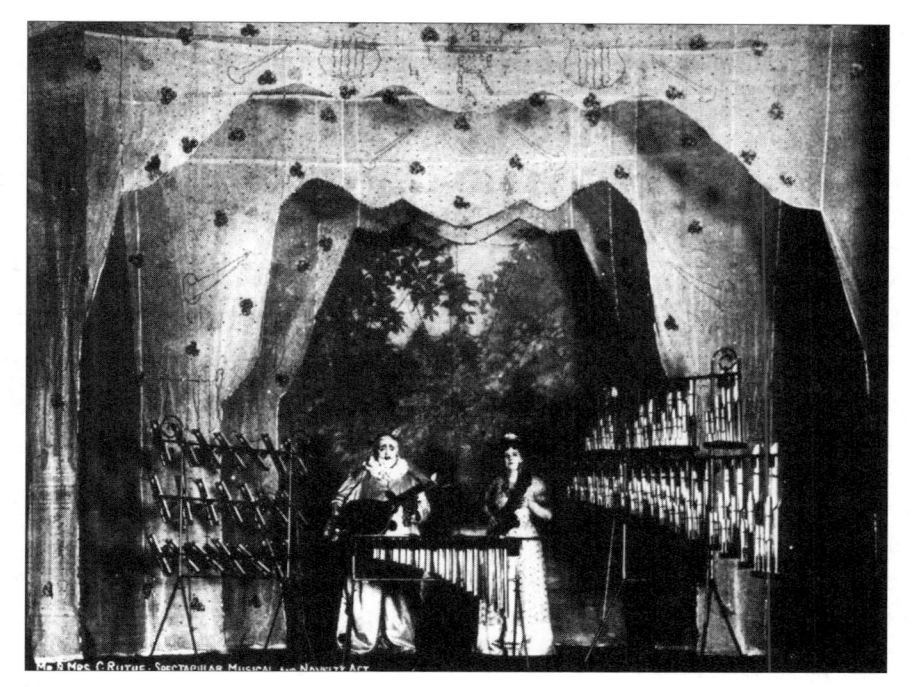

Vaudevillians Mr. and Mrs. Ruthe, who performed their "Spectacular Novelty Act" at the Davenport. (Photo: *Red Wing Daily Republican*. Courtesy the *Red Wing Republican Eagle*)

Great Wilber" and his mechanical doll, Ethel, in a program of "exceptional merit."[68] All of this was combined with motion pictures. At the Family, the comedy team of Santora and Marlow appeared with a "feature" film, Jim Bridger's *Indian Bride*.

For a time the Auditorium wafted above the battle. As its 1910-1911 season began its staple programming—touring companies, lectures, stock companies, and an occasional "highbrow" offering—continued. There were notable successes. The musical comedies *The Girl of My Dreams*, and *Bright Eyes* were heavily promoted and sell-outs.[69] But the overall quality of the touring companies deteriorated. Local newspapers tried to stay upbeat but couldn't always do it. *Seven Days* drew only a fair-sized audience and a worse review:

47

To mistake vulgarity and coarseness for humor may prove popular in New York and the other big cities of the Union, but in a town like Red Wing where people live the real human, joyous healthy life, the difference is easily discerned.[70]

"Highbrow" programs, including the Czerewonky String Quartet[71] and two appearances by Emil Oberhoffer and the Minneapolis Symphony Orchestra were artistic, but not financial triumphs. With the separateness of "high" from "low" brow well advanced, Oberhoffer's all-classical selections included works from Lizst, Wagner, Weber, Massenet, Goldmark, and Grieg.[72] The city's elite was so enthusiastic that *Daily Republican* editor Jens Grondahl wrote "Music," a poem honoring the event. It included the forgettable:

> It soothes like a drowsy confection
> It thrills like ambition new born,
> It fades, as the day into twilight,
> This magic of string and of horn.[73]

The *Daily Republican*'s review, however, noted that although the audience was "good-sized," still "it is to be regretted that every seat . . . was not taken."[74]

To rescue an unsuccessful season, the Auditorium turned, in early 1911, to vaudeville. Although plays and concerts continued, the Auditorium now also offered, at "popular" prices, wrestling between "Matsudai, the Jap" and "Young Moldoon," Professor Norwood and Eva performing hypnotism and mental telepathy, and Richard and Pringle, Georgia minstrels who appeared with Clarence Powell, the "Dean of Ethiopian Comedians."[75]

Quite suddenly, the theater "war" subsided. In May 1911, the Gem closed when Sam Roberg's lease expired and H.L. Olson rented his property to the F.W. Woolworth Company.[76] That same month, the city council, which board member Charles Betcher had urged to stop issuing vaudeville and movie licenses because the Auditorium was "entitled to some protection along this line,"[77] adopted a new licensing ordinance. The new law prohibited music in saloons and "with little discussion," increased the license fee for motion picture houses offering vaudeville from just thirty-five dollars to $200.[78] The fee did not apply to the exempt Auditorium.[79]

Robert Davenport and John Walsh correctly believed that the city hoped to put them out of business. Davenport complained to the city council to no avail.[80] Neither, however, sought legal remedy. That may have been because the exorbitant fee gave them an opportunity to quit vaudeville. For small cities, the cost of paying performers and their travel and lodging expenses was burdensome. Besides, audiences gladly paid the same admission fee for movies alone. Consequently, on June 1, 1911, when the new license fee went into effect, vaudeville, for a time, ended at the Family and Davenport.

The hiked fee arrived too late, however, to rescue the Auditorium from its first financial crisis. On August 4, 1911, the board told the city council that after taking in $4,338 in admissions, there was a deficit of $759 and that there was no money to pay outstanding bills.[81] Board Chair Charles Sheldon[82] blamed the quality of the shows, telling the city council "of late years the attractions have been growing less in quality and patronage has decreased."[83] Wilbur Scott, however, was hopeful. There was no doubt, he said, "but that the combination vaudeville and picture houses have been the means of cutting down our receipts, but as the council has placed a license on vaudeville that will in all probability put an

Auditorium posterboards (c. 1906). The Auditorium posted its own bills and received income by posting them for others. As can be seen in the picture, almost any surface was fair game for these advertisements. (Courtesy of the Goodhue County Historical Society)

effective damper on this class of amusement, I feel certain that the outlook for the coming season is fairly bright."[84] Scott also reported that the Auditorium's sideline billboard and bill posting business that grew from Taber's advertising resulted in a profit of $476.[85] Without it, the deficit would have been over $1,300.

To right finances, Scott proposed increasing the billboard business and, "At the suggestion of some of the board members I have been looking over conditions and machines with a view of running pictures in the auditorium this coming season and would recommend that the board take up this proposition."[86] A second set of suggestions proposed reducing expenses. Board president Sheldon spoke of combining the jobs of city assessor and Auditorium manager. Money could also be saved, he said, although he recommended against it, by reducing insurance coverage on the building, then estimated to be worth $78,000, to less

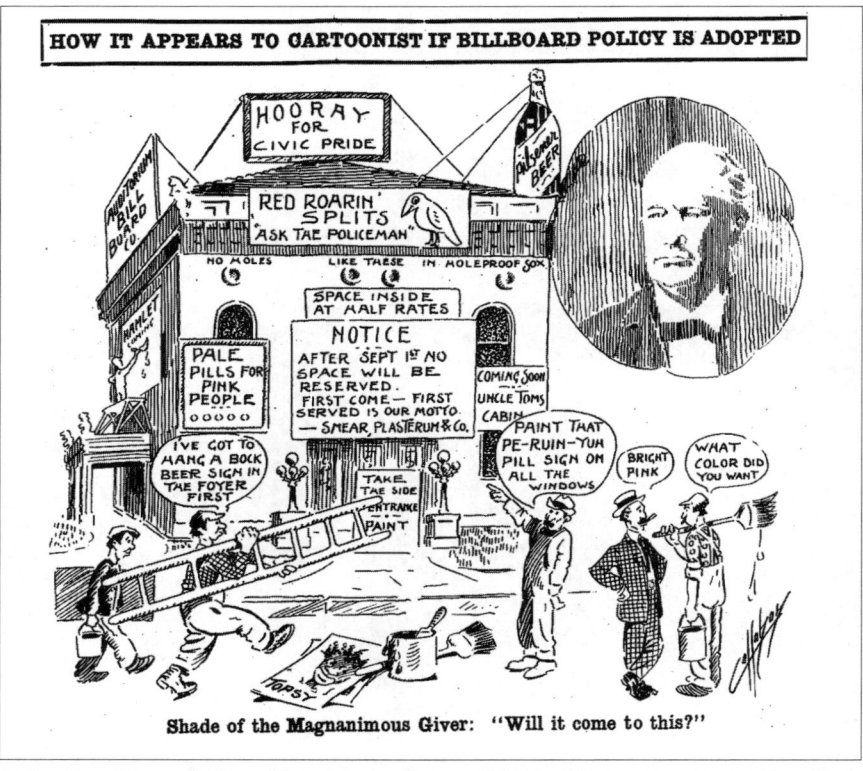

Daily Republican "Billboard" political cartoon (1911). (Photo: the *Red Wing Daily Republican*. Courtesy of the *Red Wing Republican Eagle*)

than the already inadequate $40,000 policy then carried.[87] Finally, Sheldon reminded the council that the city was obligated to provide janitorial service if the Auditorium board couldn't.[88]

The council took no action and instead scheduled a joint council-board meeting for August 15. The following day, however, the *Daily Republican* editorially attacked the billboard business. Civic spirit, Jens Grondahl wrote, ". . . cannot in any way be reconciled with the recommendation of the Auditorium board." Pointing out that many eastern cities banned billboards as eyesores and invoking progressive "city beautiful" concepts, Grondahl concluded that billboards were a "backward step" and the proposal to add more of them "sacrilegious, a contradiction to everything for which the Auditorium stands." If billboards were necessary to save the Auditorium, Grondahl concluded, ". . . better let the Auditorium die than to lower the tastes and standards of the community."[89] Although Grondahl favored maintaining high standards, he failed to reconcile his ideals with the popularity of the likes of "Matsudai the Jap."

When the board and city council met together, board Chairman Charles Sheldon, a partner with John Rich in the Red Wing Sewer Pipe Company, and not a relative of T.B. Sheldon, explained that the board had no choice but to ask the council for help. In Sheldon's words, they were "simply up against it."[90] Unfortunately, the meeting was characterized by "petty hostilities,"[91] bickering, and politics. One alderman, Fred Seebach, masterfully sidestepped the responsibilities of both the board and council. "I firmly believe," he said, "that the entire trouble lies with management. A man of theatrical experience is necessary. Mr. Scott is a gentleman and a fine fellow, but I prefer engaging the services of an experienced man and pay him good money for his work."[92] It was a cheap shot.

Mayor A.P. Pierce blamed everyone but himself. He castigated the board for setting prices that shut the "common man . . . out of the playhouse . . ."[93] and accused wealthy locals of abandoning the Auditorium for the Twin Cities.[94] He faulted the terms of the Sheldon gift. Because arrangements were hurried, Pierce said, the council didn't understand the implications. Finally, Pierce complained that the council should have imposed restrictions on vaudeville and the movies earlier. "The moving picture business has grown and the council has let these theaters go on to the detriment of the Auditorium,"[95] the mayor charged.

Sheldon's Gift

Finger pointing didn't pay the Auditorium's accumulating bills. Although there was general agreement that more billboards, "paste and paper" as the mayor called it, were part of the answer, motions to have the city pay for a janitor and to combine the city assessor and theater manager positions went nowhere. The board, but not all aldermen, opposed reducing the building's insurance coverage. When it came to who would cover the unpaid bills, City Attorney Charles Hall said it was the city's responsibility. The council majority, however, stared at their shoes while referring the matter to the finance committee.[96]

As the council and board bickered, they sideswiped but didn't confront an important issue. In one year, Mayor Pierce said, the Auditorium's entire profit resulted from a Minneapolis Apollo Club choral concert "at which time all expenses were paid by individuals and the proceeds turned over to the house."[97] Wilbur Scott chimed in that had it not been for program advertising the Auditorium would have operated in the red every year of its existence. In the beginning, he said, merchants were happy to purchase advertisements, a form of coerced philanthropy. But as attendance fell to the point where, as board member Hiram Howe said, attendance at some of the best shows would not form "a cor-

T.B. Sheldon Memorial Auditorium (c. 1910). (Courtesy the Minnesota Historical Society)

poral's guard,"[98] ads sold poorly. In Taber's final year, Scott claimed, money was lost on programs.[99] The inescapable fact, even as local leaders trumpeted confidence, was that the Auditorium from its first day forward depended on subsidy. Although Sheldon's trustees contemplated the need, they failed to provide a cash reserve and instead saddled a credulous city council with ultimate responsibility.

In the absence of advertising revenues, two other possible subsidy sources existed. One was taxpayer support. But the mayor and city council balked, despite the requirements of the gift deed, because that would necessitate everyman subsidies for entertainments the wealthy enjoyed disproportionately and because the city council was relentlessly parsimonious. Private philanthropy was an alternative. Sheldon gave $80,000. The 1911 shortfall was a paltry $500. Yet no one stepped forward as some or someone had subsidized the Apollo Club. If the city's elite sat on its hands and the city council cringed, the board and Wilbur Scott would have to cobble together another solution. To be sure, raising ticket prices, which would exclude a larger number of potential patrons and reduce attendance further, wasn't the answer.

Following the inconclusive meeting, *Daily Republican* editor Jens Grondahl groped for a solution. Billboard advertising, cheapened entertainments or entering the motion picture business, were wrongheaded. The Auditorium, Grondahl wrote, could not "possibly benefit by moving picture entertainments at five and ten cents."[100] To him, neither poor management nor motion pictures were the problem. Even if motion picture theaters were a threat, Grondahl thought that it would be difficult to eliminate them because they were lawful and their owners had invested in their businesses. Just as important, he wrote, people should be allowed to see the five- and ten-cent shows provided they are "clean and edifying, because such entertainments have become a part of the life of the middle and unmoneyed classes."[101] To Grondahl, the problem was vaudeville and, agreeing with Mayor Pierce, the council blundered when it failed to prohibit it. Though it was late in coming, the punitive license fee, he hoped, would drive it out. In writing this, Grondahl, a man who praised unfettered competition, sidestepped an uncomfortable dilemma.[102] Also absent was any suggestion of philanthropy from the "moneyed" class. Indeed, philanthropy remained an "elephant"[103] casting a fat shadow for decades.

The city's other newspaper, the *Daily Eagle*, was more specific but tripped over its logic. Editor Nels P. Olson agreed that poor management wasn't to blame. He also claimed, "The plain fact is that the city has no business in the amusement field. The city should get out of it as quickly as possible by leasing the house . . . to private parties who make a specialty of that line of business." A private lease, Olson concluded, was "the only practical way and will have to be adopted in the end."[104] It was not management but it was. Olson proved to be prescient but wrong that a lease would prove salutary.

In the end, the city council recommended, weakly, that the board borrow to cover its deficit.[105] If the Auditorium's finances did not improve in six months, the council agreed, it would reconsider a $500 annual subsidy.[106] With that "guarantee"[107] in hand, the board received a loan from the Goodhue County National Bank[108] and hoped for a successful upcoming season.

Following the dust up, the board and Scott ignored Grondahl's objection to "cheapened" entertainments. In the fall of 1911, Scott booked a comic drama, *At Sunrise*, with an admission scale from just twenty-five to fifty-cents[109] and considerable vaudeville.[110] When the vaudeville was passable, the newspapers wrote kind reviews. *The Miles Theatre Road Show*, for example, was entirely acceptable with the exception of some "stale jokes by a darkey performer."[111] Occasionally a newspaper pitted artistic sensibility against its propensity to plug the Auditorium. When Mock Sad Alli's repertoire and vaudeville troupe played, the *Daily Republican*'s review was brutal. Noting that fewer than 200 people attended opening night, the paper charged that dreadful attendance was expected because of the many repeat appearances of these "cheap actors." If they were any good, the paper said, they "wouldn't go barn storming all their lives at ten, twenty, and thirty cents." The paper even panned the troupe's "monotonous" dog act. Still, boosterism triumphed. Having blasted Alli's troupe, the paper nonetheless urged citizens to show "loyalty by turning out tonight and filling the house even if the entertainment is mediocre and a little stale, because the Auditorium needs and deserves support."[112]

The Auditorium's theatrical season that fall opened with a return of *In Old Kentucky*, a popular play with "Rollicking Fun" and "Inimitable Pickaninnies."[113] It was also long of tooth. When advance man Norman Peel visited Red Wing to sing the show's praises, he had already spent nine seasons with a company that presented a single play.[114] Soon after, *The Three Twins* arrived for a repeat performance. The audiences for both plays were "good sized" but smaller than at their first appearances.[115] Meanwhile, motion picture business was brisk.[116] In early September, on a single Thursday evening, 2,000 patrons, one in four citizens, attended the Family and Davenport theaters where a Mutt and Jeff comedy and automobile racing films were all the rage.[117]

The Auditorium's vaudeville monopoly was short-lived. Although profit was increasingly in the movies, the Auditorium's competitors apparently believed that offering motion pictures alone was risky.[118] When his license came up for renewal, Robert Davenport complained that the annual vaudeville fee in Winona was just ten dollars while in LaCrosse there was no fee at all. As a result, Davenport wrested from the council a modest reduction to $150 for a combined motion picture and vaudeville license and he took it.[119] Vaudeville soon began again at the Davenport. Meanwhile, as movies continued their evolution toward feature films, theaters such as the Davenport made inroads on the "high class" terrain of "legitimate" theaters by showing such multi-reel films as *Hamlet*.[120] In a turnabout, ten-cent houses now wooed audiences with "highbrow" culture.

At the same time, the Auditorium made good on Scott's plan to enter the motion picture business. The battle was re-engaged. The Auditorium began regular picture shows, 4,000 feet, four reels, of the "latest and best pictures," shown every night except Sunday. *Hamlet* be damned. The first program included Bison Pictures' standout *A Race for a Bride*, in which "two cowpunchers are in love with a girl," there's a horse race, and "Jack wins the race and a bride." An equally stunning second reel, *His New Dress Shirt*, was a "pretty little comedy showing the troubles of a young married woman who attempts to launder a shirt to please her husband. She fails, but is forgiven."[121] The Auditorium's condemnation of cheap entertainment while turning to it drew a screed from Davenport. "If that is considered high-classed and refined," Davenport exclaimed, "goodness help the rest! I will have to get for our kind the cheap ones."[122]

By December 1911, all three theaters combined films with vaudeville and variety acts. When the Family offered an eight-piece orchestra along with its picture show,[123] the Davenport presented "Beautiful Aimee Wonderful," a dancer,[124] and the Auditorium, alongside its picture show advertised "The Sensational Leoras" a trapeze and contortionist troupe.[125] Through that winter and into the

SHELDON'S GIFT

spring of 1912 it continued. When the Davenport presented "Happy Hooligan and his Funny Comedy Tight Wire Stunts," the Family countered with "Hindoo Magic" featuring Princess Zazzar. At the Auditorium, films, variety acts, and stock companies were interrupted occasionally by a New York touring show such as *Green Stockings*. Although top seats were two dollars, the balcony was now just a quarter.[126]

As theaters skirmished, Auditorium finances failed to improve.[127] In May, the council's finance committee reported that the Auditorium had not made money since the return of vaudeville and the start-up of regular picture shows. The council then, reluctantly, approved a $500 annual allocation—but not specifically for a janitor as called for in the 1904 agreement—for fear of setting a precedent.[128] In May and June the council continued to wrestle with theater problems. Although some councilmen pushed for an even higher vaudeville fee of $300, in the end fees for the Family and Davenport, despite yelps from Robert Davenport, remained at $200 while the Auditorium paid nothing. At the same time, in response to complaints from Alderman C.E. Friedrich that picture shows spurred children on a "downward course" the council attempted unsuccessfully to regulate Sunday movies and created a short-lived board of censorship comprised of the mayor, chief of police, and the council's licensing committee.[129]

With high costs, three-way competition, and a hostile city council, the Davenport and Family fared no better than the Auditorium. That led to change. In the midst of the vaudeville war, Jack Walsh opened a new theater in Faribault, the Empress, and sold the Family to Frank Tyrell of St. Paul.[130] By the end of the summer of 1912, Robert Davenport, who had waged pitched battle with the Auditorium, sold his theater (but not his building) to F.E. Daigneau, who also owned movie houses in Austin and Mankato.[131] Daigneau promptly renamed the theater the Pastime. Name changes and management shuffles changed nothing. Three competitors offered near-identical entertainments in a place that Mayor Pierce called a "poor theater town." Red Wing remained gripped in ruinous theatrical warfare.

Celluloid

Notes

[1] Summer traveling shows in this period began to mention projected films in their advertisements. See also Lucile M. Kane and John A. Dougherty, "Movie Debut: Films in the Twin Cities, 1894-1909," *Minnesota History* 54 (winter, 1995): 344-45, 357. In 1899 merchant sponsors of a Red Wing street fair projected films on a building wall free to the public. See "The Street Fair Oct 3, 4, and 5," *Red Wing Republican* (Weekly), August 30, 1899.

[2] Motion picture equipment was installed at Rochester's Grand Opera House, a theater that also presented repertoire and variety entertainment, in 1900. See Harriet Hodgson, *Rochester: City of the Prairie* (Northridge, California: Windsor Publications Inc, 1989), 89. Also see Lucile M. Kane and John A. Dougherty, "Movie Debut: Films in the Twin Cities, 1894-1909," *Minnesota History* 54 (Winter, 1995): 350.

[3] Within a short time that situation reversed and live performance became filler for movies.

[4] "Vaudeville House Opened to Public," *Red Wing Daily Republican*, September 4, 1906. The program changed every three days. There were three performances daily: Matinee, 7:45, and 9:15.

[5] "Most Stubborn Fire for Years," *Red Wing Daily Republican*, November 27, 1906.

[6] Charles Musser with Carol Nelson, *High Class Moving Pictures: Lyman H. Howe and the Forgotten Era of Traveling Exhibition, 1880-1920* (Princeton: Princeton University Press, 1991), passim. Howe appeared at the Auditorium as late as the early 1920s.

[7] The name derived from the Greek "odeon," a building where musical performances took place. Thus, "nickelodeon" was literally an "odeon" that charged a nickel.

[8] Lucile M. Kane and John A. Dougherty, "Movie Debut: Films in the Twin Cities, 1894-1909," *Minnesota History* 54 (Winter, 1995): 350.

[9] Kirk J. Besse, *Show Houses: Twin Cities Style* (Minneapolis: Victoria Publications, 1997), I, passim.

[10] David Q. Bowers, *Nickelodeon Theaters and Their Music* (Vestal, New York: Vestal Press, Ltd., 1986), 43. In 1909 there were at least fifteen in the Twin Cities. See Lucile M. Kane and John A. Dougherty, "Movie Debut: Films in the Twin Cities, 1894-1909," Minnesota History 54 (Winter, 1995): 350.

[11] David Q. Bowers, *Nickelodeon Theaters and Their Music* (Vestal, New York: Vestal Press, Ltd., 1986), 116.

[12] Advertisement, *Red Wing Daily Republican*, July 3, 1907.

[13] David Q. Bowers, *Nickelodeon Theaters and Their Music* (Vestal, New York: Vestal Press, Ltd., 1986), 116. A theater's square footage divided by six determined roughly the number of seats possible. In the case of the White Vaudette, a thirty-foot frontage by a fifty-foot depth yielded 1,500 square feet and 250 seats.

[14] "Report of the City Clerk, Red Wing, Minnesota, May 1, 1907-April 30, 1908," *Red Wing Daily Republican*, August 21, 1908.

[15] "Additional Locals," *Red Wing Daily Republican*, July 5, 1907.

[16] David Q. Bowers, *Nickelodeon Theaters and Their Music* (Vestal, New York: Vestal Press, Ltd., 1986), 45, 101.

[17] Advertisement, *Red Wing Daily Republican*, July 5, 1907.

[18] Advertisement, *Red Wing Daily Republican*, January 1, 1908.

[19] David Q. Bowers, *Nickelodeon Theaters and Their Music* (Vestal, New York: Vestal Press, Ltd., 1986), 6.

[20] Lucile M. Kane and John A. Dougherty, "Movie Debut: Films in the Twin Cities, 1894-1909," *Minnesota History* 54 (Winter, 1995): 355.

[21] David Q. Bowers, *Nickelodeon Theaters and Their Music* (Vestal, New York: Vestal Press, Ltd., 1986), 101.

[22] Bessie Abott is sometimes identified as Bessie Abbott. Her publicity photos, however, identify her as "Abott." See http://thestory.org/photo-galleries/pickens-hall/bessie-abbott.jpg.

[23] "Marvels of the Age at White Vaudette," *Red Wing Daily Republican*, October 31, 1907.

[24] David Q. Bowers, *Nickelodeon Theaters and Their Music* (Vestal, New York: Vestal Press, Ltd., 1986), 45.

[25] Advertisement, *Red Wing Daily Republican*, January 10, 1908.

[26] "Red Wing Progress," *Red Wing Daily Republican*, January 18, 1909.

[27] David Q. Bowers, *Nickelodeon Theaters and Their Music* (Vestal, New York: Vestal Press, Ltd., 1986), 51.

[28] Advertisement, *Red Wing Daily Republican*, August 21, 1908. Because Minnesota banned prize fighting in 1892, fight films were popular. See Lucile M. Kane and John A. Dougherty, "Movie Debut: Films in the Twin Cities, 1894-1909," *Minnesota History* 54 (Winter 1995): 354.

[29] Minutes, Red Wing City Council, June 5, 1908.

[30] Franklyn Curtiss-Wedge, *History of Goodhue County Minnesota* (Chicago: H.C. Cooper, Jr., and Company, 1909), 601.

[31] David Q. Bowers, *Nickelodeon Theaters and Their Music* (Vestal, New York: Vestal Press, Ltd., 1986), 45.

[32] Ibid.

[33] Ibid., 18.

[34] Minutes, Red Wing City Council, June 5, 1908.

[35] Advertisement, *Red Wing Daily Republican*, July 3, 1908.

[36] Advertisement, *Red Wing Daily Republican*, August 20, 1908.

[37] "Red Wing Idea Averts Panic," *Red Wing Daily Republican*, February 26, 1909.

[38] "Auditorium Notes," *Red Wing Daily Republican*, July 12, 1907. At first, the film segments were hand-colored. Subsequently a faster, stenciling system was developed. As a result,". . . by 1909 it was possible to see 'sound movies in color,' but the 'sound' was apt to be unsynchronizedand the color was anything but a subtle blend of tonal shadings." David Q. Bowers, *Nickelodeon Theaters and Their Music* (Vestal, New York: Vestal Press, Ltd., 1986), 91.

[39] Ralph G. Taber, "Letter to the Editor," *Red Wing Daily Republican*, July 13, 1907.

Celluloid

[40]"Moving Pictures were Pleasing," *Red Wing Daily Republican*, July 18, 1907.

[41]"Auditorium Notes," *Red Wing Daily Republican*, August 13, 1908.

[42]"Auditorium Notes," *Red Wing Daily Republican*, August 15, 1908.

[43]There are many histories of film sound. A good place to begin is J. Douglas Gomery. "The Coming of the Talkies: Invention, Innovation, and Diffusion," in Tino Balio (ed.), *The American Film Industry* (Madison: University of Wisconsin Press, 1976), 193-211; Also see J. Douglas Gomery, *The Coming of Sound: A History* (New York: Routledge, 2005)

[44]"Auditorium Notes," *Red Wing Daily Republican*, August 20, 1908.

[45]For a description of Rochester's Metropolitan Theater (1902) see Harriet Hodgson, *Rochester: City of the Prairie* (Northridge, California: Windsor Publications Inc, 1989), 89. Like the Auditorium, the Metropolitan became primarily a movie house. It was razed in 1936.

[46]"Auditorium Notes," *Red Wing Daily Republican*, August 20, 1908.

[47]Advertisement, *Red Wing Daily Republican*, July 2, 1908.

[48]Advertisement, *Red Wing Daily Republican*, August 15, 1908. These admonitions demonstrated the same objections that the elite had to disrepectful lower-class behaviors at "highbrow" entertainments.

[49]"Moving Picture Men to Meet," *Red Wing Daily Republican*, January 11. 1909.

[50]That "highbrow" stories were adapted to the movies early on demonstrates public familiarity with that culture. At the same time, the burgeoning demand for films meant that producers sought out any subjects that could readily be adapted to film, "highbrow" or "low."

[51]Advertisement, *Red Wing Daily Republican*, August 20, 1908.

[52]"Auditorium Board Report," *Red Wing Daily Republican*, August 6, 1910.

[53]Advertisement, *Red Wing Daily Republican*, October 21, 1909.

[54]"Auditorium Board Report," *Red Wing Daily Republican*, August 6, 1910.

[55]Advertisement, *Red Wing Daily Republican*, November 5, 1910.

[56]Advertisement, *Red Wing Daily Republican*, December 2, 1910.

[57]Advertisement, *Red Wing Daily Republican*, November 22, 1910. The building is now identified as the *Daily Eagle* due to façade work done by N.P. Olson after 1916.

[58]George W. Johnson quoted in "Advancement of the Movies Marvelous," *Red Wing Daily Eagle*, November 2, 1936.

[59]See Geoffrey C. Ward, *Unforgivable Blackness: The Rise and Fall of Jack Johnson* (New York, Random House, 2004) and Ken Burns' PBS documentary (Florentine Films, 2005) by the same title.

[60]"Stop Views of Reno Fight," *Red Wing Daily Republican*, July 7, 1910.

[61]Advertisement, *Red Wing Daily Republican*, November 9, 1910. Because The *New York Herald* held rights to the film, some entrepreneurs "re-staged" the fight and sold the film as original. David Q. Bowers, *Nickelodeon Theaters and Their Music* (Vestal, New York: Vestal Press, Ltd., 1986), page 101 says that most audiences, "never knew the difference." The 1900 census identified fourteen "colored." See *Twelfth Census of the*

SHELDON'S GIFT

United States, Taken in the Year 1900, Vol. I (Washington, U.S. Census Office, 1901).

[62] Advertisement, *Red Wing Daily Republican*, May 23, 1911.

[63] Advertisement, *Red Wing Daily Republican*, May 19, 1911.

[64] In 1912 the Davenport offered, on one program, three reels of the Chinese Revolution. See Advertisement, *Red Wing Daily Republican*, July 13, 1912.

[65] Advertisement, *Red Wing Daily Republican*, March 4, 1912.

[66] George W. Johnson, proprietor of the Family and then the Metro arrived in Red Wing in 1915. He was, however, well aware of the vaudeville "war" in 1911-1912. See "Four Reel Film Feature Sensation 20 Years Ago," *Red Wing Daily Eagle*, November 2, 1936.

[67] Advertisement, *Red Wing Daily Republican*, May 3, 1911.

[68] Advertisement, *Red Wing Daily Republican*, May 20, 1911.

[69] "The Girl of My Dreams," *Red Wing Daily Republican*, October 11, 1910; "Bright Eyes was Pleasing," *Red Wing Daily Republican*, January 17, 1911.

[70] "Seven Days at Auditorium," *Red Wing Daily Republican*, November 19, 1910.

[71] "An Evening of Great Artists," *Red Wing Daily Republican*, February 11, 1911.

[72] "Symphony Orchestra," *Red Wing Daily Republican*, December 10, 1910.

[73] Jens K. Grondahl, "Music," *Red Wing Daily Republican*, December 13, 1910.

[74] "An Evening of Rare Delight," *Red Wing Daily Republican*, December 13, 1910.

[75] Advertisement, *Red Wing Daily Republican*, May 30, 1911.

[76] "Local News," *Red Wing Daily Republican*, May 5, 1911; The Woolworth store opened July 11, 1911.

[77] Minutes, Red Wing City Council, April 1, 1910.

[78] Editorial, *Red Wing Daily Republican*, August 17, 1911; "License Fees Advanced," *Red Wing Daily Republican*, May 29, 1911. By comparison, liquor licenses (20) were $500. This fee wasn't increased.

[79] "Three New Board Members," *Red Wing Daily Republican*, November 15, 1910.

[80] Minutes, Red Wing City Council, June 2, 1911; "Seek Light on Ordinances," *Red Wing Daily Republican*, June 11, 1911.

[81] "Auditorium Is Facing Deficit" *Red Wing Daily Republican*, August 5, 1911.

[82] Charles Sheldon was unrelated to T.B. Sheldon.

[83] "Asks Advice of City Council," *Red Wing Daily Republican*, August 5, 1911.

[84] "Auditorium Is Facing Deficit," *Red Wing Daily Republican*, August 5, 1911.

[85] Ibid.

[86] Ibid.

[87] "Picture Shows Cause of Play House Deficits," *Red Wing Daily Republican*, August 16, 1911.

[88] "Asks Advice of City Council," *Red Wing Daily Republican*, August 5, 1911.

[89] "Do Not Kill Civic Spirit," *Red Wing Daily Republican*, August 5, 1911.

[90] "Picture Shows Cause of Play House Deficit," *Red Wing Daily Republican*, August 16, 1911.

[91] Editorial, *Red Wing Daily Republican*, August 17, 1911

Celluloid

[92] "Picture Shows Cause of Play House Deficit," *Red Wing Daily Republican*, August 16, 1911.
[93] Ibid.
[94] "Council Tackles City's Elephant," *Red Wing Daily Eagle*, August 16, 1911.
[95] "Picture Shows Cause of Play House Deficit," *Red Wing Daily Republican*, August 16, 1911.
[96] Ibid.
[97] "Council Tackles City's Elephant," *Red Wing Daily Eagle*, August 16, 1911.
[98] Ibid.
[99] "Picture Shows Cause of Play House Deficit," *Red Wing Daily Republican*, August 16, 1911.
[100] Ibid.
[101] Editorial, *Red Wing Daily Republican*, August 17, 1911.
[102] Ibid.
[103] During the period from about 1911 to 1918 the Auditorium was frequently referred to by N.P. Olson as an "elephant."
[104] Editorial, "The Auditorium Problem," *The Red Wing Daily Eagle*, August 16, 1911.
[105] "Give Auditorium Financial Support," *Red Wing Daily Republican*, August 30, 1911.
[106] "Order Arrest of Trainmen," *Red Wing Daily Republican*, September 2, 1911.
[107] "$500 Janitor Hire," *Red Wing Daily Eagle*, August 31, 1911.
[108] "Auditorium Has Prosperous Year," *Red Wing Daily Republican*, February 6, 1915.
[109] Advertisement, *Red Wing Daily Republican*, September 11, 1911.
[110] Advertisement, *Red Wing Daily Republican*, September 23, 1911.
[111] "Local News," *Red Wing Daily Republican*, September 26, 1911.
[112] "Small Crowd at Mediocre Show," *Red Wing Daily Republican*, September 13, 1911.
[113] Advertisement, *Red Wing Daily Republican*, August 18, 1911.
[114] "Management Not Blamed for Deficit," *Red Wing Daily Eagle*, August 18, 1911.
[115] "Three Twins at Auditorium," *Red Wing Daily Republican*, October 14, 1911.
[116] "Small Crowd at Mediocre Show," *Red Wing Daily Republican*, September 13, 1911. There was more to this story. The previous year the *Daily Republican* criticized the Mock Sad Alli troupe for presenting a "suggestive" song. In response, in 1911 Mock Sad Alli had not permitted the Auditorium to advertise his show in the *Daily Republican*. This disturbed the *Daily Republican* greatly and led the newspaper to suggest that failure to advertise in their newspaper was an additional cause of the small attendance at this show. See "Repertoire Failure Closes Engagement," *Red Wing Daily Republican*, September 14, 1911.
[117] "Big Crowds See Picture Shows," *Red Wing Daily Republican*, September 1, 1911.
[118] "Do Away with Saloon Lunch," *Red Wing Daily Republican*, November 11, 1911. At about the same time the city's twenty saloon owners asked the city to ban free saloon lunches. The saloon owners argued that the lunches were expensive for the owners—one saying he spent over $1,000 a year on them compared to $500 for a liquor license. Also, banning them would promote family life and get the men home

earlier. When aldermen said the matter was up to bar owners they were told that self-regulation was tried but failed miserably.

[119]"Council Lowers Vaudeville Fee," *Red Wing Daily Republican*, November 16, 1911.

[120]Advertisement, *Red Wing Daily Republican*, September 6, 1911.

[121]Advertisement, *Red Wing Daily Republican*, November 25, 1911.

[122]Advertisement, *Red Wing Daily Republican*, November 13, 1911.

[123]"Local News," *Red Wing Daily Republican*, November 25, 1911.

[124]Advertisement, *Red Wing Daily Republican*, December 4, 1911.

[125]Advertisement, *Red Wing Daily Republican*, December 5, 1911.

[126]Advertisement, *Red Wing Daily Republican*, April 6, 1912.

[127]"Aldermen Don War Paint at Meeting of Council," *Red Wing Daily Republican*, March 2, 1912.

[128]Minutes, Red Wing City Council, May 3, 1912. Also see "City to Assist Auditorium," *Red Wing Republican* (Weekly), May 8, 1912.

[129]"Claims Picture Show Immoral," *Red Wing Republican* (Weekly), May 29, 1912; "City May Start Street Paving," *Red Wing Republican* (Weekly), June 19, 1912; The issue of Sunday movie showings was settled in favor of film exhibitors two years previously by the Minnesota Supreme Court in *State v. Chamberlain* (1910). See "Picture Shows Open on Sunday," *Red Wing Daily Republican*, August 29, 1910.

[130]"Local News," *Red Wing Daily Republican*, May 19, 1911; "New Manager of Theater," *Red Wing Daily Republican*, October 30, 1911.

[131]"Local News," *Red Wing Daily Republican*, August 28, 1911.

Chapter Four

The Set-Up

"The movie game has not been rosy what with three theaters in town."
~*Red Wing Daily Eagle* (May 1916)

"Auditorium Board Makes New Deal: Rejects Experienced Man at $75, Hires Beginner at $100." ~*Red Wing Daily Eagle* (May 1916)

"Under the new arrangement I believe the moving picture problem in Red Wing will be solved." ~George W. Johnson (February 1919)

"... A band of men who constituted its board were free to go ahead and plan some system whereby the playhouse might be lifted from the red bath into which it had become immersed and give it a change of ink." ~Elmer W. Olson (August 1936)

With the Auditorium planted squarely in the motion picture business by 1912 and with the three competitors clinging to vaudeville, competition was keen. Nationwide, and in Red Wing, theaters changed hands at a break neck pace. By early 1915, the Family had been operated by Paul Eichinger, J.B. Schmidt, and C.E. VanDuzee,[1] E.A. Bierman,[2] and Martin Igo, a real estate broker and investor from Rochester. Across the street, the Davenport, now the Pastime, changed hands as well. Within two years, F.E. Diageneau was gone and the Pastime was in the hands of Axel Nielsen, another newcomer. Rapid turnover and consolidation in an industry so new wasn't surprising. Although some proprietors acquired skills and accumulated capital sufficient to allow them to purchase additional theaters, failure was common. Competition was fierce, and despite the advice offered in trade magazines, it was easy to overestimate the audience, stay too current with the films and thus pay too much or especially, to employ too much help.

Changes in the film business nationally made survival for independent theaters in towns like Red Wing even more difficult. Importantly, movie "product" changed dramatically. In the earliest years, theaters typically ran three or four one-reel and occasional multi-reel "feature" programs. By 1913, with the release of *The Squaw Man* (seventy-four minutes), features had arrived. In early 1914, the Pastime showed *David Copperfield* (sixty-seven minutes) and began advertising itself as the "House of Features." What was more, fewer people attended movies for the sake of seeing a picture show. Now they came because of the "photoplay" subject and title and increasingly because of "stars." In 1914, for example, the Auditorium presented a four-reel comedy romance, *An American Citizen*, starring John Barrymore, and in early 1915, the Family heralded John's equally famous sister Ethel in *The Nightingale*.[3] This transition to stars and multi-reel story lines heightened competition as theaters booking the most popular stars attracted the largest audiences.

Change in the nature of films was accompanied by change in the way they were distributed. In the very early days, theaters procured films from traveling salesmen and catalogs. By 1908, however, national film exchanges had opened offices in Minneapolis, which quickly became the hub of Midwest film business. Transactions were straightforward at first. Exchanges purchased films and theater owners rented them on a flat-rate basis.[4] As film popularity grew, new competitors entered the industry as equipment manufacturers, producers, and distributors. This across-the-board competition caused old-line companies, including Edison and Biograph, to attempt to control the industry by setting aside differences and establishing the Motion Picture Patents Company. For exhibitors, the upshot was the imposition of a royalty charge for the use of patented equipment. When it failed to gain an industry hammerlock, the MPPC bought up film distributors nationwide and substituted its own General Film Corporation.[5] In Red Wing, the Family, in advertising the Edison comedy *The Janitor's Flirtation*, announced that it was the "home" of the General Film Corporation.[6] The MPPC, however, faced defiance and legal challenges

The Set-Up

from independent producers and distributors. Already weak and ineffective, it was defeated in the courts as an unreasonable restraint of trade in 1915.

By that time, as distributors added new layers of complexity and control, the days of uncomplicated film rentals ended. Many films no longer leased at a simple flat rate. Instead, better pictures now rented as a percentage of their gross receipts (frequently thirty percent). As a result, "windfall" profits to exhibitors resulting from films that drew a surprisingly large crowd became less likely. More importantly, by 1917 Adolph Zukor's Paramount Pictures had implemented "block" and "blind" booking, strategies soon mimicked by other distributors. Paramount's films were especially desirable for theaters such as the Auditorium that sought to offer only multi-reel features staring Hollywood's biggest names—Mary Pickford, Douglas Fairbanks, and William S. Hart—names "owned" by Paramount. To obtain those desirable features, theaters were required to purchase Paramount's films in "blocks" of a dozen to over a hundred films, most of which were second rate, in order to secure a few top draws. Within each block, the best films rented on a gross percentage basis while lesser films rented at flat rates as low as just fifteen or twenty dollars. What was more, films were often booked "blind," meaning that at the time of booking they were nothing more than a number, a general description such as "comedy," and possibly the name of a star. Theaters were not required to show the latter films, but they were required to pay for them. Besides, distributors awarded and priced film blocks within a market area such as Red Wing based upon the size and prestige of a theater and whatever other factors they chose. For the Auditorium, which sought to present only the finest films, these terms presented a serious financial challenge.[7]

Despite fierce competition and rising business costs, films were attracting a growing base of middle class patrons—people who earlier regarded picture shows, as Jens Grondahl, wrote, as for the "unmoneyed" class. Because of that growth, many entrepreneurs were eager to try the movie game. One was forty-two-year-old George Johnson who had operated family businesses, none of them theaters, in Willmar and Crookston, Minnesota. In early 1915 Johnson borrowed $1,600, enough to purchase the 290-seat Family Theater, but not the building, from Martin Igo. Promising that his pictures would be "first class all the way," Johnson, his wife, Etta, their five children, and George's parents, moved to Red

Wing where the Johnsons lived above the theater. The children, especially the two boys, Theodore, a piano player, and Urban, a trap drummer, became the backbone of the Family's "orchestra." The girls and George's father also worked at the business in order to reduce costs.[8] Still, as Johnson recalled many years later, "It took pretty tight pinching to make a go of it," and, even so, the theater was too small to make a decent profit.[9]

A year later, in 1916, a series of events fundamentally altered the Red Wing moviescape for the next seventeen years and influenced it for twenty more. It began when the Family's building owners decided to sell their property to Nels P. Olson, publisher of the *Red Wing Daily Eagle*. Johnson, having lost his lease, faced relocation or closure in a city that had, by all accounts, at least one too many movie houses. As the *Daily Eagle* put it, "The movie game has not been rosy what with three theaters in town." It was a problem, the paper said, that had "worried a dozen proprietors of the two smaller theaters."[10]

After months of negotiation, Johnson purchased the Pastime, now renamed the Metro, from Axel Nielsen.[11] At the time, Johnson claimed that he had "lined up the World, the Big Four, the Metro, and the Equitable feature films and will also continue the General Service which has been so popular."[12] After closing briefly for redecorating, the Metro re-opened on May 3, 1916, with *My Lady's Slipper*, a Vitagraph feature about the French Revolution.[13]

With Johnson ensconced at the Metro, Nielsen made for the Auditorium where he proposed what Robert Davenport had offered a few years before. In his rejected proposal, Davenport offered to lease the Auditorium and guarantee the board a profit.[14] Nielsen, however, was unwilling to assume any risk, telling the board only that if they hired him as manager for more than the seventy dollars per month paid Scott, he would guarantee a profit of $1,200 a year over and above expenses.[15] Greater profits would be divided between the Auditorium (forty percent) and himself (sixty percent).[16] How Nielsen planned to accomplish this wizardry he didn't say.[17]

Astonishingly, and even though one board member, Hiram Howe, threatened to quit if the arrangement went through, the board accepted Nielsen's offer. Although most board members charged that the Auditorium was an "elephant," Howe urged patience, saying that finances were improving. He pointed out that

THE SET-UP

with the abandonment of vaudeville the outstanding debt was reduced to $2,000. What's more, he said, the Family's closing was a hopeful sign.[18]

Because of Howe's objection and because others feared legal trouble, City Attorney Charles Hall was consulted. The proposed arrangement, Hall said, was repugnant to the trust deed requirement to hold surpluses for the Auditorium's benefit. As for Nielsen, the board could hire him at reasonable compensation if they wished, but profit sharing was contrary to public policy and illegal.[19] The board groused, accepted Hall's opinion, sacked Scott and hired Nielsen. Although there was street talk of circulating a petition to retain Scott, who had seven years experience, nothing came of it. The *Daily Eagle's* headline said it best: "Auditorium Board Makes New Deal: Rejects Experienced Man at $75, Hires Beginner at $100."[20]

Although Nielsen had motion picture experience and the Auditorium increasingly saw itself as a movie house, compared to Scott he was woefully unproven, especially when it came to booking live performances. Somewhat surprisingly, under Nielsen, the Auditorium undertook two of the most ambitious "highbrow" events in its history. In January 1917 it presented the San Carlo Opera Company in Verdi's *Il Trovatore*. Tickets were $2.00, $1.50, and $1.00—a high scale.[21] The following winter the San Carlo returned with Donizetti's *Lucia Di Lammermoor*. Although neither was a sell out, the *Daily Republican* called the latter a "brilliant artistic and musical success." The lead, Miss Elvig Vaccari, the paper glowed, sang with a "bird-like" quality and her "F above high C was reached with a delightful and clear tone."[22]

By the time America entered the Great War in 1917, it was clear that Nielsen hadn't delivered. Measured by financial self-sustainability, the Auditorium was no better off than under Scott. Since Nielsen's plan was "trust me," the board shouldn't have expected better. As finances worsened, the board became more secretive, arguing that openess would put the Auditorium at a competitive disadvantage. It was a claim that boards would fall back upon for many years to come.

~⋅∫~

In the early morning hours of February 22, 1918, a tragic and peculiar event occurred. The previous evening, a Thursday, the Auditorium presented *So Long Letty*. Starring Gladys Lockwood as Letty and with many chorus girls and an orchestra, it was a typical musical road show. The performance ended at 11:00 P.M. The orchestra left the building shortly thereafter—possibly in search of one of Red Wing's twenty saloons. Stagehands remained to pack costumes, props, and sets. By 12:30, stagehands and cast had left the building. Manager Nielsen was the last to leave at 1:00 A.M.[23] About these facts there is no disagreement.

At 2:00 A.M. young men identified in one account as "several" and in another as "two," walking home, probably from a saloon, saw the building afire. After forcing entry through the stage door, they groped through the smoke, laid hands on a fire hose, and began fighting the blaze. Realizing quickly that the fire exceeded their abilities, one of the men sprinted down the alley toward the fire department two blocks east. On his way he came upon police officer Anderson. Anderson and the young man sounded the alarm and then raced back to the burning theater.[24]

Red Wing firefighters waged a frigid battle against the roaring fire until 5:00 A.M. Damage from fire, smoke, and water was extensive. The interior was in ruins. All seats, curtains, ornamental plasterwork, scenery, the two large Peter Claussen oil paintings, and the chandelier were ruined. Saved in the fire were the projection equipment and, it was reported, the Auditorium's books and financial records.[25] In the morning light, officials estimated the loss at between thirty and fifty thousand dollars. That the damage was so extreme was chiefly because an asbestos fire curtain separating the orchestra pit and the stage from backstage wasn't lowered. That "misjudgment on someone's part" as the *Daily Eagle*'s account said, resulted in the fire rising to the fly and working its way toward the front of the house through the rafters, causing extensive damage to the upper balcony.[26]

That the conflagration didn't result in total ruin was indisputably due to the actions of the passersby. As to the cause, Fire Chief Fred Rethschlag was certain the fire began in the orchestra pit and might have resulted from a cigarette dropped by a careless orchestra member. Defective wiring did not cause the fire.[27] The chief was at a loss, however, to explain "a second fire, absolutely separated from the main blaze," a fire that did not cause extensive damage. That fire began in the front stairway leading from the manager's office to the basement restroom. That it was a second fire was certain, the chief said, because the heat from the initial fire had not reached that spot. At the origin of the second fire, firemen picked up oil soaked cotton waste and that

THE SET-UP

immediately gave rise to the thought that "incendarism" was responsible.[28] Axel Nielsen however, explained that the waste was used to "clean an old stove" and must have been left in the area by workmen. Otherwise, it was reported, "manager Nielsen was at a loss to explain how the fire occurred."[29]

Chief Rethschlag was cautious. Although he did not believe the fires, which he said smoldered for a couple of hours before being discovered, were deliberately set, he added that "two fires breaking out in two separate parts of the house at the same time look suspicious."[30] While Rethschlag was guarded, others openly attributed the cause to arson. On the day after the fire the *Daily Republican* ran a photograph of the Auditorium over the caption "Building Attacked by Fire Fiend."[31] A day later the *Republican* reported that "an investigation to determine the cause of the fire . . . is underway by the local authorities and the state fire marshal's office may be called in to assist in the probe. . . . The fact that two separate fires broke out in the building naturally arouses suspicion that they were set."[32]

Despite the uncertainty, arson wasn't investigated. No mention of the probable cause appeared in either newspaper from that day forward nor was the matter discussed by the city council. It is difficult to explain why this was so. Fred Rethschlag, age fifty-five, had been chief for only two years but had many years of

The Auditorium balcony following the 1918 fire. (Courtesy of the Goodhue County Historical Society)

69

firefighting experience. He determined where the fires started and with equal certainty ruled out electrical failure. Yet he was unable to pinpoint a cause. Nor, although the names of three citizens who offered firemen coffee was reported,[33] did anyone identity the young men who discovered the blaze. Officer Anderson said that, in the excitement, he had failed to ask. Yet the young men, having endangered themselves, should have been hailed as heroes. How was it possible to fail to identify them? Why wasn't the state fire marshal asked for assistance?

Most mysterious were Axel Nielsen's explanations. The stagehands reported that when they left the building at 12:30 A.M. there was no smell of smoke. Chief Rethschlag estimated that the fire smoldered for approximately two hours before discovery. That would place the time that the fires began at around midnight—an hour after the orchestra players exited the pit. Yet Nielsen saw nothing suspicious when he left just an hour before the fires were discovered.

Financially, there was bad news. The Auditorium, valued at $78,000, was insured for less than half that. Although the board demanded that the insurers "pay up" the full amount or repair the damage, they refused. The Auditorium, they said, must first prove its claims. In the end, insurers paid $27,500. With that and a verbal understanding that the city would help out, the restoration began.[34]

Auditorium stage and boxes following the 1918 fire. (Courtesy of the Goodhue County Historical Society)

The Set-Up

Architect Lowell Lamoreau and the Elliot Construction Company were re-engaged. By mid-April repairs were underway and the entire Auditorium was a "sea of scaffolds."[35] In June, the city council allocated $3,000 per year for the next three years ($9,000) to make up the difference between insurance and the expected repair costs.[36] In return, the city demanded that the city treasurer be given control of the Auditorium's funds as called for in the 1904 agreement, a power the city hadn't exercised, and required that, henceforth, the board meet in the office and presence of the city clerk who would record minutes.[37] The latter occurred; the former was ignored.

As restoration continued, Axel Nielsen assured citizens that despite wartime problems in booking good acts, stock companies were available.[38] A grand reopening was promised for early fall but delayed both by an inability to secure a good show and then, in October, because theaters closed due to the influenza pandemic.[39] Finally, on November 26, the Auditorium reopened. The program that evening was not a live performance but rather a moving picture, albeit a good one, Oliver Morosco's *Tom Sawyer* starring Jack Pickford.[40] The restoration was magnificent. The walls and ceilings were a mottled blue and cream. The ornamental plasterwork was finished in bronze, blue, and red with plum-colored plush drapes in the boxes. The new seats were well upholstered, quieter, and comfortable. Good-old-boy backslapping ensued. The curtain raised to reveal, on stage, the Auditorium board. Speeches were given. A noted actress, Bertha Galland, who once played Red Wing, was quoted. Making her way to the top of Barn Bluff where she surveyed the city below, she exclaimed that "Red Wing is a jewel box with the Auditorium as a jewel within it." City Attorney Charles P. Hall, who was for decades Red Wing's patriotic elocutionist and whose musical composition, *Loyal Red Wing*, was performed at the rededication,[41] addressed "The Spirit of Red Wing." His oration skillfully united *Tom Sawyer*, Red Wing, and Wilson's Great War in an all-American mélange.[42]

Unfortunately, primary records that might help explain the Auditorium's great fire don't exist and many questions remain unanswered. Why didn't the city demand full insurance coverage? Why, when evidence pointed to arson, didn't the police, the board, the city council, or the fire chief, demand an investigation? If the fires were set, by whom and why? Why did manager Nielsen fail to inspect the building or notice fires smoldering? Why did Nielsen fail to lower the asbestos fire curtain? How could a manager ignore oily rags on a restroom stairway on the evening of a significant performance?

If arson was committed that cold February night, Axel Nielsen had means and opportunity. But for what motive? Perhaps the board planned to dismiss him. If so, why didn't the board push for an investigation? Fires are known to conceal financial malfeasance. But if "cooking the books" (literally) was the aim, the fires were a flop since the financial records, or so newspapers reported, were spared only to later disappear forever.[43]

A tempting scenario focuses on the Auditorium, the city's 'elephant,' as a money-losing proposition. The deed of gift terms specified that if the theater were destroyed and insurance was insufficient to cover re-building, then upon agreement of a council majority and fourth-fifths of the board the insurance proceeds and whatever amount could be salvaged from the Auditorium would fund another memorial to Sheldon. That proviso's existence raises the possibility of a failed plot involving Nielsen. Still, there is no corroborating evidence and no councilman or board member stood to benefit personally. If Nielsen wasn't party to arson, he was careless, incompetent or both. Why then did the board retain him when Scott, an experienced manager, was fired for little reason?

Ironically, having inexplicably kept Nielsen on for ten months, on the day of the grand re-opening, the board sacked him. They didn't say so directly; boards often don't. The *Daily Republican*, however, reported that the board believed it needed to take a direct hand in management. Board president Fred Kroeger, a millwork executive with no theatrical experience, was now in charge. It was reported that Nielsen, ". . . who has served so faithfully, may remain with Mr. Kroeger for an indefinite period. Mr. Nielsen, however, has plans . . . which may not enable him to assist Mr. Kroeger beyond a certain time."[44] The newspaper's conclusion was baffling:

> There is a feeling among board members, which cannot conceal itself, that the arbitrariness of any individual member must be avoided and that the atmosphere must be clarified to bring about the best results. The members themselves are silent when it comes to matters for publication, but the situation is felt by those who come in contact with Auditorium affairs.[45]

The Set-Up

T.B. Sheldon Audiitorium board, 1918. Left to right: top: Hiram Howe, Ben Gerlach, F.H. Kroeger; bottom: Manager Axel Nielsen, Theo Thompson, and N.P. Olson. (Photo: *Red Wing Daily Eagle*. Courtesy the *Red Wing Republican Eagle*)

In hiring a new manager, the board didn't stray from the entrepreneurial schemes proposed by Davenport and then Nielsen. In February 1919, George W. Johnson, proprietor of the Metro, was hired. In taking up his new job, Johnson announced that he would also manage the Metro.[46] "Under the new arrangement," Johnson said confidently, "I believe the moving picture problem in Red Wing will be solved."[47] "Problem," as everyone knew, was shorthand for competition.

In taking over at the Auditorium, Johnson noted that patrons should be aware that films would, henceforth, occasionally move from the Auditorium to the

SHELDON'S GIFT

Metro for an additional run.[48] What neither Johnson nor the board revealed publicly was of greater import. That a film might migrate from one theater to another was possible not because Johnson as Auditorium manager also owned the Metro, but because the board now leased the Metro from Johnson. The Auditorium and Metro became one enterprise, controlled by the board and operated by George W. Johnson, its employee.

Beginning on March 1, 1919, and for the next sixteen years the Auditorium leased the Metro and shared significant costs between the two theaters. Importantly, the two theaters shared films as a way to diminish the effects of block-and-blind booking. The best films, the "high class" films with the biggest stars, pictures rented as a percentage of gross receipts, played the Auditorium. The Metro showed the rest. Not a film frame was wasted for having been paid for but not shown. The Auditorium became a film "chain" unto itself. To accommodate live performances, good films, those for which the distributor specified play on particular days of the week, occasionally moved to the Metro.

No news accounts mentioned the "arrangement." Board minutes are lost or destroyed. Still, the genesis of the set up can be traced to *Daily Eagle* publisher N.P. Olson who urged in 1911 that the city should leave the Auditorium, "to private parties who make a specialty of that line of business."[49] In 1919, with Olson a key member, the board determined to lease the Auditorium to George W. Johnson. But city attorney Charles P. Hall, who three years earlier rejected the scheme to give Nielsen a percentage of profit, objected. As Olson's son, Elmer, wrote years later,

Metro owner and Auditorium manager George W. Johnson (c. 1920). (Photo: *Red Wing Daily Eagle*. Courtesy the *Red Wing Republican Eagle*)

The Set-Up

"... at the time the set up was made a certain city attorney [Hall] said, 'it can't be done,' and was told that it wasn't for him to say whether it could or could NOT be done, but HOW to do it [emphasis in original]. And he found a way."[50] Hall upended the plan. Rather than the board leasing the Auditorium to Johnson, the board hired Johnson and leased the Metro. Hall's objection, that a city employee not benefit other than by salary, was satisfied.

Years later, when the "set up" unraveled, Elmer Olson defended his father's board in a way that exposed the heart of American pragmatism, Progressivism, free enterprise, and lip service to the rule of law. In 1936 Olson wrote:

> When the Auditorium was a strictly losing proposition—which it certainly was back in the days when it and competing motion picture theaters were losing money hand over fist—nothing much was said about it. Nor were there many who were so deeply concerned over the legality of this or that activity that concerned it. Therefore a band of men who constituted its board were free to go ahead and plan some system whereby the playhouse might be lifted from the red bath into which it had become immersed and give it a change of ink.
> That Auditorium board which devised a system whereby it eliminated competition and yet gave to the patrons good pictures at a low price, blinked once or twice at the strict wording of this or that law and went straight ahead to success. Perhaps the process wasn't exactly according to the letter of the law, the city charter, or even the constitution of the United States. But certainly the plan worked, and out of two or three theaters that were starving to death, along with their managers, emerged two theaters, each catering to a certain clientele but both serving the public well, at reasonable price and with profit to both.[51]

There are few better statements of ends justifying the means or of what Progressivism became—the knowledge that stifling competition was profitable. Early Progressivism, an outgrowth of Populism preached by the likes of "Fighting" Bob La Follette and Teddy Roosevelt (both of whom were revered in Red Wing), sought to bust the trusts and enforce competition. After 1912, however, both Roosevelt's New Nationalism and Woodrow Wilson's New Freedom pruned Progressivism of its remaining Populist roots by favoring friendly government regulation over unfettered competition. As played out in the merger of the Auditorium and Metro, the new Progressivism denoted a small city's recognition of what industry's captains long knew, that unbridled competition led to ruin. Efficiency, control and cooperation in one's self-interest were profitable values.

Sheldon's Gift

Notes

[1] "Local News," *Red Wing Daily Republican*, August 19, 1912. Charles E. Van Duzee was a Twin City film distributor. See Lucile M. Kane and John A. Dougherty, "Movie Debut: Films in the Twin Cities, 1894-1909," *Minnesota History* 54 (Winter, 1995): 355.

[2] "Local News," *Red Wing Daily Republican*, April 14, 1914.

[3] Advertisements, *Red Wing Daily Republican*, February 6, 1915; April 1, 1914; April 3, 1914.

[4] For comments on the development of film exchanges in Minneapolis see Lucile M. Kane and John A. Dougherty, "Movie Debut: Films in the Twin Cities, 1894-1909," *Minnesota History* 54 (Winter, 1995): 355-57.

[5] On the MPPC see Tino Balio, "Struggles for Control: 1908-1930," and Jeanne Thomas Allen, "The Decay of the Motion Picture Patents Company," in Tino Balio, ed., *The American Film Industry* (Madison: University of Wisconsin Press, 1976), 103-109; 119-134.

[6] Advertisement, *Red Wing Daily Republican*, April 2, 1914.

[7] On early block and blind booking practices see Richard Koszarski, *An Evening's Entertainment: The Age of the Silent Feature Picture, 1915-1928* (Berkeley: University of California Press), 71-72; Tino Balio, "Struggles for Control: 1908-1930," in Tino Balio ed., *The American Film Industry* (Madison: University of Wisconsin Press, 1976), 109-113.

[8] Johnson's family history is at http://users.acelink.net/mrrockydog/FTM/ dat8.htm.

[9] "Advancement of Movies Marvelous," *Red Wing Daily Eagle*, November 2, 1936; "Reminiscences of Old Theater Days Bring Smiles," *Red Wing Daily Eagle*, November 2, 1936.

[10] "Family Theater Buys Out Metro," *Red Wing Daily Eagle*, May 2, 1916.

[11] "Reminiscences of Old Theater Days Bring Smiles," *Red Wing Daily Eagle*, November 2, 1936. Johnson noted that the building remained owned by Robert Davenport. Johnson later purchased the building.

[12] "Family Theater Buys Out Metro," *Red Wing Daily Eagle*, May 2, 1916.

[13] Advertisement, *Red Wing Daily Eagle*, May 4, 1916.

[14] "Roxie Resigns from the Board," *Red Wing Daily Eagle*, March 1, 1912.

[15] "New Manager of Auditorium Named," *Red Wing Daily Eagle*, May 18, 1916.

[16] "Legal Opinion in Auditorium Case," *Red Wing Daily Eagle*, May 20, 1916; "Manager Cannot Share in Profits," *Red Wing Daily Republican*, May 20, 1916.

[17] "New Manager at the Auditorium," *Red Wing Daily Republican*, May 18, 1916.

[18] "New Manager of Auditorium Named," *Red Wing Daily Eagle*, May 18, 1916.

[19] "Legal Opinion in Auditorium Case," *Red Wing Daily Eagle*, May 20, 1916.

[20] "Auditorium Board Makes New Deal: Rejects Experienced Man at $75, Hires Beginner at $100," *Red Wing Daily Eagle*, May 22, 1916; "Nielsen Manager of Auditorium," *Red Wing Daily Republican*, May 22, 1916.

The Set-Up

[21] "Grand Opera at the Auditorium," *Red Wing Daily Republican*, January 17, 1917.

[22] "Brilliant Event at Auditorium," *Red Wing Daily Republican*, February 14, 1918. The San Carlo company presented a significant repertoire. When it played at the Metropolitan Opera House in St. Paul for several days following its Red Wing appearance it also presented *Faust* and *Rigoletto*.

[23] "Auditorium Gutted by Early Morning Fire; Fixtures, Seats and Scenery are Ruined," *Red Wing Daily Eagle*, February 22, 1918; "Auditorium Badly Gutted By Flames," *Red Wing Daily Republican*, February 22, 1918.

[24] "Auditorium Badly Gutted By Flames," *Red Wing Daily Republican*, February 22, 1918.

[25] Those records, including the minutes of the Auditorium board, however, have disappeared. The Auditorium Board minutes, beginning with meetings held in the office of the Red Wing City Clerk, date from April 16, 1919, the first meeting conducted in the office of the city clerk.

[26] "Auditorium Gutted by Early Morning Fire; Fixtures, Seats and Scenery are Ruined," *Red Wing Daily Eagle*, February 22, 1918.

[27] Ibid.

[28] Ibid. If boiled linseed (flax) oil was used to clean the "old stove" and oil soaked rags were left in a container, (which was not mentioned in news accounts) then spontaneous combustion might have been possible under "just right" circumstances. If that were indeed the cause of the second fire it does not explain Nielsen's carelessness.

[29] "Auditorium Badly Gutted By Flames," *Red Wing Daily Republican*, February 22, 1918.

[30] "Auditorium Gutted by Early Morning Fire; Fixtures, Seats and Scenery are Ruined," *Red Wing Daily Eagle*, February 22, 1918.

[31] Photo caption. *Red Wing Daily Republican*, February 22, 1918..

[32] "Seek Adjusted Loss at $30,000," *Red Wing Daily Republican*, February 23, 1918.

[33] "Auditorium Badly Gutted by Flames," *Red Wing Daily Republican*, February 22, 1918.

[34] "Insurance Paid on Auditorium," *Red Wing Daily Republican*, April 13, 1918.

[35] "Local News," *Red Wing Daily Republican*, April 16, 1918.

[36] Minutes, Red Wing City Council, June 27, 1918; "Council Votes to Aid Auditorium," *Red Wing Daily Republican*, June 28, 1918;

[37] "City to Handle Theater Funds," *Red Wing Daily Republican*, March 29. 1919.

[38] "Auditorium Will Have Good Shows," *Red Wing Daily Eagle*, June 20, 1918.

[39] As the Auditorium was rebuilt, America was struck by the first wave of the Spanish influenza pandemic that ultimately claimed the lives of over 600,000 Americans. Schools and theaters were closed, reopened and then closed again.

[40] The film was released by Paramount which was already the Auditorium's prime supplier. *Tom Sawyer* was directed by William Desmond Taylor (famously murdered in a case never solved).

[41] Ruth Nerhaugen, "Fires Nearly Destroy Theater," *Red Wing Daily Republican Eagle*, August 30, 1988.

[42] "Beauty of Reconstructed Auditorium Is Revealed," *Red Wing Daily Republican*, November 27, 1918; "Red Wing's Theater Is Re-Opened to Public," *Red Wing*

Sheldon's Gift

Daily Eagle, November 27, 1918.

[43]"Auditorium Badly Gutted by Flames," *Red Wing Daily Republican*, February 22, 1918.

[44]"Board President to be Active," *Red Wing Daily Republican*, November 27, 1918.

[45]Ibid.

[46]"Assumes Charge of Auditorium," *Red Wing Daily Republican*, February 11, 1919.

[47]"Assumes Charge of the Auditorium March 1," *Red Wing Daily Republican*, February 26, 1919.

[48]"G.W. Johnson New Theater Manager," *Red Wing Daily Republican*, March 6, 1919.

[49]Editorial, "The Auditorium Problem," *Red Wing Daily Eagle*, August 16, 1911.

[50]"Aimless Amblings by Ambrose," *Red Wing Daily Eagle*, October 12, 1935.

[51]"Aimless Amblings by Ambrose," *Red Wing Daily Eagle*, August 10, 1936.

Chapter Five

Boom Boosters and Bust-Up

"... many people in town think that Johnson makes too much money already."
~Walter E. Koehler (October 1935)

"The $5,000 salary is all bunk. I can get $3,300 without doing a thing. I am willing to be fair but will not accept $6,000 as both salary and rental."
~George W. Johnson (October 1935)

"The Auditorium setup is really detrimental to us. We can't legally get any of its profits and we cannot collect taxes on the building or its equipment."
~Alderman Milt Warren (October 1935)

Under the two-theater "set up," the details of which were not mentioned in board minutes or discussed publicly until 1935, the Auditorium's reversal of fortune was staggering. Of the $9,000 the city promised for reconstruction, only the first $3,000 was paid. The second and third installments were unneeded. Already by 1921 the board had invested a $10,000 surplus in city municipal bonds and repaid the city's $3,000 rebuilding contribution. Additional bond investments followed.[1]

There were numerous reasons for the rapid turnabout. Just as in a movie multiplex today, salaries and advertising costs were shared, and Johnson was unquestionably a good manager. Subletting block-booked films to the Metro was advantageous. Perhaps more than any other reason for the financial turnabout, however, was the overwhelming increase in movie popularity following World War I. Although probably overstated to enhance credit ratings, the movie industry reported fifty million moviegoers per week in 1926 and a whopping 95,000,000 in 1929 (when the total U.S. population was just 120,000,000).[2] Movie attendance nevertheless grew swiftly. In Red Wing, George Johnson for a time reported theater attendance in local newspapers. On Sunday, March 2, 1919, for example, Johnson said that over 1,500 patrons attended the two theaters.[3] By the mid-1920s, based upon average monthly gross income of $4,500 and average ticket prices of twenty cents, the Auditorium and Metro sold 20,000 to 25,000 tickets were per month.[4]

    The stampede to film was especially notable among middle class audiences who came to accept fully the legitimacy of movies as central to their culture and as their primary entertainment. The Auditorium, no longer regarded as a European opera house but rather as a small city incarnation of the movie palace, invited residents to self-identify as metropolitans. Also, with affordable admission prices and considering Red Wing's relatively large factory worker population, the opulent Auditorium became an icon for a "classless, homogenized, consumerist society."[5]

    Some cause for the rush to movies is also attributable to passage, in October 1919, of the Volstead Act. Under it, and for over a decade, alcohol manufacture, sale, and use were prohibited, i.e., Prohibition. No one would argue that law enforcement was strict or effective, that people stopped drinking alcohol or that home brew and wine making did not become popular avocations. Still, in Red Wing, where once there were twenty saloons, now there were none. When people went "out," movies cornered their market.

    While "high class" films played the Auditorium, "sure seaters," films that audiences attended simply because they were low cost entertainment, played the Metro. Paramount's best pictures, headlined by established "stars" and distributed as Artcraft films, played the Auditorium. Paramount's many lesser films, usually starring Hollywood newcomers and distributed as Realart Productions, appeared at the Metro. By mid-decade the Metro also became home to hundreds of westerns starring the likes of Buck Jones, Hoot Gibson, and Tom Mix and to serials. In 1922, for example, the Metro offered the fifteen-part *Hurricane Hutch*, "an absolutely clean serial, free from gun play."[6]

Boom Boosters and Bust-Up

Whatever the quality, there were plenty of movies. Producers released 854 domestic films in 1921. Although the number fell to under 600 between 1923 and 1925, it rose again to almost 700 in 1928.[7] Film turnover was astounding with four film changes per week common. In 1919, the Auditorium in one week presented six different films. None were double features. Only D.W. Griffith's *The Great Love*, starring Lillian Gish, played two days.[8]

Importantly, middle class audiences, if not always impressed by dramatic merit, were especially drawn in by improving technical qualities—above all sound and color.[9] In the 1920s the Auditorium, now successful financially, fed the growing market by keeping pace with technological improvements.

In 1926, the Auditorium purchased, for a whopping $13,561.76, a magnificent Kilgen theater organ, an instrument capable, as silent film accompaniment, of producing a surfeit of sounds from train whistles to sirens to bomb blasts.[10] As it would turn out, however, the organ was obsolete when

Metro, 1926. The photo was taken upon the occasion of the visit to Red Wing by Swedish Crown Prince Gustav Adolf and his wife, Princess Louise. (Courtesy of the Goodhue County Historical Society)

installed. That same year the greatest technological improvement of the decade was unveiled when Warner Bros. released *Don Juan*. Although only the musical selections "talked" by way of a 33⅓ r.p.m. synchronized disc recording, the film is usually cited as the first talking "feature." Al Jolson's *The Jazz Singer*, also a Warner Bros. Vitaphone picture with "talking" musical selections, followed in 1927. The disc system, however, suffered from many of the same problems that had plagued "talking" movies for twenty years. For those reasons, sound films from 1927 to 1929 were typically vaudeville-like short subjects. Outstanding surviving examples of these films include George Burns' and Gracie Allen's *Lambchops*, (1929) and Harry Wayan's *Debutantes* (1929), a musical short featuring an all-female orchestra.[11]

    Although the Auditorium did not install sound at either theater until 1929, the board was nonetheless an "early adopter." Only twenty American theaters were wired for sound when *The Jazz Singer* was released in 1927. In 1929 just 800 were sound equipped while 22,000 remained silent.[12] Resistance was twofold. Sound equipment was costly as were sound film rental fees. For those reasons even some large theater chains believed that sound was a fleeting fad.[13] That the Auditorium board was willing to invest in sound equipment so early signified its commitment to Hollywood films and its financial wherewithal.

    The local sound era began at the Metro in January 1929 with a two-evening experiment with Sync-chro-phone, a sound-on-disc system capable only of short subjects.[14] In August, the Auditorium announced that it would offer sound regularly on its newly purchased DeForest Phonofilm, a system that accommodated either sound-on-disc or the vastly superior sound-on-film.[15] Its first showing was Maurice Chevalier in *Innocents of Paris*, an all-singing and all-talking feature. Within weeks the Auditorium presented *On With the Show!*, a talkie in two-color Technicolor featuring a young Ethel Waters singing "Am I Blue," and for which adult admission was raised to fifty cents.[16] Shortly thereafter, the Metro purchased a disc system capable only of "shorts."[17] Early the next year, however, the Metro installed an Elec-Tro-Phone, another already out-of-date disc system but one capable of showing features.[18] Its first all-talking feature was *Salute*, a forgettable film, despite John Ford's direction, centered on the Army-Navy football game.[19]

Boom Boosters and Bust-Up

As attendance rose and the two theaters enjoyed increased prosperity, the number of live performances, although they did not disappear, continued their decline. Lectures, never a large attendance draw, were all but eliminated by radio. Although the Auditorium hosted such notable performers as Mme. Bourskaya, a Metropolitan Opera mezzo,[20] and a Civic Music League briefly sponsored highbrow concerts, such offerings dwindled further.[21] In the first half of the 1920s stock companies, whose diminishing post-war quality contributed to their demise, visited but were poorly patronized. By the end of the decade "talkies" killed them dead.[22]

On Broadway, meanwhile, the sort of musical productions favored by earlier Red Wing audiences thrived. Notables of the decade included *Rose Marie, The Student Prince, Vagabond King*, and *Showboat*.[23] Touring companies occasionally played Red Wing as happened when *Blossom Time*, the Franz Shubert story, appeared in 1925. Hailed as ". . . an exquisite musical delight," it was also "one of the rarest treats Red Wing has seen for many years."[24] Indeed, touring companies were rare. Rising costs and second-rate performers reduced sharply their number and quality.[25] Even local reviewers complained about mediocre stories, poor performances, and, at a scale of $2.00 to fifty cents, high prices.[26]

In an important way, however, the traveling companies that once thrilled Auditorium audiences staged a comeback. With the advent of reliable sound on film, Broadway musicals quickly found their way to Hollywood. With the addition of two-color and then three-color Technicolor, musicals turned to film have more often than not been blockbusters since. There is no better early example of this progression than Florenz Ziegfeld's "fabulous all-talking, all-singing, super screen spectacle," *Rio Rita* (RKO, 1929). That show opened on Broadway (494 performances) in February 1927, and, thirty months later, a two-hour sound film version, whose last half hour was in two-color Technicolor, was released. *Rio Rita* played the Auditorium in January 1930, the same month as *Glorifying the American Girl*, a Rudy Vallee film that also incorporated two-color Technicolor, and *So Long Letty*, a film version of the stage comedy that played the Auditorium the evening of its 1918 fire.

Along with musicals, Broadway drama was alive. On the New York stage in 1920-1921 there were 157 productions and in 1927-1928, 200.[27] Although much output was commercial melodrama and comedy, serious drama, notably in the plays of Eugene O'Neill, fared well. Outside New York, Little Theater companies took on serious drama. These troupes, sometimes professional, were as often non-profit semi-professionals nearly indistinguishable from community theater yet devoted to serious drama. By 1926, a *Variety* writer claimed there were 5,000 such companies.[28] When Little Theater began in nearby Faribault, the *Republican*, mentioning that it sought "to serve community, keep alive better drama, and afford opportunities for self-expression," urged it for Red Wing. Little Theater, an editorialist wrote, was not expensive, required just forty or fifty backers, and would become a "unique cultural asset."[29] Not surprisingly, the flush Auditorium, enthralled by movies, showed no interest.

Although serious theater never developed a Red Wing audience, light fare community theater revived. From the mid to late 1920s The Attic Players staged several productions. Their most ambitious, in 1926, was Harry James Smith's popular 1919 four-act comedy, *A Tailor-Made Man*.[30] Ironically, by the time the local theater group staged it, the play was already a 1922 United Artists film. Although the Attic Players were given free Auditorium use, the board didn't offer financial support. Indeed, despite remarkable financial success after 1919 the board was content to see its golden calves benefit local tax relief and other civic projects.

Profits were substantial. Although the city vowed in 1919 to take charge of the Auditorium's finances,[31] the board continued to manage and invest its funds and revealed little to the city council and less to the public. Still, a surviving cash ledger and testimonial evidence make a rough accounting possible. As the "set up" unraveled in 1935 amid charges and counter charges, it became clear that over sixteen years the Auditorium profited by more than $300,000. Although so large a sum seems inordinate considering the Auditorium's earlier struggles, that amount is plausible. Annual gross income throughout the period averaged $55,000 or more for the combined theaters.[32] Film costs for the Auditorium, even if all films were leased at thirty percent of gross income, were $16,000 and the Metro's flat rates less than $3,000. Johnson's salary and rent accounted for $6,380 and additional salaries—for ticket takers, secretary, ushers, and janitorial services—could not have been more

Boom Boosters and Bust-Up

than $15,000. Importantly, because the Auditorium was re-built in 1918, maintenance and replacement costs during the "set up" years were low. If such an estimate is accurate, then a profit of $15,000 a year or $225,000 to 250,000 over the period is certain. What's more, not all Auditorium features were leased at the top thirty percent rate, the board paid no taxes, and Johnson tried to keep costs at forty percent of gross income. Even if costs were close to fifty percent of gross, a net profit of more than $300,000 is probable. Although the Depression years were less profitable, in 1935 the Metro alone netted over $4,000 a year. Had the Metro been no more profitable throughout the period, it alone accounted for nearly a quarter of total profits. In addition, from pasting posters and billboards other than its own, the Auditorium continued to receive a modest income.

Of its more than $300,000 profit up to 1935, the board retained over $100,000 as a maintenance and improvement fund.[33] In the same period, the board spent an additional $75,000 or more on capital improvements, primarily its organ and sound equipment. By 1935 sound systems were already updated once at a total cost for both theaters of $30,000 or more. The board installed refrigerated air conditioning,[34] purchased a strip of land to the theater's east for $2,750,[35] and made minor upgrades at the Metro. In addition, in 1930 contractor F.O. Green, for a considerable and unrevealed sum, constructed a second lobby toward Third Street in order to accommodate patrons awaiting the second evening show.[36]

An additional $125,000 was given away. Beginning in 1927, a flush board agreed when member Hiram Howe proposed, the board passed, and the city accepted, an unrestricted $5,000 gift.[37] That began a series of contributions, frequently used to reduce the city's bond debt, that totaled $54,000.[38] Additional gifts were made at the height of late 1920s financial high spirits. For some time, the city desired a municipal swimming pool. Such structures were a relatively new phenomenon and an idea that suited Red Wing's progressivism, civic mindedness, and competitiveness toward other municipalities. It was also acknowledged that Red Wing's swimming spots, the Mississippi River and nearby Lake Pepin, were a health danger, a hazard locals blamed on upstream contributions of untreated wastewater and not on their own raw sewage.[39] The project, reliably reported to cost over $45,000 for the pool and bathhouse, remained unfunded until March 1930 when it was rumored that the Auditorium would contribute the entire cost.

Sheldon's Gift

After a "star chamber" board meeting whose secretiveness the *Daily Republican* later attributed to "some technicalities in the city charter . . . relative to the Auditorium Board using its funds for any other purpose than the theater . . . ."[40] the city got its pool "without burdening the taxpayer."[41] Altogether the combined general contributions of $54,000, pool gifts of more than $45,000, and "another $25,000 to the water board"[42] meant that between 1927 and 1935 the board contributed at least $125,000 for purposes and projects unrelated to the Auditorium.

Contributions, understandably, were enormously popular with councilmen, city officials, and presumably taxpayers. When he became mayor in 1931, Fred Seebach was so smitten with the idea that he made three board appointments, as one appointee later recalled, with an explicit understanding that the board's gifts would increase. Seebach's appointees were auto dealer R.S. "Staff" Curran, bookstore owner and Chamber of Commerce President Walter E. Koehler, and Red Wing Milling Company executive John Dengler. Already by 1933-1934, local interest had turned to identifying a site for constructing a municipal athletic field and there is no doubt that city officials looked to the Auditorium for money.[43]

Against community-wide enthusiasm for the Auditorium's civic largesse were a handful of dissenters including City Attorney Thomas Mohn. Mohn, who was mayor from 1923 to 1925, became city attorney in 1926. In 1935 the council again, by a vote of eight to one over Plato Sargent, elected Mohn to a new one-year term.[44] Although Mohn didn't object publicly to the earliest board gifts, he opposed the swimming pool contribution. Also, on at least two occasions, he chastised the board. In 1927 he told members they could not invest Auditorium funds outside the State of Minnesota except for public bonds. Mohn later advised that if members made contracts with themselves such action would constitute felonious self-dealing.[45] When reelected in 1935 Mohn told the council explicitly that Auditorium contributions, "direct or indirect," were illegal under the terms of Sheldon's gift. Not surprisingly, Mohn's opinion was unpopular with the city council[46] and the board, which believed that a $100,000 "sinking fund" was as much as would ever be needed for repairs, replacements, and improvements.[47]

Boom Boosters and Bust-Up

Another party who undeniably harbored doubts about the board's largesse was Auditorium manager and Metro owner George W. Johnson. Although Johnson managed both theaters well, he received scant tangible reward. In 1931 he accepted a contract that gave him a $5,000 annual salary and $1,380 rent for his Metro for a total of $6,380. In addition, the board paid for Metro repairs and improvements. Then, in 1934, in response to the Depression, the city reduced all salaries, including Johnson's. Johnson was handed a $5,280 contract, to run until May 1, 1936, that left his lease payment unchanged but reduced his salary to $3,900. In arguing that the contract was fair, the board noted that Johnson remodeled the Metro, a building he now owned, at his own expense, closing the theater's setback open entryway in order to expand the lobby and create a small retail space that he rented as a dress shop.[48] In addition, Johnson installed a candy counter and retained its profits.[49] Johnson, however, was dissatisfied. To him, the board profited because of him and his Metro. What's more, the board was miserly in making Metro repairs and improvements. In 1932, for example, two citizens asked the board to make proper toilets available at the Metro in order to "eliminate some of the nuisance now existing at the side and rear of the property."[50] Although the board agreed to look into the matter, it did nothing.

A crisis arose in the sweltering summer of 1935 when Johnson attempted to renegotiate his contract with a profit-centered board that failed to understand that he held a fist-full of high cards, including, at age sixty-three, a willingness to retire. The board proposed a new contract, to take effect May 1, 1936, paying Johnson $6,000—$4,200 in salary and $1,800 in rent, $380 less than his 1931 agreement.[51] Although Johnson retained dress shop rent, the board, which eschewed candy income for the next fifteen years, demanded he close the concession counter. Johnson rejected the offer.[52]

On October 4, the city council reviewed and initially accepted a proposed 1936 budget that included, at a time when such fees were typically $50 to $100, a $1,500 Metro license fee.[53] In discussion, the finance committee, to circumvent Mohn's opposition, described the fee as a disguised gift from the Auditorium to the city.[54] As questions arose, however, the committee revealed that the fee was to be levied only if Johnson failed to renew his lease. Johnson was being coerced. To say the least, the claim that the fee was intended to dodge Mohn now lacked veracity.[55]

Sheldon's Gift

When the ruse was plain, Alderman Charles Wendler and Mayor John Kappel leapt to Johnson's defense. Wendler, claiming he glimpsed a "nigger in the wood pile," said it was clear to him that the Auditorium planned to eliminate the Metro because Johnson couldn't survive with a $1,500 annual fee. Kappel, appalled by this "rotten deal," agreed. Their complaints were ignored. In the end the council resolved, four to three, over Mohn's objection to the legality of a gift or to an exorbitant license fee, whichever it was, to keep the $1,500 fee in the budget. [56]

About town the fracas inspired a gossiper's field day that caused the board to invite the council to a joint "clear the air" meeting.[57] And what a meeting it was. Charges and counter charges flew. There was backpedaling. It was *opera comedia*. It went on and on. Three hours of non-stop talking. In the absence of President William Krise, Walter Koehler[58] did the board's talking. In an about face Koehler insisted that the license fee occurred as a board response to a city finance committee request for gifts.[59] Council finance chairman Milt Warren agreed and added, falsely, that his committee was unaware of Johnson's contract dispute.[60] Koehler, adopting Mohn's legal opinion as his own, reminded the council that "Under the terms of the gift, which made possible construction of the Auditorium, the board cannot legally make outright gifts to the city."[61] Koehler did not say how a sham transaction passed legal muster.

Koehler also insisted that the dispute with Johnson was minor and that the board didn't intend to fire him. That was true enough. The board worried that Johnson would quit, take back his Metro, deprive the Auditorium of its outlet for unwanted films, and engage in direct competition. At the same time, the board doubted that Johnson could be successful operating his aging, second-class theater independently and refused to agree to the terms he demanded. Johnson, board finance head John Dengler said, wrongly believed that the Metro could command higher rent. The Metro's profits were distorted, he said, because of the cheap films it acquired from the Auditorium. Dengler also assumed that, if the Metro operated independently, block-booking contracts would put it in the same rough spot as an independent Auditorium.[62] "We've been fair," Koehler added. "In fact, many people in town think that Johnson makes too much money already."[63]

Later, probably at Wendler's insistence, George Johnson spoke. His appearance was unusual because the board, obsessively secret, hadn't even allowed Johnson

Boom Boosters and Bust-Up

to attend its meetings. When council president Henry Tiedeman said that such behavior was senseless, John Dengler shot back, "That is our plan from now on," meaning that the manager would henceforth attend board meetings.[64] When he spoke, Johnson acknowledged the theaters' interdependence. Under block booking, Johnson explained, "percentage" pictures played the Auditorium while the others, renting for just twelve to twenty dollars, played the Metro. In 1935, Johnson said he had thus far paid $9,258 for percentage films but only $2,299 for flat-rate pictures.[65] To Johnson, the question was fair rental. Any business, he said, that netted $4,280 a year, the Metro's profit, was worth more than just $115 in monthly rent, especially when he, Johnson, was responsible for property taxes. Moreover, Johnson claimed better offers. One theater chain, RKO, he submitted, happily proposed annual rent of $3,300. "The $5,000 salary is all bunk, Johnson said. "I can get $3,300 without doing a thing. I am willing to be fair but will not accept $6,000 as both salary and rental."[66] What Johnson did not say, and the board didn't understand, was that because the Metro showed a wide array of films, low cost and high, block booking was less of a disadvantage than it was for the Auditorium whose self-image depended on showing expensive films exclusively. More importantly, if the Metro became part of a theater chain, the problems of block booking would largely disappear.

As the meeting ended, Walter Koehler, in a brief exchange, revealed that the board had proposed to purchase the Metro for $20,000. When Johnson, amazingly, said he knew nothing of it, Koehler repeated the offer but there the discussion ended.[67] Although the subject of purchasing the Metro never appeared in board minutes, Koehler's remarks left no question that a public board intended to expand its "business" in order to thwart competition and secure a market for excess films. City Attorney Thomas Mohn was horrified.

Although bitter words were exchanged, especially when Milt Warren yelled at Wendler for "preaching" municipal ownership and then turning his back to taxpayer well-being,[68] all agreed on the fundamental issue—money. "The Auditorium setup is really detrimental to us." Warren said. "We can't legally get any of its profits and we cannot collect taxes on the building or its equipment." In a prescient remark, he added, "If an outsider operated the theater for himself we would get a nice return in taxes." Warren even wondered aloud if the Auditorium couldn't build a new theater of its own.[69] Henry Tiedeman, who wanted a $5,000 contribution toward an

SHELDON'S GIFT

athletic field, hoped Johnson and the board could come to terms. "We don't want any competition in the theater business here," he said.[70] Wendler added that "If the set up is busted, it is just too bad. I'd be very displeased personally."[71] Taking credit for the "set up," Wendler added, "About twenty-five years ago, I urged just such a combine as now exists, but I was laughed at."[72]

Neither of the city's newspapers questioned the merits or legitimacy of Auditorium largess. At the *Daily Eagle*, Elmer Olson, whose father, N.P., was a "set up" originator, wrote that just as a solution was found in 1919 a way could be found whereby the Auditorium,

> prospering because of that little hook up framed in a dimly lighted office that night so many years ago, can give of its profits to relieve the tax load of the citizens of Red Wing for whom the gift of the Auditorium was originally intended. Now that the Auditorium is in a position to pay some dividends on that investment, who is to step forth and say it can't be done? Not your Old Scrivener.[73]

The three-hour meeting ended with backslapping. An upbeat *Republican* remarked that, "Incidentally, it was the first time [the meeting] that matters pertaining to the operation of the municipal theater were made public, the Auditorium board under charter provisions being a law unto itself and not being responsible to any other body or forced to divulge any details as to its acts."[74] Still, nothing was resolved. The $1,500 license fee remained in the budget. At one point John Dengler told the council, confrontationally, "It is not customary for the board to make its records public. You have them now. What are you going to do about it?" When a councilman asked how much money the board had in its "sinking" fund, Dengler refused to say.[75]

Notes

[1] Minutes, T.B. Sheldon Auditorium Board, November 14, 1922; September 13, 1921; March 13, 1922; March 19, 1924.

[2] For industry attendance figures see Cobbett S. Steinberg, *Film Facts* (New York: Facts on File Inc., 1980), 42. The argument that attendance could not possibly have been so high is made by Lary May, *The Big Tomorrow: Hollywood and the Politics of the*

90

Boom Boosters and Bust-Up

American Way (Chicago: University of Chicago Press, 2000), 121.

[3] "Local News," *Red Wing Daily Republican*, March 3, 1919.

[4] T.B. Sheldon Auditorium Board, "Financial Reports Auditorium Board/Cash Receipts and Deposits 1918-1944," Minnesota Historical Society.

[5] See Thomas Cripps, *Hollywood's High Noon: Moviemaking and Society Before Television,* (Baltimore: The Johns Hopkins University Press, 1997), 17.

[6] Advertisement, *Red Wing Daily Republican*, January 22, 1922.

[7] Cobbett S. Steinberg, *Film Facts* (New York: Facts on File Inc., 1980), 42. This was indeed a prodigious number. In the next twenty years, although supplemented by imports, domestic film production leveled off to 500 or fewer films per year.

[8] Advertisement, *Red Wing Daily Republican*, March 31, 1919.

[9] If middle class audiences weren't particular about the content and quality of films, that fact may legitimize Hollywood's blind-and-block booking which fed huge quantities of films to the theaters. See Thomas Cripps, *Hollywood's High Noon: Moviemaking and Society before Television,* (Baltimore: The Johns Hopkins University Press, 1997), 64.

[10] Minutes, T.B. Sheldon Auditorium Board, March 9, 1926; March 8, 1927.

[11] Program, Seventy-fifth Anniversary Celebration of Talking Pictures, (Minneapolis: The Heights Theater, n.d.[2005]).

[12] Cobbett S. Steinberg, *Film Facts* (New York: Facts on File Inc., 1980), 40.

[13] Kirk J. Besse, *Show Houses: Twin Cities Style* (Minneapolis: Victoria Publications, 1997), 44.

[14] "Sound Movies Will Be Shown at Metro," *Red Wing Daily Eagle*, January 3, 1929.

[15] "Best of Sound Pictures Will Be Shown Here," *Red Wing Daily Republican*, August 1, 1929.

[16] Advertisements, *Red Wing Daily Republican*, August 2, 1929; October 4, 1929.

[17] Advertisement, *Red Wing Republican* (Weekly), October 2, 1929.

[18] "Talkie Equipment to be Installed at Metro Theater," *Red Wing Daily Eagle*, February 22, 1930

[19] "Metro Talkies," *Red Wing Daily Eagle*, March 12, 1930.

[20] Fred Johnson, "The Golden Years," in Barbara Tittle, Fred Johnson, Elaine Robinson, "The T.B. Sheldon Memorial Auditorium," *Goodhue County Historical Society News*, 19, 1 (March, 1985), n.p..

[21] "Concert Monday Crowning Event of Year's Course," *Red Wing Daily Republican*, March 24, 1925.

[22] Howard Taubman, *The American Theatre* (New York: Coward McCann, Inc., 1965), 129; Frank M. Whiting, *Minnsota Theater: From Old Fort Snelling to the Guthrie* (Minneapolis: Pogo Press, 1988), 98-99.

[23] Ibid., 190-191.

[24] "Blossom Time's Beauty Enraptures Red Wing," *Red Wing Daily Republican*, March 4, 1925.

[25] Howard Taubman, *The American Theatre* (New York: Coward McCann, Inc. 1965), 148.

[26] "Dunbar Follies at Auditorium," *Red Wing Daily Republican*, March 23, 1922.

Sheldon's Gift

[27] Howard Taubman, *The American Theatre* (New York: Coward McCann, Inc., 1965), 148.

[28] Dorothy Chansky, *Composing Ourselves: The Little Theatre Movement and the American Audience*, (Carbondale: Southern Illinois University Press, 2004), 5.

[29] Editorial, "For a Little Theater," *Red Wing Republican* (Weekly), April 2, 1930.

[30] [Caroline Vogel] "Souvenir Program: *Pygmalion*," (n.p., n.d. [1971]).

[31] "City to Handle Theater Funds," *Red Wing Daily Republican*, March 29, 1919.

[32] T.B. Sheldon Auditorium Board, "Financial Reports: Auditorium Board/Cash Receipts and Deposits, 1918-1944."

[33] After 1932, because of opposition to dispersals to the city, the amount grew and by 1935 was probably about $150,000.

[34] Minutes, T.B. Sheldon Auditorium Board, September 10, 1929; September 13, 1932; May 1, 1935.

[35] Minutes, T.B. Sheldon Auditorium Board, September 13, 1927. It was purchased from the Red Wing Printing Company.

[36] Minutes, T.B. Sheldon Auditorium Board, January 8, 1935; November 12, 1929; December 9, 1930.

[37] Minutes, T.B. Sheldon Auditorium Board, September 13, 1927; October 11, 1927.

[38] T.B. Sheldon Auditorium Board, "Financial Reports Auditorium Board/Cash Receipts and Deposits 1918-1944," Minnesota Historical Society.

[39] It was another twenty-five years before Red Wing acknowledged responsibility for its own contribution of raw sewage from 10,000 people and local industries.

[40] "City Theater to Pay Entire Cost of Colvill Pool," *Red Wing Republican* (Weekly), March 26, 1930.

[41] "Red Wing to Get Swimming Pool This Year," *Red Wing Daily Eagle*, March 20, 1930. Board president W.C. Krise noted that the Auditorium could not "legally" make a gift for the pool. Krise believed, however, that a sham transaction in which "it is agreed, however, to turn over a percentage of its earnings to the council," which "has control of the disposition of the funds" was acceptable.

[42] Elmer W. Olson, "Aimless Amblings by Ambrose," *Red Wing Daily Republican Eagle*, April 17, 1959.

[43] "Board of Education to Contribute toward Athletic Field Purchase," *Red Wing Daily Republican*, October 9, 1935.

[44] Minutes, Red Wing City Council, May 7, 1935.

[45] Minutes, T.B. Sheldon Auditorium Board, March 4, 1927; May 11, 1932.

[46] "City Government to Cost $120,490 in 1936," *Red Wing Daily Eagle*, October 5, 1936. The city's bond debt was always low. In January 1929 it was $171,000 and was reduced to just $113,000 later in the year. See "Local News," *Red Wing Daily Republican*, September 25, 1929. By 1936 it may have been as low as $10,000, an amount held by the Auditorium board and an amount that the city council hoped to have forgiven.

[47] Minutes, T.B. Sheldon Auditorium Board, January 12, 1932.

Boom Boosters and Bust-Up

[48] By the late 1920s the inclusion of rental shops, typically to either side of a theater's entryway, became a ubiquitous feature of small city and neighborhood theaters.

[49] Johnson's remodeling remained a sore point between him and the board. Board members argued that he made changes that were not authorized by the board. Johnson said that William Krise was well aware of the remodeling and that the work took six months, plenty of time for the board to notice and complain. In the final negotiations, the matter of who retained concession income was important, with Johnson understanding far more than the board, its bottom line importance. See "Affairs of Auditorium," *Red Wing Daily Republican*, October 12, 1935.

[50] Minutes, T.B. Sheldon Auditorium Board, January 12, 1932.

[51] Current day comparisons are difficult. Still, a conservative comparison with the Consumer Price Index suggests a $5,000 salary in 1935 was the equivalent of $70,000 in 2009.

[52] Minutes, T.B. Sheldon Auditorium Board, September 10, 1935.

[52] Minutes, Red Wing City Council, October 4, 1935.

[54] T.B. Sheldon Auditorium Board, "Financial Reports Auditorium Board/Cash Receipts and Deposits 1918-1944, Minnesota Historical Society. If the $1,500 license fee was intended as a gift it was in addition to a $6,000 contribution,in the form of surrender of city bonds held by the board,that the council accepted earlier in the year.

[55] "Auditorium Board Meets with Council, *Red Wing Daily Republican*, October 5, 1935.

[56] Minutes, Red Wing City Council, October 4, 1935.

[57] Editorial. "Turn on the Light," *Red Wing Daily Eagle*, October 7, 1935; Minutes, T.B. Sheldon Auditorium Board, October 8, 1935.

[58] Krise was said to be out of town on malting company business. It was Krise with whom Johnson had maintained a close working relationship. By 1935, however, the board was dominated by Koehler, Dengler, and Curran. Within a year, Krise was deceased and Walter Koehler was board president.

[59] Minutes, T.B. Sheldon Auditorium Board, October 8, 1935. The board inserted this explanation of the fee into its minutes after the fact.

[60] "Auditorium Board Answers 'Unfair' Charges," *Red Wing Daily Eagle*, October 12, 1935.

[61] "Affairs of Auditorium Aired Before Council," *Red Wing Daily Republican*, October 12, 1935.

[62] "Auditorium Board Answers 'Unfair' Charges," *Red Wing Daily Eagle*, October 12, 1935.

[63] "Affairs of Auditorium Aired Before Council," *Red Wing Daily Republican*, October 12, 1935.

[64] Ibid.

[65] "Auditorium Board Answers 'Unfair' Charges," *Red Wing Daily Eagle*, October 12, 1935

[66] "Affairs of Auditorium Aired Before Council," *Red Wing Daily Republican*, October 12, 1935

[67] "Auditorium Board Answers 'Unfair' Charges," *Red Wing Daily Eagle*, October 12, 1935; "Affairs of Auditorium Aired Before Council," *Red Wing Daily Republican*, October 12, 1935.

SHELDON'S GIFT

[68] "Auditorium Board Answers 'Unfair' Charges," *Red Wing Daily Eagle*, October 12, 1935.

[69] "Affairs of Auditorium Aired Before Council," *Red Wing Daily Republican*, October 12, 1935; "Auditorium Board Answers 'Unfair' Charges," *Red Wing Daily Eagle*, October 12, 1935.

[70] "Affairs of Auditorium Aired Before Council," *Red Wing Daily Republican*, October 12, 1935. Also see "Board of Education to Contribute Toward Athletic Field Purchase," *Red Wing Daily Republican*, October 9, 1935. The Athletic Field issue was resolved with construction of a city athletic field in 1938.

[71] "Auditorium Board Answers 'Unfair' Charges," *Red Wing Daily Eagle*, October 12, 1935.

[72] "Affairs of Auditorium Aired Before Council," *Red Wing Daily Republican*, October 12, 1935.

[73] E.W. Olson, "Aimless Amblings by Ambrose," *Red Wing Daily Eagle*, October 12, 1935.

[74] "Affairs of Auditorium Aired Before Council," *Red Wing Daily Republican*, October 12, 1935.

[75] Ibid.

Chapter Six

Gentleman's Agreement

"I've always had a liking for the show business, more from the business angle than otherwise."
~John Wright (April 1936)

"There are a lot of things we could spill here but are not going to do it."
~Alderman J.A. Haustein (July 1936)

"Such civic enterprises makes me proud of being an American."
~Actress Marian Talley (July 1936)

"What a jumble," ~Alderman Milt Warren (August 1936)

"It looks to me as if you were just trying to make a monkey out of me. I have been accused of swallowing the hook, line and sinker but I'll be damned if I do it in this case."
~Mayor John Kappel (August 1936)

Although everyone said they wanted to retain the "set up" and the board offered a new contract, whose terms were undisclosed, it wasn't to be.[1] On February 20, 1936, George W. Johnson resigned and announced that he would operate his Metro with the help of new partner, Edmond "Eddie" Ruben, a man described by the *Daily Republican* as a "wealthy theater owner who has had many years of experience in the motion picture business."[2]

Wealthy and experienced indeed. Ruben was the son of I.H. Ruben, of Finkelstein and Ruben, a motion picture partnership that built and operated as many as 140 theaters including Minneapolis's Minnesota, the region's largest. When Publix

(Paramount),[3] purchased his father's theaters, Ruben began his own chain, Welworth Theaters, and by 1936 owned seven Midwest movie houses. Alert to his "outsider" status, Ruben paid saccharine homage to Red Wing's superior tastes. "Truthfully," he said, he had never "witnessed such an appreciation of good entertainment and theaters as in Red Wing." Citizens could count on him, Ruben added, to be a "real booster for this progressive city."[4] Johnson too heaped obsequious praise on the city, its people, and the Auditorium.[5] And although Johnson noted that it is "not our purpose to enter into any cutthroat competition," by immediately announcing plans for extensive improvements to the Metro the two men signaled that keen competition had returned.[6]

Edmond "Eddie" Ruben, owner of Welworth Theaters and proprietor of the Metro 1936-1950 (c. 1935) (Photo: *Red Wing Daily Eagle*. Courtesy of the *Red Wing Republican Eagle*)

Indeed, Ruben and Johnson's partnership plans, for which Ruben would pay $20,000,[7] called for a complete "rearrangement." There would be a sloping concrete floor making the theater a "stadium" type with increased seating for 700 patrons. Renovation was also to include new seats, sound and projection equipment, heating and cooling equipment, and lower level lounges.[8] Although there was good reason to improve the aging Metro, Ruben's plans went well beyond simple revamping and represented the essence of moderne theaters. Its new persona was an about-face from the palaces, which, like the Auditorium, were inspired by European opera houses. In the Great Depression, as film historian Lary May says, people turned from older styles in part because those styles were aristocratic.

One 1930s architect, Ben Schlanger, described key factors in differentiating the old style from the new. New theaters, Schlanger said, rejected pretentiousness and ornamentation, which drew attention away from the film, and focused instead on content. Modern theaters were functional, efficient, less expensive, and, with between 500 and 800 seats, intimate. Where old theaters, with their balconies, were "vertical," modern theaters were "horizontal," an egalitarian design that sat everyone on the same level. No proscenium arch separated viewer from film.[9] Whether Schlanger's ideas were drawn upon explicitly or were simply "in the air," his streamline principles were at the heart of the new Metro.

Although Johnson and Ruben expressed hope for peaceful co-existence, the Auditorium board and its council allies prepared for hardball. Trouble began when Johnson asked the city council for a license in the name of Ruben's Welworth Theaters and suggested seventy-five dollars a year, the amount the Metro paid when the "set up" began and somewhat higher than the fee paid in neighboring cities. Although the license committee approved, the council balked. Talk of mugging the Metro for fifteen hundred dollars wasn't revived, but some, including councilman Milt Warren, wanted to deny the Metro a license altogether. When city attorney Thomas Mohn said there was "no way" the council could limit the number of theaters in the city the council adjourned rather than accept Mohn's opinion.[10]

Four days later, the council met again. Although council meetings required advance notice to the town's newspapers, had it not been for the *Daily Eagle* getting wind of the meeting, no reporter would have been present.[11] The session began peacefully enough when license committee chairman Charles Wendler, arguing that George Johnson was entitled to fair treatment, recommended a seventy-five-dollar-a-year fee. But J.A. Haustein and C.J. Bombach, staunch Auditorium backers, demanded to know why the license committee hadn't met with the board before making its recommendation. "We didn't need to," Wendler said. "It's city business." Haustein and Bombach were displeased. Consultation was necessary, they said, to "protect" the Auditorium from "outside" interests. Haustein also said that he'd heard that Eddie Ruben planned to expand the Metro to 1,000 seats, an enlargement that would reduce "our fine city-owned" auditorium to "second-run" features.[12]

Haustein's fears had some basis. The term "second run," although used loosely, actually referred to metropolitan areas where films moved from downtown theaters (first run) to neighborhood theaters (second run). In small cities, all releases were "first run" in their own market even though they had been released in downtown large city theaters eight to ten weeks earlier. Haustein's erroneously expressed fear was not of "second run" films but that the Auditorium might find itself showing too many second "rate" or B films. It was a matter of quality, not timing. Still, the right to exhibit major producer picture blocks wasn't determined by price alone. Where a film block was especially desirable and contained highly touted pictures, the number of seats in the theater as well as other features, such as up-to-date sound and projection equipment,[13] were considered. For that reason Haustein was correct to believe that a 1,000-seat Metro might command a disproportionate share of better films. Even though George Johnson said that the new Metro would seat only 500 to 700 patrons, when Haustein charged Johnson with planning for 1,000 seats, Johnson didn't deny it. Haustein then asked City Attorney Mohn if it was possible to license a restricted number of seats—say 600. Mohn answered yes and the meeting adjourned.[14]

In the days following, the council asked the board to recommend an appropriate license fee but the board deferred to the council. John Dengler and Walter Koehler did, however, remind aldermen that they had a "duty" to look out for the Auditorium.[15] A *Daily Eagle* editorial mused that there were two good sides to the issue. One, represented by Haustein, Bombach, and the board, was the need to protect profits, a justifiable fear of outsiders, and the specter that tax increases might be necessary if the Auditorium faltered. The other, stated by Wendler and Mayor Kappel, held that Johnson was a taxpaying businessman who could choose his partners freely and was entitled to fairness. Well, the editorial concluded, "will somebody page Solomon?"[16] In the end, compromise won out when the council unanimously approved a seventy-five-dollar license for a revamped Metro seating no more than 600, a proviso that Mayor Kappel asserted was "a slap in the face" to Johnson.[17]

As the city council tussled over the Metro's license, the Auditorium board, taking the threat of competition seriously, announced its own extensive renovations.[18] Premier theater architect Perry Crosier, whose credits included the Boulevard, Parkway, Nile, and Westgate in Minneapolis as well as theaters in Waseca, Owatonna, Wabasha, and Blue Earth[19] was hired. The essence of Crosier's plan was

Gentleman's Agreement

to remove the second balcony, identified inelegantly as "nigger heaven" in order to improve main balcony sight lines and change the projection angle to allow a doubling of the screen size. The balcony, supported by distracting pillars, was to be replaced by a new balcony supported by steel girders sunk into the theater's outer walls. On the main level, an inner foyer was to be eliminated to make room for more seats and the wood floor replaced by concrete. All of it was to be topped off by new seats, paint, draperies, decoration, and a canopy extended over the sidewalk.[20]

A key element of the plan increased seating by nearly 500 to 1,300! The alleged reason for this whopping increase was to encourage "high class" productions that were unavailable because of the theater's size,[21] an absurd rationale. Stage presentations were already rare as hen's teeth and not for lack of seats since, from its opening, the Auditorium was rarely filled. How it hoped to attract 500 more theatergoers with a stagnant population, in the midst of the Great Depression, and in an age of motion pictures and radio wasn't addressed. In truth, live performance was irrelevant. Expansion and modernization, never considered before the board lost hold of the Metro, was a direct response to Eddie Ruben. Once the city issued the Metro a 600-seat license, talk of expanding the Auditorium by 500 seats died.

The board's plans stirred a minor controversy when Arthur Taber, son of the Auditorium's first manager, Ralph Taber, protested. Writing to the *Daily Republican*, Taber said he was "astonished" to learn that the agreement with Johnson had ended. To Taber, "severance of these relations marks an almost irretrievable backward step and typifies in a large measure the pettishness of policy which is one of the contributing factors tending to make the small town smaller and the big city larger." As for the expansion, why destroy the Auditorium's architectural integrity, Taber asked, when, with two theaters in town, there was ample seating and the Auditorium claimed to be making plenty of money. Taber, predictably, was ignored.[22]

In mid-April a contract was awarded to local builder F.O. Green who bid $22,720 to an extraordinarily precise $23,619.12 from W.J. Longcor. As Green tore apart much of the Auditorium's interior, the Board fussed with subcontracts, eventually letting twenty-two of them, many locally. They were valued at $35,830 for a total project cost of $58,550.[23] And fuss they did. Elmer W. Olson chuck-

SHELDON'S GIFT

led in his "Aimless Amblings by Ambrose" column that a theater seat salesman waited hour after hour while the board engrossed itself in designs, materials, fabrics, and decorating. Convinced that the board wanted to look over his merchandise, the salesman laboriously set up seats outside the meeting room. But the board droned on until the wee hours of the morning and then, exhausted, refused to look at the seats.[24]

While the board buried itself in detail, a process that contributed to town gossip as to rising costs, Green removed the second balcony, pillars and inner lobby.[25] Sight lines and screen visibility were vastly improved. Seating capacity, with the threat of a 1,000-seat Metro eliminated, was nevertheless expanded to 1,025.[26] In addition, the renovated theater now boasted life-like Western Electric sound that "almost completely eliminated" distortion and an eighteen by twenty-four-foot glare-reducing screen.

On the eve of a grand re-opening the *Daily Eagle* admitted that there had been doubts about changing the Auditorium. Those doubts, however, were

Artist's drawing of the remodeled Auditorium (1936) showing the canopy over the sidewalk in front of F.O. Green's 1930 lobby extension. (Photo: *Red Wing Daily Eagle*. Courtesy *Red Wing Republican Eagle*)

GENTLEMAN'S AGREEMENT

Remodeled Auditorium Interior (1936). (Photo: *Red Wing Daily Eagle*. Courtesy the *Red Wing Republican Eagle*)

unwarranted, the *Eagle* concluded, because "the Auditorium emerges from the confusion of wrecking and rebuilding into an even more beautiful and certainly a more suitable structure to serve the public than ever before."[27] If praise came from many quarters, including the merchants from whom congratulatory advertising was extracted, the newspaper queried, how could a decision by high-minded volunteers be wrong? The *Eagle* even pointed to studio-generated telegrams from motion picture stars to prove the wisdom of the grand work. Good wishes came from a score of these. Most were the likes of Don Ameche's generic "My sincere wishes to you on the opening of your new theater." "As one showman to another," wrote Bing Crosby's publicist, "I hope your new Auditorium theater is a tremendous box office success. Congratulations!"[28] Actress Marian Talley, using off the mark grammar, wrote that for her "Such civic enterprises makes me proud of being an American."[29]

On the eve of the great reopening on July 24, 1936, in the hottest days of the hottest, driest summer then recorded, the board concluded that the Auditorium was re-born for the public. Although the film, United Artists' pleasant romantic comedy *One Rainy Afternoon* was an incongruous choice, the board felt confident that it had taken a big step to manage competition and rake in hefty profits. The reopening night crowd, for two performances, was a prodigious 1,750 persons.[30]

As the Auditorium raced forward with remodeling it wasted no time in engaging George Johnson's replacement.[31] In late March, thirty-three-year-old John Wright was hired. Born in Canada, Wright moved with his family to Minneapolis when his father was appointed British Counsel for the Northwest[32] and later graduated from law school. Before taking the bar exam, however, Wright became a partner in a movie theater in Webster, Iowa. It was a good career choice, Wright said, because "I've always had a liking for the show business, more from the business angle than otherwise." Pointing out that two of this brothers worked in theatrical management, (two others were attorneys) Wright concluded that show business "runs in the family."[33]

A few years after cutting his theater teeth in Iowa, Wright bought the run-down Granada in New Prague, a theater he intended to own and operate through an assistant,[34] and turned it into a successful enterprise.[35] Wright told the *Daily Eagle* that he had been considering "branching out" by purchasing additional theaters but

John Wright and wife, Myra (c. 1936). (Photo: *Red Wing Daily Republican*. Courtesy *Red Wing Republican Eagle*)

that the offer to manage the Auditorium was a great opportunity. For the Auditorium, Wright planned extensive advertising coupled with continuous showings and occasional intermission vaudeville acts.[36]

As manager, Wright confronted an immediate problem because some film contracts were held by George W. Johnson personally rather than by the Auditorium. More serious was the specter of negotiating and bidding for film blocks against Ruben's chain whose size gave it advantage. Because the Auditorium identified itself as a class-A theater, maintaining its status meant showing A-grade films almost exclusively. Wright was bound to uphold the Auditorium's reputation without causing financial ruin by purchasing too many film blocks containing undesirable movies.

To his credit, Wright took his problem to the major film studios' financial headquarters in New York. Based upon conversations there, at the film distributors' regional headquarters on "film row" (Currie Avenue) in Minneapolis, and with Eddie Ruben, a film-splitting agreement was reached. Although it was a "gentleman's agreement" that could have been abrogated by either party at any time, it was ideal and lasted for twenty years. Under it, the Auditorium had the exclusive right to contract for films from major producers—Paramount, Twentieth Century Fox, and United Artists. The Metro, largely reflecting Ruben's close existing relationship with RKO, contracted with RKO, Columbia, and Universal. The two theaters split films of the other two major studios, Warner Brothers and Metro Goldwyn Mayer, evenly. If, for example, Warner Brothers planned to release forty films of which ten were A and thirty were B features, then five A and fifteen B films, distributed alternatively by release date, were assigned to each of the two theaters.[37] Although film-splitting agreements were not unheard of, this was the only such arrangement in Minnesota.[38]

Under the agreement, the Auditorium, because of its relationship with Paramount, Twentieth Century Fox, and United Artists, received more A films than the Metro. That fact did not disadvantage the Metro. Eddie Ruben knew, and George Johnson's experience with the Metro confirmed, that in small cities there was a strong market for lesser films, especially when shown as double features. Indeed, in addition to its major films, the Metro also booked low-cost westerns, serials, and others from independent or "poverty row" producers that were not

SHELDON'S GIFT

subject to the agreement. At the same time, the Auditorium paid relatively high prices for its disproportionate number of A films and, because of block booking, found itself paying for B films it didn't care to show. Although the Auditorium justly proclaimed itself an A theater, status came at a steep price.

Although Johnson and Ruben announced that the Metro would begin remodeling in May, they postponed their project. When the Auditorium closed for remodeling, the Metro took advantage of its temporary monopoly to upgrade its image by showing a large number of A films. With Auditorium renovation complete, the Metro embarked on its own ambitious transformation. On the exterior, red and maroon "Vitrolite" set off by solid black replaced white enamel bricks that had marked the exterior since Johnson's earlier remodeling. The large red and rose-colored marquee hung over the sidewalk was a model of art deco modernity with a "dazzling array of electric and neon lights at night."[39] Inside, the new Metro was even better. The superior sound system was Western Electric's "Mirrophonic," said to be only the third such system in Minnesota.[30] To make the most of it, acoustic

Renovated Metro Exterior (1936). (Courtesy of the Goodhue County Historical Society)

GENTLEMAN'S AGREEMENT

Remodeled Metro Interior (1936). Note the wide seat rows with aisles only at the far sides. (Courtesy of the Goodhue County Historical Society)

Renovated Metro lobby (1936). (Courtesy of the Goodhue County Historica Society)

panels lined the walls and ceiling.[41] There were 520 comfortable new seats. Importantly, with just two side aisles, all seats were in the middle, giving everyone the same dead on, undistorted view. Entry was through ascending ramps on either side of the lobby made necessary because the rear eleven rows were stepped up to provide better viewing. All in all, with its streamline décor, indirect lighting, intimacy with the screen, lounges and rest rooms, the Metro became a first-rate example of the best moderne theaters of its time.[42]

Within months of its November reopening, Metro management changed. Whatever George Johnson said publicly about his intention to continue at his theater, it is certain he planned nothing of the sort.[43] Although his presence was necessary temporarily when the Metro came under an "outsider," after a respectful hiatus, Johnson, age sixty-three, announced that he would continue to own the Metro building but that Eddie Ruben solely owned the business. It was, Johnson said, a simple matter of "outside activities" demanding too much of his time.[44] From then on Johnson and his wife spent long winters tending their grapefruit orchard in McAllen, Texas, while summering in Red Wing and at a Green Lake family home.[45]

As manager for the new Metro, Ruben picked a man with theatrical experience and, ever mindful of the curse small cities could impose on outsiders, Red Wing native Edward "Eddie" Swanson. Swanson was a clarinet bandsman, had traveled with Buffalo Bill's Wild West Show, and was a natural showman. When tapped by Ruben to manage the Metro, a job that Swanson jumped at, Swanson was working for Ruben as a twin cities theater manager.[46]

With the arrival of Ruben, Wright, and Swanson and the remodeling of both theaters, movie competition, of a sort, returned. That competition had nothing to do with admission price as the theaters matched pricing. Nor did they vie for the finest pictures since each booked its agreed upon films. Competition, which appeared vigorous, focused on externals. Wright had said he was a great believer in advertising and he was. By December 1936 theater advertisements touting the excellence, suspense, zaniness, or drama of even the most mediocre Hollywood fluff comprised better than one-third of a news page at both newspapers and, on weekends, more. Combined with syndicated, "what's showing" review columns, the renovated movie houses were a Depression boon to local papers. Competition, moreover, took on other dimensions. In a city of just ten thousand,

Gentleman's Agreement

both theaters offered two evening shows, daily matinees, continuous showings from 2:00 P.M. on Sunday, and "Bank Night," giveaways.[47]

~~§~~

In May 1936, as Auditorium renovation began, board president W.C. Krise, age seventy-seven, died suddenly. Mayor Kappel named, and the city council approved, C.C. Bracher, a former mayor, meat market owner and civic stalwart, to fill the vacancy. Within the board, members elected bookstore owner Walter E. Koehler to succeed Krise as president and John Dengler as vice president. Koehler and Dengler, and their ally "Staff" Curran, men who strongly opposed city attorney Mohn's opinions, controlled the board.[48] Unfortunately for this board faction, Koehler's term expired in just three months, and mayor Kappel, who blamed Koehler for Johnson's resignation, determined that he wouldn't re-appoint him. Instead, on July 10, Kappel named mortician E.C. Erb. Although the Sheldon trust deed didn't require council confirmation of mayoral appointees, city ordinance did. To Kappel's dismay, and for the first time, the council rejected, six to three, his appointment. With that a new ruckus that deepened divisions and led to long lasting discord began.[49]

Although aldermen opposing Erb agreed that he was an upstanding fellow, they objected to his appointment, they said, because they didn't want to make changes with the Auditorium in the midst of renovation. Kappel countered that he talked with many people in town and that even "business men are in favor of making a change." Shouting ensued and J.A. Haustein, who earlier told Kappel to "shut up" demanded names. Kappel demurred. Haustein, saying that "there are a lot of things we could spill here but are not going to do it," defended the board and claimed that no rumors could be proved. Haustein then nominated Koehler for re-appointment. However, city attorney Mohn, citing the mayor's authority to make appointments, forbade it. Mayor Kappel said, "I'll take my stand and stick to it."[50] For the moment that's where it ended.

On August 7, Mohn told the council that in his legal opinion the contract under which the city accepted the Auditorium called for a five-person board appointed by the mayor. Koehler's term was expired, and there was no provision for holdover appointments as some aldermen argued. Citing a Minnesota Supreme

Court ruling, Mohn stated that where a term was fixed a vacancy occurred at the end of that term. "In this case," Mohn said, "the term of the member expired as of August first. It ended then, there is no holdover. There is no member holding that position now. Is that plain enough?"[51]

Mayor Kappel saw Mohn's point, but optometrist Joe Haustein didn't. Haustein argued that Koehler was the man the board itself wanted to lead it. When Kappel said, "I don't know about that," Haustein cut him off. "I'm talking now," said Haustein, who went on to say that many businessmen thought everything was fine. Kappel countered with, "I've had, God knows how many compliment me for my stand and tell me to stick to it." C.J. Bombach shot back at the mayor, "Now I don't like the way you're acting in this matter. You aren't doing yourself a bit of good. And I'll tell you that to your face. This is spite work and it's about time you got down off from that horse." In the end it was plain that Kappel didn't have the votes to confirm Erb and that Alderman Milt Warren's words, "What a jumble," were especially apt.[52]

Book and stationery store owner Walter E. Koehler served on the Auditorium board from 1931 to 1936 (c. 1935). Koehler was instrumental in creating the Chief theater. (Photo: *Red Wing Daily Republican*. Courtesy of the *Red Wing Republican Eagle*)

Two days after the bitter meeting, an unidentified spokesman for the council majority said that, "We have decided to fight this thing to a finish." These councilmen then urged Koehler to continue on as board president because "the burden of proof that the ruling [Mohn's opinion] is correct is on the opposition." Another alderman added that a special council meeting might be necessary because, "There are numerous angles to the situation that have been kept covered perhaps too long." A special meeting, he said, "would have some queer and perhaps interesting angles."[53] That meeting took place on August 11. Although some councilmen thought there were issues that could be "threshed over," most believed that positions had hardened and that both Kappel and the Council majority would "stand pat."[54]

A compromise proposed by Alderman William Mossberg suggested that the mayor appoint Koehler with the understanding that if, after six months, the Auditorium's affairs were not in order, the entire board would resign. The mayor had none of it. When Tiedeman, Kappel's ally, called for Erb's confirmation, the motion failed. Kappel, perturbed, said, "It looks to me as if you were just trying to make a monkey out of me. I have been accused of swallowing the hook, line and sinker but I'll be damned if I do it in this case."[55]

When a resolution aimed at keeping Koehler on the board as a "hold over" was introduced, Mohn began to say "the Supreme Court has held . . ." but Bombach cut him off and called the vote. Not surprisingly, it passed.[56] Summing it up, Milt Warren said he believed it wasn't necessary to abide by the attorney's opinion. If the council adopted a resolution that someone thought was illegal then "it's up to them to take it into court and test it." Expressing a view that ends justify means, Warren said that the "set up" was, in a strict sense, illegal. "But it worked. And the city benefited. Who contested that? Who's to contest this if it is for the best interest of the city?"[57]

As the spat continued, gossipers questioned the board's competency, the profligacy of the money spent on the Auditorium overhaul, and the council's ability to resolve issues—important or otherwise. To restore confidence, councilman Tiedeman asked the board for an itemized accounting for its remodeling. "I have been approached on the subject of remodeling the Auditorium," he said, "and I had to admit that I didn't know how much was spent and how it was spent. People seem to think we should know." Surprisingly, Tiedeman's request wasn't opposed. The Board, the *Daily Eagle* reported, "has already ordered a complete checkup of the entire project, required affidavits from all contractors as to amounts spent and how, and was planning to make this report to the council unasked."[58] Coming from a board that hadn't revealed financial data, the response was incredulous. The report, which the board termed the "audit," though no independent auditor was hired, remained "underway" for some months. That delay contributed to ongoing council quibbling with the majority determined not to approve an appointment until the "audit" was complete.

Sheldon's Gift

In November, an impatient Mayor Kappel appointed longtime labor leader Frank Koester to the board. When Milt Warren demanded to know why the mayor was determined to "spring something like this . . ." Kappel answered that it was "because two of you fellows hatched up one on me the other time." Fur flew. Haustein, chimed in. "We refused to agree to any board member's dismissal because there was a big change going on at the Auditorium. You said they wasn't [sic.] going to make a go of it. It's not settled yet. Under the circumstances I wouldn't vote to confirm anybody, not even my own brother."[59] In December, Kappel again appointed Koester. This time the labor community, because no representative of labor had ever sat on the board, backed Kappel.[60] At the January council meeting forty representatives of the Trades and Labor Council showed up only to see Koester's nomination again fail six to three.[61] At the same meeting, the council, confident that hard times had passed, voted to restore the city pay cut that had been a contentious issue with George Johnson. There was one exception. The council voted, again six to three, to reduce City Attorney Thomas Mohn's salary from $1,200 to $900. Tiedeman objected, saying you got what you paid for. But Joe Haustein declared, without naming any names, that he had consulted with other cities and that $900 was good enough.[62] Mohn was spanked.

In February 1937, the board presented its long-awaited self-audit and a glimpse, but only that, into its financial affairs. For doing this, the board was praised mightily by the *Daily Eagle* because, the paper noted, the board wasn't required to report to the council and this was the "first time any such board has done so."[63] More importantly, the report 'fessed up little and raised as many questions as it answered.

In its self-proclaimed "audit," the board told the council that remodeling expenses totaled $66,000. Admitting that that amount was more than projected, the board nonetheless asserted that its "sinking fund" remained at $102,730,[64] suspiciously just $2,700 above the $100,000 mark that the board asserted was as much as would ever be needed. More interesting were figures presented to demonstrate recent success. Although the board refused, for competitive "business reasons," to offer details,[65] it claimed that in just five months operating expenses were reduced from forty-six percent to forty percent, film expenses fell from thirty-two and one half percent to twenty-seven percent (of gross), that ticket sales increased twelve percent, and that profits were up by a whopping sixty-two percent. Truly amazing. To begin, George Johnson was widely credited with having brought the Auditorium from disaster to prosperity. Was it possible for new management to have worked such a miracle in so short a time? Was it possible with the Auditorium focused on A films and without an outlet for excess B's? There was, to be sure, the possibility that attendance increased simply because the fall and winter seasons were the best theater-going months of the year and because patrons were eager to attend the spiffed up theater. Not surprisingly, the vague report was received enthusiastically. The *Daily Eagle*, the next day, reported that the council "eulogized" the board. High praise and backslapping all around.[66]

Good feelings were short lived. The council majority claimed for months that once the "audit" was complete and the board cleared of wrongdoing that the mayor's appointment could go forward. Councilman Tiedeman reminded the others that the board had just four members and that its president, Walter Koehler, had no standing. Silence. It was broken when Mayor Kappel again nominated Frank Koester. At that Bill Mossberg insisted that no vacancy existed because Koehler was a "holdover." So there. Again the mayor's appointment failed—six to three. "Promises don't seem to amount to much with this council," Kappel said. But Joe Haustein, claiming, "I didn't promise anything" explained that because the "audit" was so excellent it was impossible to make any change in the fine group of fellows who headed up the Auditorium. "We as aldermen," Haustein said, "are responsible for this auditorium. If it was our own private business not a man of us here would think of breaking up the combination after hearing this report."[67]

That spring the controversy spilled over to city elections. Mayor Kappel filed for re-election and council president C.J. Bombach, whose seat was not up for re-election, ran against him. Frank Koester, the mayor's pick for the board, filed against Ed Anderson in the second ward. In the first, former councilman Charles Wendler ran against Haustein. In the April election, Kappel easily defeated Bombach, Wendler lost to incumbent Haustein by just four votes, and Ed Anderson defeated Koester. Little had changed.[68]

On the eve of the election an anonymous letter, likely attributable to Wendler,[69] charged that the Auditorium's finances were being handled in a "questionable manner" and that the board wasn't, as its "charter provision" required, turning over revenues to the city treasurer. The board cried foul, saying that the board's accounts were open to city officials and that an annual "certified" audit was submitted to the city council. That was true, but barely. The board was generally uncooperative with city government, and its argument that secrecy was for "competitive" reasons was balderdash. From 1919 until 1935, competition didn't exist, yet the board shared nothing with the council. After 1936, with the film-splitting agreement in place, minimal competition existed. Nor, prior to its 1937 audit by Raglan and Associates of Minneapolis had the board engaged outside auditors.

Still, tensions eased. On May 5, 1937, the *Daily Eagle* reported that with the "audit" complete, Walter Koehler "retires gracefully from the board." The newspaper claimed, in tortured prose, "Mr. Koehler was president of the board when the end of his term came and he presided at the meeting until the old board adjourned sine die."[70] At that, Thomas Mohn must have snarled. At the May council meeting Mayor Kappel appointed, without opposition, thirty-two-year-old electrician and unionist Bernard Schilling. At the same meeting, having previously reduced Mohn's salary, and hoping for legal opinions more to its liking, the council chose, five to four, William C. Christianson over Thomas Mohn to be city attorney.[71] In coming days, the newspapers fell over themselves to praise Koehler. The *Eagle* noted that there was disparagement but that "any active program is bound to arouse criticism." The point was that Koehler "had the courage to stick to his job until it was proved beyond contradiction that the program . . . had received the acid test of operation and results."[72]

It was quiet again. Briefly.

Notes

[1] Minutes, T.B. Sheldon Auditorium Board, January 14, 1936.
[2] "Johnson Resigns as Manager of Auditorium; Will Remodel Metro at Cost of Over $20,000," *Red Wing Daily Republican*, February 21, 1936.
[3] Kirk J. Besse, *Show Houses: Twin Cities Style* (Minneapolis: Victoria Publications, 1997), 30.
[4] "Ruben Son of Noted Theatrical Family in N.W." *Red Wing Daily Eagle*, November 2, 1936.
[5] "Johnson Resigns as Manager of Auditorium; Will Remodel Metro at Cost of Over $20,000," *Red Wing Daily Republican*, February 21, 1936.

Gentleman's Agreement

[6] Ibid.
[7] Conservative comparison figures to today suggest that the renovations cost between $700,000 and $1.5 million To compare prices over time see the Economic History website at www.eh.net
[8] "Johnson Resigns as Manager of Auditorium; Will Remodel Metro at Cost of Over $20,000," *Red Wing Daily Republican*, February 21, 1936.
[9] Ben Schlanger, "Changes in Theater Planning Factors," *Motion Picture Herald*, November 19, 1932, reprinted in May, *The Big Tomorrow: Hollywood and the Politics of the American Way* (Chicago: University of Chicago Press, 2000), 116-117.
[10] "License for Metro Theater Held Up by City Council," *Red Wing Daily Eagle*, March 7, 1936.
[11] "Council Indicates It Will Impose Restrictions on Second Movie House Here," *Red Wing Daily Eagle*, March 11, 1936.
[12] "Auditorium Should Get First Consideration Board Warns," *Red Wing Daily Republican*, March 11, 1936.
[13] Ernest Borneman, "The United States Versus Hollywood: The Case Study of an Antitrust Suit," in Tino Balio, *The American Film Industry* (Madison, University of Wisconsin Press, 1976), 332-345.
[14] "Council Indicates It Will Impose Restrictions on Second Movie House Here," *Red Wing Daily Eagle*, March 11, 1936.
[15] "Auditorium Should Get First Consideration Board Warns," *Red Wing Daily Republican*, March 11, 1936.
[16] Editorial, "Page Solomon," *Red Wing Daily Eagle*, March 12, 1936.
[17] "Welworth Theater Gets License: Seat Capacity Limited," *Red Wing Daily Eagle*, April 4, 1936.
[18] "Auditorium to be Remodeled," *Red Wing Daily Republican*, March 28, 1936.
[19] "Perry Crosier Planned Change," *Red Wing Daily Eagle*, July 23, 1936; "Minutes," T.B. Sheldon Auditorium Board, March 27, 1936.
[20] "Auditorium to be Remodeled," *Red Wing Daily Republican*, March 28, 1936.
[21] Ibid.
[22] Arthur P. Taber, Letter to the Editor, *Red Wing Daily Republican*, April 6, 1936.
[23] "Minutes," T.B. Sheldon Auditorium Board, April 20, 1936.
[24] Elmer W. Olson, "Aimless Amblings by Ambrose," *Red Wing Daily Eagle*, May 8, 1936.
[25] "Complex Task in Remodeling Faced Green," *Red Wing Daily Eagle*, July 23, 1936.
[27] "1,025 Seats in Theater Add to Capacity," *Red Wing Daily Eagle*, July 23, 1936.
[27] Editorial "Congratulations," *Red Wing Daily Eagle*, July 23, 1936.
[28] "Movie Stars Wire Congratulations to Auditorium on its Reopening," *Red Wing Daily Eagle*, July 23, 1936.
[29] "Stars of Movie World Shower Congratulations upon City," *Red Wing Daily Eagle*, July 23, 1936.
[30] "Close to 2,000 on Hand at Opening of New Auditorium," *Red Wing Daily Republican*, July 25, 1936.

[31]Minutes, T.B. Sheldon Auditorium Board, March 29, 1936.
[32]"John Wright of New Prague to be New Auditorium Manager," *Red Wing Daily Republican*, April 3, 1936.
[33]"Love of Theater Runs Strong in Wright Family," *Red Wing Daily Eagle*," July 23, 1936.
[34]"John Wright of New Prague to be New Auditorium Manager" *Red Wing Daily Republican*, April 3, 1936.
[35]"Love of Theater Runs Strong in Wright Family," *Red Wing Daily Eagle*," July 23, 1936.
[36]"New Prague Theater Owner Is New Auditorium Manager," *Red Wing Daily Eagle*, April 3, 1936.
[37]Supplemental Partial Transcript of Proceedings, John Wright, October 3, 1961, *John Wright and Associates v. Harold R. Ullrich et. al* (Civ. No. 3-59-169) United States District Court for the District of Minnesota, Third Division, 676-679.
[38]*Paramount Pictures, et. al. v. James F. Lynch*, Ramsey County Attorney, et. al,, Attorney General Case Files, Minnesota Historical Society, 101FS, 2F, Box 72.
[39]"Mottled Vitrolite Is Used for Metro Front," *Red Wing Daily Eagle*, November 2, 1936. Vitrolite was a pigmented structural glass used for exterior and interior vertical surfaces. It was manufacturedby Libby Owens Ford and was extremely popular for moderne architecture.
[40]"Sound System in New Metro Best and Latest Type," *Red Wing Daily Eagle*, November 2, 1936.
[41]"Metro Takes Rank With Finest Show Houses in State," *Red Wing Daily Eagle*, November 2, 1936.
[42]"Metro Rebuilding Begun Today; Work to Take Six Weeks," *Red Wing Daily Eagle*, September 21, 1936.
[43]Mary Gwen Owen Swanson Oral History. February 4, 1975, Goodhue County Historical Society, I.5.34. Swanson relates that Eddie Ruben told Eddie Swanson that he had purchased the Metro and asked Swanson if he would like to manage it. As a Red Wing native and employee of Ruben, Swanson surely knew about the purchase as soon as it was announced in March 1936. He would not have been told about it by Ruben later in the year. Certain it was that Swanson was tapped for the manager's job at the Metro in the spring of 1936.
[44]"George Johnson Quits Metro Firm, Rubin [sic.] Sole Owner," *Red Wing Daily Eagle*, May 4, 1937.
[45]Johnson Family Genealogy @ http://users.acelink.net/mrrockydog/ FTM/dat8.htm
[46]"Ed Swanson Will Manage New Metro," *Red Wing Daily Eagle*, November 7, 1936; Mary Gwen Owen Swanson, Oral History, February 4, 1975, Goodhue County Historical Society I.5.34.; "Traveled With Wild West Show," *Red Wing Daily Republican*, April 8, 1912.
[47]"Movie Fans to See Best at the Metro," *Red Wing Daily Republican*, May 1, 1936.
[48]The other two members, Gerlach and Bracher, did not necessarily oppose the majority. Their views were simply not stated publicly.
[49]"City Council Rejects Mayor's Theater Appointment," *Red Wing Daily Eagle*, July 11, 1936.

Gentleman's Agreement

[50] Ibid.
[51] "Koehler Off Board, City Attorney Declares," *Red Wing Daily Eagle*, August 8, 1936.
[52] Ibid.
[53] "Council Majority Says It Will Stand Pat on Koehler," *Red Wing Daily Eagle*, August 10, 1936.
[54] "Special Meeting of Council to Study Theater Problem," *Red Wing Daily Eagle*, August 11, 1936.
[55] "Council Acts to Keep Koehler on Theater's Board," *Red Wing Daily Eagle*, August 12, 1936.
[56] Ibid.
[57] Ibid.
[58] "Council Requests Remodeling Cost at Auditorium," *Red Wing Daily Eagle*, September 5, 1936.
[59] "Auditorium War Flares Up in City Council," *Red Wing Daily Eagle*, November 7, 1936.
[60] "Council Rejects Mayor Appointee for Third Time," *Red Wing Daily Eagle*, December 5, 1936.
[61] "Labor Delegation Opens Auditorium Board Argument," *Red Wing Daily Eagle*, January 9, 1937.
[62] "$5,000 Pay Cuts Restored by City Council," *Red Wing Daily Eagle*, January 9, 1937.
[63] "Auditorium Board Eulogized by City Council on Audit," *Red Wing Daily Eagle*, February 6, 1937.
[64] Ibid.
[65] Only finance committee chairman Milt Warren, a strong board backer, was said to have been shown the figures.
[66] "Auditorium Board Eulogized by City Council on Audit," *Red Wing Daily Eagle*, February 6, 1937.
[67] Ibid.
[68] "Mayor, Three Aldermen, Retained by Voters," *Red Wing Daily Eagle*, April 27, 1937.
[69] "Auditorium Board Members Resent Campaign Letter," *Red Wing Daily Eagle*, April 24, 1937. The Eagle said that the letter was circulated by a former councilman. Charles Wendler was the only candidate who fit that description.
[70] "Koehler Thanked for his Services on Theater Board," *Red Wing Daily Eagle*, May 13, 1937.
[71] "Council Elects W.C. Christianson as City Attorney," *Red Wing Daily Eagle*, May 5, 1937.
[72] "Thanks for Service," Editorial, *Red Wing Daily Eagle*, May 13, 1937.

Chapter Seven

Chief

"... it won't be long before they'll be as numerous as 3.2 beer parlors."
~City Council President C.J. Bombach (June 1937)

"Who is behind this thing?" ~Mayor John Kappel (August 1937)

"I would like to know who is back of this third playhouse and will not vote on the ordinance until I have the information." ~Alderman Enoch "Nickie" Johnson (August 1938)

"There is no reason to be afraid of competition for America has thrived on competition."
~Arthur Arntson (September 1938)

In 1936, when the "set up" unraveled, there was talk of the economic horror to befall the existing theaters should a third movie house establish itself in Red Wing. Two and a half years later, in January 1939, that theater, the Chief, opened its doors on Bush Street where the old Becker Building, home to Albert Oelkers Round Up, a 3.2 joint, and a Chinese laundry had stood. Its first film was Warner Brothers' *Men Are Such Fools*.

The Chief's architect, C.W. Sunden, designed a structure, described as wholly "modernetic,"[1] that was not only streamline moderne but incorporated elements of "native" lore. In the lower level lounge, hand-painted murals portraying romanticized Indian life and produced by unidentified non-Indian St. Paul artists, adorned the walls.[2] Throughout was special beige, blue, and maroon Crestwood carpet that resembled an Indian blanket.³ Advance publicity noted that Hazen Wacouta, the last living descendant of Chief Red Wing, praised the new theater's beauty and authenticity.⁴

The Chief's 540 seats were set on a gradually sloped main floor and an equal-sized rear stadium-style section—a layout known as "parquet and ramp."⁵ Entry was through a center corridor with stairways on either side rising to the elevated rear. It was claimed that every seat was good and that was true. Wall coves concealed indirect lighting. The Chief boasted that its Super Simplex Projection,⁶ Simplex 4-Star Sound, and Acousticon for the hearing-impaired gave it the best sound and picture reproduction in the city.⁷ Streamline design was also evident on the façade where 800 feet of neon and two hundred light bulbs emblazoned a giant vertical "CHIEF." The exterior's special feature, however, was its beige and wine "carrara," a cast stone produced by the American Artstone Company of New Ulm.⁸ First-nighters were greeted by manager Orville Reich, a local young man who was called to the glamour of "show business" in 1936 when he became John

New Chief Theater (1939). (Photo: *Red Wing Daily Republican.* Courtesy *Red Wing Republican Eagle*)

Wright's assistant at the Auditorium.[9] Considering the anxiety shown over its coming, and its central role in the crisis that arose twenty years later, the new Chief was heralded as a welcome addition to Red Wing commerce.

During the "set up" years, the town gossiped about unnamed parties seeking to establish a third Red Wing theater. Those rumors were revived in early 1936. From a business perspective the idea of opening a new movie house had some merit. Motion picture attendance was rising[10] due to economic optimism, the knowledge that movies represented bargain priced entertainment, and new technologies including advanced sound, three-color Technicolor, and production techniques. Nationally, movie theaters increased modestly from 15,273 in 1935 to 18,192 in 1938.[11] In the Twin Cities, eight new theaters opened between 1936 and 1940.[12] In Red Wing, recreational choices were many but entertainment was limited, and taverns, reopened with Prohibition's repeal, were yet viewed as inappropriate for respectable women. There, a night at the movies followed by a visit to the Palace of Sweets ice cream shop was an entertainment mainstay. George Johnson lent credibility to the notion that movie entrepreneurs eyed Red Wing when he told the city council that a new Metro would give pause to outside theater men.

Still, there were cautions. Red Wing's population grew insignificantly from 9,629 in 1930 to just 9,962 in 1940.[13] On top of that, nearby cities, Faribault (population 14,527) and Albert Lea (population 12,200) supported just two theaters each.[14] Only Owatonna (population 8,694), where two houses were under the same ownership, supported three.[15] Nationally, some movie men suggested that a city could support 100 seats per 1,000 population.[16] By that measure Red Wing could support just 1,000 seats (the Auditorium). Some capacity could be added because of surrounding towns. Still, Red Wing's immediate trade area included theater towns Lake City, Zumbrota, and Ellsworth, Wisconsin. In tiny nearby Plum City, Wisconsin, the Works Progress Administration built a municipally owned movie theater in 1937.[17] Whatever guidelines one used, a third theater crowded the limits of sustainability. More important was the question of why a theater owner would want to face Red Wing's anti-competitiveness. Observing the lengths to which the board and council went to shield Auditorium profits and the roadblocks thrown at Johnson and Ruben, it is only remotely possible that theater entrepreneurs eyed Red Wing—unless an "invitation" guaranteed success.

Although the gentleman's agreement blunted competition, it didn't solve what the Auditorium, branding itself an A theater, identified as a problem, an excess of B films. Under the "set up" the Auditorium sent inferior films to the Metro. That "overflow" screen was no longer available. In the mid-1930s, moreover, Hollywood film production rose. Most of those films, including those of the major studios, were secondary or low budget B's. These movies, which typically ran less than ninety minutes, were ideally suited to double billings and to the "studio system." They allowed production companies to "try out" rising talent and keep contracted, salaried actors as well as writers, stagehands, set designers, and other salaried workers productive. These movies, as well as short features, were bundled in inseparable blocks with a few A films. Among the production companies, only United Artists and "poverty row" producers, whose films were exclusively B, marketed films individually.

A surfeit of B films posed little problem for the Metro. With already a dozen theaters, Welworth held negotiating advantages. More importantly, the Metro's successful business model meant that it happily offered B's, genre, and westerns along with A features. The Auditorium's initial plan to gain an outlet for unwanted films was to purchase the Metro. When city attorney Thomas Mohn foiled that scheme, the Auditorium had little choice but to show a wider array of A and B features. Ironically, that modified plan may have contributed to the Auditorium's improved profitability after John Wright became manager. In the end, however, image and long-standing belief trumped actual profit.[18]

In June 1937, H.C. Berry, also identified as J.C. or John C. Barry and Harry Berry, said to be "proprietor" of the Interstate Amusement Company, requested a city "permit" for a Plum Street theater.[19] Berry explained that he wanted to know the council's attitude "at once" before he spent money turning the site, which then housed the Hooley market and the Roosevelt tavern, into a theater. In discussion, Council President C.J. Bombach hoped that the number of movie houses could be limited. "If we don't," he said, "it won't be long before they'll be as numerous as 3.2 beer parlors."[20] To that, newly elected city attorney William Christianson, while agreeing that it would be difficult to deny licenses, commented that it would be possible to adopt ordinances so restrictive that an applicant could not comply. Although the council argued briefly whether there was a difference between a license and permit, a "permit" was granted due, amazingly, to support from Auditorium stalwarts Haustein and Warren.[21] Whether Berry received a "permit" or a license was irrelevant. It did matter that Harry Lilyblad, owner of the Plum Street address for which the "permit" was issued, told the *Daily Republican* that he hadn't spoken with theater representatives and that his current tenants held valid leases.[22]

Just two months later Berry announced that the Interstate Amusement Company was now doing business as the Gopher Amusement Company, had purchased the Becker Building on Bush Street, and planned to renovate it, at a cost of approximately $20,000, as a small theater that would purchase and show the Auditorium's "excess" films.[23] A few days later, Berry asked the City Council to transfer his "permit" to the new location, a request that hit an immediate "snag." One councilman wanted to "know who is behind this thing and what's it all about." Alderman Tiedeman, chairman of the license committee, said he was "in the dark." "At the last meeting," Tiedeman said, "we didn't know who was to have the license. If the Auditorium is hooked up with it, I don't know."[24]

Berry said only that under the Auditorium "hook up"[25] the new theater would "use the surplus pictures booked by the Auditorium under its contract."[26] Mayor Kappel demanded to know, "why this thing is being kept in the dark?" and "Who is putting up the money for your playhouse and why not make the Auditorium connection plain?" Berry answered that he was a principal investor but also had "four or five backers in Minneapolis."[27] Mystified, the council postponed approval of Berry's request until the licensing committee met with the Auditorium board to "attain an understanding."[28]

With the council bewildered and Berry mum, the *Daily Republican* examined the Minnesota secretary of state's incorporation filings for the Interstate and Gopher companies. Interstate listed nine incorporators, all said to be Minneapolis men. The Gopher Amusement Company, its "successor," listed four incorporators, one man, Joseph A. Hosp, and three Minneapolis women. Neither company listed H.C. or J.C. Berry or Barry. It was little wonder council members were confused.[29] Although the *Daily Republican* investigated, it failed to dig below the surface or, if it did, to report the results. It might have reported that none of the Interstate incorporators were known to be in the film business and that the Gopher Amusement Company's president, Joseph A. Hosp, was an attorney in practice with Auditorium manager John Wright's two brothers, Gordon and Lyle. Two of the three women listed as Gopher incorporators were employees of the same firm and another a neighbor of one of them.[30] Hosp and the others, including the mysterious Mr. Berry, were "fronts." None, including Berry, was likely to have had any financial interest in the company.

On the afternoon that the *Daily Republican* reported the incorporators' names, license committee chairman Henry Tiedeman asked the Auditorium's permission to grant a license to the Gopher Amusement Company. To that hat-in-hand request, board President John Dengler explained dismissively that the board had already reached a verbal agreement with Mr. Berry whereby the Auditorium would purchase all films and sublet the lesser products to the new theater. With that assurance, Tiedeman promised to recommend a license on condition that a written agreement existed between the board and the new theater.[31]

When a *Daily Republican* reporter tried to cover Tiedeman's meeting, the board told him its meeting was a closed "executive session" that would be followed by an open meeting in "an hour or so." After watching "a complete performance of *Wee Willie Winkie*, a newsreel, a musical comedy and three previews," the reporter wrote the next day, "the board was still closeted in the cellar." This was curious, the stood-up reporter thought, since city attorney Christianson and Henry Tiedeman had left an hour earlier! No open session occurred, and when the meeting finally broke up, an unidentified board member told the reporter that the "Auditorium board was not financially interested in the new venture, *so far as he knew* [emphasis added]."[32]

The *Republican* had scarcely hit the streets when a hastily produced contract between the Auditorium and the new theater, prepared by John Wright and an unidentified Twin City attorney, most likely Hosp, and signed by H.C. Berry, was handed to the council. Under its terms, the Gopher Amusement Company agreed to sublet all films offered to it by the Auditorium while the Auditorium retained the best (about 130 films per year). If the Auditorium offered insufficient films, the new theater would secure them from "poverty row" producers and major studio re-releases. After Mayor Kappel, seeking political advantage, asserted that the "... contract was gotten up at my request, to protect the Auditorium," the council approved a seventy-five-dollar-per-year license for a 600 seat (maximum) theater.[33]

Nearly a year later, however, construction of the Chief hadn't begun. Finally, in July 1938, Berry told the city council that the Gopher Amusement Company was eager to begin work at the Bush Street site if the council would renew its license.[34] The license application, signed by H.C. Berry on behalf of the Interstate Amusement Company, a company that disappeared a year earlier, was approved.[35] At the same meeting the council heard a proposed ordinance, the outcome of discussions begun in 1937, aimed at keeping additional theaters out of Red Wing. Stating that any new theater had to be at least 300 feet from any other playhouse, gas station, paint shop, or other fire hazard, the regulation would have disqualified most if not all of downtown. The ordinance would not apply, however, to existing playhouses or to the Gopher Amusement Company.[36] Although fear of a third theater drove planning for the restriction, with a third theater now welcome, a fourth show house became the fear. "There has been talk of a fourth theater here," Alderman Joe Haustein said. "It is going to hurt us." Alderman Arnold Kosec, agreeing, pointed out that the city needed a new measure that "should go farther than the state law" to protect the Auditorium from competition. Former mayor Bracher, now an Auditorium board member, confirmed that the board favored the proposed ordinance and City Attorney Christianson added, "We cannot keep another theater out of the city, but we can draw up a restrictive ordinance which promoters will find hard to live up to."[37]

Council newcomer Enoch "Nickie" Johnson, a Red Wing fixture as well known for his dance band as for his furnace business, was perplexed. Uninterested in a fourth theater, Johnson demanded to know why the council granted a third license. Grumbling that he "... never saw a time when our two theaters could not take care of the crowds," Johnson said he "would like to know who is back of this third playhouse and will not vote on the ordinance until I have the information." With that, the proposed ordinance was deferred, perhaps because no one wanted to talk to Johnson about who was behind the new theater.[38] And it wasn't mentioned again.

On August 23, in a startling turnabout, local papers reported that the third theater would not be operated by outsiders after all. Instead, locals doing business as

CHIEF

the Red Wing Theater Company now owned it. Amazingly, the new company's head was the board's former controversial president Walter Koehler, a man who earlier denied that the board had an interest in the new theater. Koehler said that he and his partners, physicians L.E. Claydon and R.B. Graves—nominees for "least likely B movie house operators of the year"—had purchased, "the entire interests of outside parties." That was not entirely true. Leo Molitor, a theater owner from Norwood, Minnesota, whose business connection wasn't specified, was a board member.[39] A "silent" partner in the project, it was learned years later, though he said his investment of $7,500, a considerable sum, was merely a "loan," was Auditorium manager John Wright.[40] H.C. Berry wasn't mentioned then or in Red Wing again. The new theater, Koehler affirmed, would "co-operate" with the Auditorium by buying its surplus films. Because the city already had two "Class A" theaters, Koehler said, there was a good opportunity for a "[Fifteen] cent house." Koehler added that the old Becker building would be razed and that the wholly new theater was projected to cost $50,000.[41]

Although the "change of ownership" to Koehler unquestionably surprised many, it didn't take the board, with the probable exception of newcomer Bernard Schilling, or its aldermanic allies unawares. Board members earlier favored purchase of the Metro and were angered at Mohn's rebuff. They sought, as the board did in 1919, to create a new "set up" that circumvented legalities. Although "outside" investors might have participated in the initial Interstate Amusement Company plan, the successor Gopher Amusement Company was a subterfuge. The use of Wright's brother's law firm to "front" the new corporation, a later revelation that Wright invested in the enterprise, and the fact that Myra Wright, Jack's wife, joined the new company's board of directors[42] places John Wright, if not at the center of the plan, then as its key facilitator.

An assertion by Walter Koehler in mid-1938 that the Auditorium board wasn't involved in the new theater financially was probably truthful. It is likely, however, that despite apparent legal and conflict-of-interest questions, the board initially planned to use Auditorium funds, probably in the form of a loan or private bond purchase, to establish the privately owned new theater. That transaction never occurred. Rising construction costs to $50,000 for a larger project may have catapulted it beyond the Auditorium's means. The board may have been warned off by city attorney Christianson or by potential legal problems, troubles that surfaced just days after the announcement of Koehler's interest in the new theater.

Third theater opposition did not die with the announcement of local ownership. One unidentified councilman said, "We are going to blow this theater business wide open and find out what it is about—if these rumors have any foundation and who are the persons back of the new theater project."[43] To head off uncomfortable questions, board members claimed, in a highly unusual "interview," with the *Daily Eagle* that the impetus for a contract with a third theater came not from the board but from its Minneapolis auditor, J.K. Raglan Company. They, the *Daily Eagle* reported, told the board that it should "do something about disposing of second-run films which accumulate, pointing out that a cash saving could be made in this manner." Quoting from the 1937 audit, the newspaper said, "Operating only one high-class house without any outlet for low-grade and unpopular films means that such films, when paid for, cannot be liquidated and constitute an additional expense." The report concluded that solving this problem would allow the Auditorium to build up attendance and retain popular films for longer runs without incurring new advertising costs. Suggesting that an additional profit of $5,000 per year could be had, the report urged that, ". . . this matter in all its phases be given immediate, careful attention by the board."[44]

The board told the *Daily Eagle* that realizing it had six months of excess films available[45] had naturally led it to study the auditors' recommendation carefully. Then, when the Gopher Amusement Company announced it would open a new theater in Red Wing, the board had logically pursued the opportunity to share films.[46] Rubbish. The accountants' 1937 report wasn't completed until months after H.C. Berry announced that his company's purpose in opening a theater in Red Wing was to absorb "excess" Auditorium films and the board had explained the "facts of life" to council president Henry Tiedeman.

The Trades and Labor Council spearheaded opposition. In September 1938, a labor delegation led by former Alderman Charles Wendler charged that a third theater would damage the Auditorium and demanded, on behalf of taxpayers, that the council rescind its license even though such action would cost jobs.[47] To quiet labor, local Attorney Arthur E. Arntson, who represented Koehler's Red

Chief

Wing Theater Company, replied that a new theater would make a place of beauty out of an old eyesore and help the Auditorium realize additional profit. "There is no reason to be afraid of competition for America has thrived on competition," Arntson asserted.[48] That was pure hyperbole. From its beginning the Auditorium did everything possible to stifle competition. Afterwards, the *Eagle* reported that unions dropped their complaint when told that local labor would construct the new theater.[49] That wasn't true. Rather, the council simply accepted and filed the labor protest.[50]

Although the board undoubtedly believed it was true, and theaters in Rochester and Faribault had film-sharing agreements,[51] facts didn't support its claim that the Auditorium would profit by subletting excess films. To begin, it wasn't certain that the Auditorium could attract larger audiences by showing fewer but higher quality pictures on longer runs. Although Hollywood studios employed that strategy in metropolitan theaters, in small cities it generally remained true that within three days everyone with an interest in a picture, regardless of quality, had seen it. Moreover, although the board believed profitability and film sharing were linked, under John Wright profits increased without it![52] Those gains were largely due to generally increasing attendance everywhere. But it is also likely that profitability improved because the Auditorium was forced, without film sharing, to show more low-cost B films.[53]

With opposition stifled, construction began.[54] When the Chief opened under young Orville Reich, John Wright's assistant, it meant in truth that Wright managed two theaters. Effectively, the film sharing "set up" was back. Red Wing was also a three-show-house town for the first time since 1916. From the day it opened, the Chief became, as intended, a temple of B's, westerns, serials, and A's in re-release. With its low cost flat-rate films, it was, apparently, successful financially. Profitability aside, the Chief, from its premier onward, gained a reputation as a home to lesser films. The Chief's reputation was cemented when it presented "adults only" fare such as *The Birth of a Baby*, a film billed as educational but whose advertising was lurid, and Hedy Lamarr's infamous *Ecstasy*, whose promotions shouted that U.S. Customs earlier banned it. It was a reputation that later, when affection for B's soured, and despite new programming, the Chief couldn't surmount.

Sheldon's Gift

Notes

[1] "Work on New Theater to Begin Monday," *Red Wing Daily Republican*, July 30, 1938; "Building of a New Theater to Start Early Next Week," *Red Wing Daily Eagle*, July 30, 1938.

[2] "Attractive Lounge Promises to be Popular Place," *Red Wing Daily Republican*, January 20, 1939.

[3] "Treading on Air Feeling for Patrons," *Red Wing Daily Republican*, January 20, 1939.

[4] "Attractive Lounge Promises to be Popular Place," *Red Wing Daily Republican*, January 20, 1939; "New Chief Theater to Open Saturday Night," *Red Wing Daily Republican*, January 20, 1939.

[5] "New Chief Theater to Open Saturday Night," *Red Wing Daily Republican*, January 20, 1939.

[6] "Projection to be Finest in New Theater," *Red Wing Daily Republican*, January 20, 1939.

[7] "Sound System Selection Made After Long Study," *Red Wing Daily Republican*, January 20, 1939; "Hard of Hearing Can Enjoy Pictures with Acousticon," *Red Wing Daily Republican*, January 20, 1939.

[8] "Advertisement," *Red Wing Daily Republican*, January 20, 1939.

[9] "Orville Reich to Manage New Theater," *Red Wing Daily Republican*, January 4, 1939.

[10] Cobbett S. Steinberg, *Film Facts* (New York, Facts on File, Inc., 1980), 46; Lary May, *The Big Tomorrow: Hollywood and the Politics of the American Way*, (Chicago, University of Chicago Press, 2000), 121. May suggests that the industry inflated attendance figures to secure financing and believes that the reported audience of ninety million per week in 1929 was closer to thirty-seven million. During the Depression, with the exception of 1933, attendance gradually rose to reach fifty-four million by 1939.

[11] Cobbett S. Steinberg, *Film Facts* (New York, Facts on File, Inc., 1980), 40.

[12] Kirk J. Besse, *Show Houses: Twin Cities Style*, (Minneapolis, Minnesota: Victoria Publications, Ltd., 1997), 55ff.

[13] Bureau of the Census, *Sixteenth Census of the United States*, Vol. I (Washington, U.S. Government Printing Office, 1940), 539-554.

[14] Bureau of the Census, *Sixteenth Census of the United States*, Vol. I (Washington, U.S. Government Printing Office, 1940), 539-554; *Tribune* (Albert Lea, Minnesota), 1937-1939, passim; *Faribault* (Minnesota) *Daily News*, 1937-1939, passim.

[15] *The Daily People's Press* (Owatonna, Minnesota), 1937-1939, passim.

[16] Ben Schlanger, "Motion Picture Theaters," *Architectural Record*, 81 (February, 1937), 17-20, Excerpted in Greg Waller, Ed., *Movie Going in America: A Sourcebook in the History of Film Exhibition* (Malden, Massachusetts: Blackwell Publishers, 2002), 221-223.

[17] Mrs. Edward Eccles, *Plum City Centennial, 1857-1957* (n.p., Helmer Printing Co., n.d.), 9.

[18] After Eddie Ruben assumed ownership of the Metro he offered to share films with the Auditorium, an offer that the Auditorium board ignored.

[19] Red Wing newspapers identified Berry as J.C. and H.C. and Howard J. and Howard C. Barry. In part this may have resulted from inattentive reporting. I consistently refer to this person as H.C. Berry, the name he signed when applying to the city for a theater license in 1938.

[20] "Permit for Third Movie House Is Issued by Council," *Red Wing Daily Eagle*, June 5, 1937; "Council Grants Permit for New Theater," *Red Wing Daily Republican*, June 5, 1937.

[21] Ibid.

[22] "Council Grants Permit for New Theater," *Red Wing Daily Republican*, June 5, 1937.

[23] "Third Movie Theater Assured for Red Wing," *Red Wing Daily Eagle*, August 2, 1937; "Buy Bush Street Property for New Theater," *Red Wing Daily Republican*, August 2, 1937; Title Transfer. August Becker and Wife to Gopher Amusement Company, Goodhue County Register of Deeds, H-8, 103, September 9, 1937.

[24] "Third Theater for City Hits Snag at Session of Council," *Red Wing Daily Eagle*, August 7, 1937.

[25] "Defer Action on Licensing New Theater," *Red Wing Daily Republican*, August 7, 1937.

[26] "Third Theater for City Hits Snag at Council Session," *Red Wing Daily Eagle*, August 7, 1937.

[27] "Defer Action on Licensing New Theater," *Red Wing Daily Republican*, August 7, 1937.

[28] "Third Theater for City Hits Snag at Council Session," *Red Wing Daily Eagle*, August 7, 1937.

[29] "Theater Firm Names Bared," *Red Wing Daily Republican*, August 10, 1937.

[30] Ibid.

[31] "Minutes," T.B. Sheldon Auditorium Board, August 10, 1937.

[32] "Favor Strict Contract for New Theater," *Red Wing Daily Republican*, August 11, 1937.

[33] Ibid.

[34] "New Theater for Red Wing Is Proposed," *Red Wing Daily Republican*, July 26, 1938; "Work on New Theater to Begin Monday," *Red Wing Daily Republican*, July 30, 1938..

[35] Minutes, Red Wing City Council, August 5, 1938. Berry's application was dated July 30, 1938.

[36] From the time the Interstate Amusement Company became the Gopher Amusement Company there was newspaper confusion regarding the appropriate name to use, and they were often used interchangeably. It is clear that the Becker Building was purchased by Gopher. Title Transfer. August Becker and Wife to Gopher Amusement Company, Goodhue County Register of Deeds, H-8, 103, September 9, 1937.

[37] "Theaters to be Regulated by Ordinance," *Red Wing Daily Republican*, August 6, 1938.

[38] Ibid.

SHELDON'S GIFT

[39] "Three Local Men to Operate Third Movie House Here," *Red Wing Daily Eagle*, August 23, 1938; "New Theater to be Locally Owned," *Red Wing Daily Republican*, August 23, 1938. The theater license was reported as issued to Molitor. The notice of incorporation listed Graves but not Clayton on the new Red Wing Theater Company board of directors.

[40] John Wright Testimony, Supplemental Partial Transcript of Proceedings, *John Wright and Associates, Inc., Plaintiff, v. Harold R. Ullrich et. al., Defendants*, Civ. No. 3-59-169 United States District Court for the District of Minnesota Third Division, 203 F. Supp. 744, 1962, 67-69.

[41] "Three Local Men to Operate Third Movie House Here," *Red Wing Daily Eagle*, August 23, 1938

[42] Goodhue County Minnesota, Register of Deeds, Deed No. 141733, June 9, 1948, Book Z-8, 425. Myra Wright signed as board secretary.

[43] "Fireworks at Council Meeting Next Friday," *Red Wing Daily Republican*, August 30, 1938.

[44] "Council Expected to Study Theater Tangles Tonight," *Red Wing Daily Eagle*, September 2, 1938.

[45] Ibid.

[46] "Audit Urges Outlet for Unused Films," *Red Wing Daily Republican*, September 2, 1938.

[47] Minutes, Red Wing City Council, September 2, 1938; "Labor Council is Opposed to Third Movie House Here," *Red Wing Daily Eagle*, August 30, 1938; "Argue Third Theater; Council Does Nothing," *Red Wing Daily Republican*, September 3, 1938.

[48] "Argue Third Theater; Council Does Nothing," *Red Wing Daily Republican*, September 3, 1938.

[49] "Labor Groups Drop Theater Opposition," *Red Wing Daily Eagle*, September 3, 1938.

[50] "Argue Third Theater; Council Does Nothing," *Red Wing Daily Republican*, September 3, 1938; "Minutes," Red Wing City Council, September 2, 1938.

[51] "Court Decision Wanted in Audiorium [sic] Controversy," *Red Wing Daily Eagle*, September 8, 1938. In one exchange the council asked why, if film sharing was profitable, the Auditorium did not share films with the Metro. Although Eddie Ruben had at one time offered to share films, the board said that the Metro had rejected the idea. When new board member Arthur Hernlem offered to contact the Metro again his offer was rejected.

[52] Ibid.

[53] Cobbett S. Steinberg, *Film Facts* (New York, Facts on File, 1980) 47-48.

[54] "Contract Is Let for Third Theater Job," *Red Wing Daily Eagle*, September 8, 1938; "Progress with Theater," *Red Wing Daily Republican*, September 17, 1938.

Chapter Eight

Longcor's Complaint

"The Auditorium was getting along nicely, to the benefit of all concerned, including the taxpayers, until a bunch of fixers started meddling. And now look what you've got!"
~Elmer W. Olson, "Aimless Amblings by Ambrose" (August 1938)

"If the attorney general had, upon adequate showing, refused to act, another result might obtain. But that is not before us."
~Justice Clifford L. Hilton, Minnesota Supreme Court (January 1940)

"What do you want? We've got a manager here who is making money for you and he doesn't get the salary you get at the post office and yet he does five times the work."
~Frank Ferrin to Arthur Hernlem (April 1940)

In January 1938, Auditorium manager John Wright met with contractor William J. Longcor, whose considerable local accomplishments included the Carnegie Lawther Library, Post Office, United Methodist Church, First Lutheran Church, Daily Republican, Goodhue County National Bank, and the Goodhue County Courthouse. In May 1936, Longcor submitted a general contractor bid for Auditorium remodeling but lost narrowly to F.O. Green.

At their meeting, Wright asked Longcor to draw plans and submit a bid to reconstruct the Auditorium's concrete balcony floor because either Perry Crosier's design or F.O. Green's work resulted in a sightline problem. Although the board was unhappy with some aspects of Green's earlier work, why Green was not told to re-

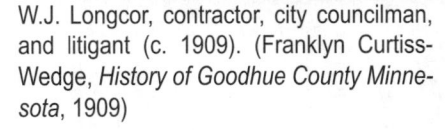

W.J. Longcor, contractor, city councilman, and litigant (c. 1909). (Franklyn Curtiss-Wedge, *History of Goodhue County Minnesota*, 1909)

Thomas Mohn (c. 1930), Red Wing mayor (1923 to 1925) and city attorney (1926-1937) (Courtesy the Goodhue County Historical Society)

do his work isn't known. The board quickly accepted Longcor's $726 bid on February 28. Days later, without reason, the board canceled the project.[1] Longcor, arguing that he prepared plans and turned away other work, demanded payment. The board offered just seventy-five dollars, designated as the cost of plans, and promised that if it later undertook the project it would hire Longcor.[2]

Unhappy, Longcor visited with Tom Mohn, his attorney of many years standing. For civic and personal reasons, both were angry. Longcor believed he was doubly stiffed. In the first instance, he narrowly lost a bid only to see the project overrun its budget by several thousands of dollars. Then, when the city council called the board to account it settled for a secretive self-audit. Now the same rascals had stung him again. Mohn was equally discontent. As city attorney, his Auditorium opinions were disregarded, resented, and cost him his position.

Longcor's Complaint

To be sure, Mohn and Longcor had personal reasons to be disgruntled. Together they shared a head-shaking disbelief at the preposterous circumstances leading to the awarding of a third theater license. Councilman "Nickie" Johnson and the Trades and Labor Council may have been confused, but Mohn and Longcor surely knew that the board and Jack Wright were up to their armpits in a subterfuge. They also knew that the mysterious Mr. Berry fronted for others and that although the board did not intend to purchase the new theater directly, it very likely intended to "invest" in it, a scheme that was revamped when the theater's costs ballooned.

On June 14, 1938, Mohn filed suit in Goodhue County District Court on Longcor's behalf demanding $726, the amount Longcor said was due him. Meanwhile, Mohn and Longcor considered other action. If legal recourse was sought, action that predictably would be regarded as hostile locally, who would take it? Mohn, a former mayor and city attorney, was the wrong man for the suing or the lawyering. Longcor, age seventy, nearly retired and without concerns for his business future, volunteered. That settled, Mohn and Longcor, perhaps not yet knowing what precise action to take, consulted R.H. deLambert of the St. Paul law firm Todd, Stone, and deLambert.

On August 23 local newspapers reported that the Gopher Theater Company "handed over" its interests to Walter E. Koehler's new company.[3] Three days later, on August 26, Longcor, represented by deLambert, filed two new actions. In the first Longcor demanded, on behalf of taxpayers, that the City of Red Wing return $54,000 in documented gifts that the Auditorium gave it between 1927 and 1938.[4] Another $40,000 or more, not clearly documented and given for a swimming pool and other purposes, was excluded.[5] The total was consistent with an amount that John Wright quoted to the city council in 1940, with George Johnson's assertion that cumulative Auditorium profits during his tenure were over $300,000, and with statements made later by a former board member. As to why Longcor sued rather than asking the City and Auditorium to set matters right, his complaint said it all:

> It would be an idle gesture for plaintiff or anyone else to demand of said T.B. Sheldon Auditorium Board or the City of Red Wing that such Board or said City bring an action for the return of said funds because the Board and the

Sheldon's Gift

City were and are parties to the conspiracy and the execution thereof which caused said funds to be so misappointed.[6]

That same day Longcor filed a second suit against the Auditorium and former board members Dengler and Koehler. That complaint was in three parts. The first demanded a full Auditorium accounting because, it said, financial operations were conducted in secret and the board had refused to turn over its funds to the city as called for in the 1904 agreement. A second allegation charged that the board spent $66,000 on its 1936 remodeling, a project that was never accounted for fully, despite the board's assertions, and that the expenditure was "extravagant and unreasonable." A third accusation, aimed at the third theater, alleged:

> ... that some of the present members of the Board [Curran] and said Dengler and Koehler [former board members] are financially interested in the establishment of another motion picture theater ... to be operated by them for their gain, and are endeavoring and attempting to obtain and use $20,000 or more of said Auditorium funds for such purpose ... all in violation of their duties and fiduciary relationships to said charity, contrary to statutes of this state ... and against public policy; that the establishment and operation of such proposed new theater would be a competitive enterprise, taking away from said Auditorium ... that unless enjoined and restrained, members of said Board will carry through and complete the understanding and scheme hereinbefore referred to and use and misappropriate a large part of the Auditorium funds.[7]

On August 27, the board huffed publicly that it welcomed an airing of the "ridiculous" charges. Addressing only the demand for repayment of $54,000, the board admitted that full disclosure might show that "technically" it had violated the trust deed. However, because its contributions aided taxpayers no one should object. Local newspapers echoed that view. The *Daily Eagle* admitted editorially that the Auditorium's funds couldn't be, "used for any other purpose than the care, maintenance, and conduct of said auditorium as is herein provided." But the larger issue, the newspaper claimed, was that an end to distributions meant higher taxes. If citizens lose if Longcor wins, the editorial concluded, what is the purpose of the suit?[8]

That fall, while the Chief was built, the *Daily Eagle* took dead aim at Longcor, and, without naming him, Thomas Mohn, for rocking the gravy boat. To

Longcor's Complaint

Elmer Olson, in his "Aimless Amblings by Ambrose" column, taxpayer relief was always good. Unfortunately, he wrote, the Auditorium board, selfless volunteers all, found themselves "in bad." "It would be interesting to know," he asked, knowing the answer, "just what lineup is behind [the attack]."[9] Wondering whether resentment of the "set up" was behind the lawsuits, Olson turned to the last days of the Auditorium-Metro combination:

> Then came a split of the combination which has proven so fortunate for some persons and the city-owned theater. Why was the split necessary? Because someone [Thomas Mohn] knew better than those who had made the plan work what should be done and insisted on its being done. With the rumpus that followed there developed a split also in civic leadership and open threats were made to some aldermen that in due time the city would be called upon to return the money it had been given by the Auditorium board. Those threats are now being made good, it appears. Who is responsible? And won't the taxpayers, who stand to lose in the long run, feel just dandy toward them when and if they get the low-down on the situation.[10]

Olson concluded that:

> There are many things that just exist and get along fine and dandy if let alone. Doctors have learned that a greater majority of wounds, if left to their own devices, will heal much quicker than if continually meddled with. The Auditorium was getting along nicely, to the benefit of all concerned, including the taxpayers, until a bunch of fixers started meddling. And now look what you've got![11]

At the city council, Mohn and Longcor, unnamed, came in for abuse. J.A. Haustein charged that, "Someone is back of that suit who is not interested in the welfare of Red Wing. It certainly isn't the fellow who signed his name to the complaints." Haustein scoffed at the idea that the suit was a taxpayer complaint when the taxpayer (Longcor) paid just seventy-three cents a year in tax.[12]

Although Longcor's contract dispute was on the district court's calendar for the fall term,[13] it was settled out of court. On November 16 the board discussed Longcor's $726 claim and offered him $150 and a contract to perform the balcony work for two dollars per hour with the total number of hours not to exceed 288—$726. An additional provision called for Longcor to begin work before January 15, 1939. Only R.S. "Staff" Curran objected.[14] Longcor had no trouble complying. On January 2, the Auditorium closed. Longcor began work employing local labor[15] and finished six weeks later. The reopening film was *Jesse James*.[16]

Meanwhile, Longcor's attorneys and the city agreed to resolve the $54,000 "donations" suit prior to litigating the other matters. On September 14, 1938, City Attorney Christianson filed a motion to dismiss. Because affidavits of prejudice were filed against local judges Charles P. Hall and W.A. Schultz, Judge Alfred Stolberg heard the motion. As expected, Christianson argued in his "demurrer,"[17] that even if Longcor's accusation was true[18] he had no legal right to sue to enforce the terms of Sheldon's gift[19] because sole responsibility for bringing an action in charitable cases lay with the state's attorney general. Stolberg promptly denied the city's motion, ordered the city to answer Longcor's complaint, and set a date to hear oral arguments.[20]

As anticipated, the city appealed and Stolberg certified the case to the Minnesota Supreme Court. Nearly a year later the supreme court, in a unanimous ruling, reversed Judge Stolberg.[21] Justice Clifford L. Hilton spoke for the court. In his opinion, Hilton reviewed the conditions of Sheldon's gift and its requirement to credit all revenues to the "Auditorium Fund." "The provision that the income was to be used for the benefit of the Auditorium only is clearly a valid condition," Hilton wrote. "On a gift for a public purpose where it is contemplated that the benefit is to insure [sic, inure?] to several generations, a restriction of this character is often vital to the successful accomplishment of the objective sought."[22] Here, however, the issue was whether Longcor could sue on his own behalf or on behalf of taxpayers.

The question was not substance but procedure and turned on whether Sheldon's gift was a charitable trust or a simple conditional gift, not in trust, for a public purpose. DeLambert argued for Longcor that it was the latter. Although charitable trusts were recognized in common law, Minnesota law stated that no trusts were valid unless supported by statute. The legislature enacted a statute authorizing charitable trusts in 1927, some twenty-five years after Sheldon's gift. In addition to authorizing charitable trusts, the 1927 law assigned enforcement to the state attorney general.[23] Because charitable trusts were not legal in 1904, deLambert argued that Sheldon's trustees did not create one. Instead, they made a

Longcor's Complaint

simple conditional gift—the only gift they could make legally. Therefore, the 1927 law regarding charitable trusts was irrelevant and Longcor had a right to sue as one of a large class of Sheldon beneficiaries.

Judge Hilton, who was Minnesota attorney general when the legislature enacted the charitable trust statute,[24] agreed with deLambert that Sheldon's gift was in fact a gift with conditions. For Longcor, so far so good. Nevertheless, when Hilton asked if Longcor could sustain his action his answer was "no." Judge Stolberg erred. Longcor, as a resident and taxpayer did have an interest in the affairs of the Auditorium but it was an interest no greater or less than that of any other taxpayer and resident. To Hilton, there was no distinction between a charitable trust and a gift for a public purpose. In either case, the proper party to enforce its provisions, having been given that power by statute, was the state attorney general.

To Hilton, the fact that a citizen might benefit from enforcement of a charitable gift did not entitle them to sue when the attorney general could act on their behalf. The 1927 law gave enforcement power to the attorney general simply because that official presumably acted in the public interest. Private parties, on the contrary, might act irresponsibly, without adequate investigation, or for a non-public reason. It didn't matter to Hilton that the law setting forth this rationale was enacted in 1927—it applied to all public gifts. To draw any other conclusion, he said, would "create an arbitrary and artificial difference between the two situations."[25]

Although Longcor appeared to have lost, it wasn't over. "The scope of the attorney general's power to act or refuse to act," Hilton added, "is not before us." Still, in this case there were legitimate public matters that justified "permitting a responsible officer insuring the continuance of that benefit to the community when it is jeopardized by conduct of certain individuals." "If," Hilton wrote, ". . . the attorney general had, upon adequate showing, refused to act, another result might obtain. But that is not before us."[26] What was more, Hilton concluded, should the attorney general fail to act "upon adequate showing"[27] then Longcor was welcome to return to the courts. Longcor was set back but not defeated. Indeed, the court decided only that Longcor's first avenue for complaint was through Attorney General J.A.A. Burnquist, to whom deLambert wrote, "In the event of your failure to bring such action, Mr. Longcor, as such citizen, resident, and taxpayer of the City of Red Wing will bring such action for the purposes above stated."[28]

Sheldon's Gift

Unlike the board, city council, and the *Daily Eagle*, not everyone believed that an eventual outcome favoring Longcor was unbearable. A *Daily Republican* editorial pointed out that whatever actions Burnquist took it was generally understood that the board's gifts to the city were "unsound legally." Still, the newspaper said, Auditorium profits could be used consistent with its purpose. It thought, for example, of more programs in cooperation with the city's schools, subsidizing extraordinary live musical and dramatic performances, and involving citizens to help identify other possibilities.[29] Not surprisingly, the board ignored those suggestions.

Joseph Alfred Arner Burnquist, a former Republican governor and the only governor to become attorney general later, surely did not want Longcor's case. Burnquist returned to politics in 1938 in a Republican sweep. A political creature through and through, Burnquist was busy inventing a new political future for himself by ferreting out corruption and, because state office holders were then elected every two years, had already begun his 1940 campaign. For Burnquist, there was nothing to be gained politically by pursuing city repayment of the Auditorium's gifts. Merit aside, there was no doubt where Red Wing citizens stood. As the *Daily Republican*, which accepted the illegality of the gifts emphasized, "*Should the state take a hand in the matter and win a decision it will mean that taxpayers of the city will have to dig down into their pockets to repay the money, the entire amount received from the Auditorium having been expended years ago* (emphasis in original)."[30] More, Red Wing and Goodhue County were Republican strongholds. Why risk votes over a principle? Still, if he refused to act, he created a needless political vulnerability. Burnquist compromised. He sent investigators to Red Wing but took no immediate action.

Meanwhile, in cafes, drugstores, and bars, Longcor's case rekindled gossip about the Auditorium's finances. Rumors hotfooted their way to city councilmen who summoned enough courage to ask the Auditorium for a financial report. They got it because, as board president C.C. Bracher said, "There is nothing to hide."[31] But the audit was given to the council only for its brief and temporary perusal and wasn't made public for fear it would be seen by competitors.[32] As Jack Wright put it, "some of those figures, if placed in the right hands, could do plenty of damage."[33]

Longcor's Complaint

The board also agreed to meet with the city council to discuss the "upset conditions" and unfounded talk that, as Wright said, ". . . is highly injurious to one of the finest institutions of its kind in the country." Most of the three-hour meeting was devoted to a glowing financial report from Wright who reported that although business in 1939 was relatively poor, the theater enjoyed net profits of $16,000 since he became manager. It also held a reserve of $124,000, an amount well in excess of the $100,000 the board believed it ever needed. All this, he added, was despite having spent "between $83,000 and $90,000 on remodeling and gifts to the city since 1936. Since reported gifts to the city were just $5,500 from 1936 to 1939, Wright's statements meant either that the board spent a minimum of $77,000 on remodeling, an amount significantly greater than Longcor charged, or that it made unreported gifts.[34]

Wright argued that the Auditorium would be more profitable if legal "technicalities" could be sidestepped to allow it to purchase the Metro from Eddie Ruben, who Wright said he had heard was willing to sell. The Auditorium, Wright said, was "handicapped" because it was competing with a "chain theater . . . that has a big advantage as regards bidding on pictures . . . ."[35] When asked whether the Chief was also a competitor, Wright said that it was not because the Auditorium controlled its movies.[36]

In retrospect, Wright's remarks about the Metro and Chief were questionable. In the first instance he failed to mention that under the 1936 gentleman's agreement the theaters didn't bid against one another. Instead, they negotiated film prices with the distributors assigned them. It was doubtless true that the Metro, because of Ruben's buying power, paid less for films. But that difference did not result in price competition. As for the Chief, although the Auditorium controlled its film purchases, the third movie house added another theater to a stagnant population. The Chief presented a somewhat different product but was, despite Wright's claim, a competitor.

Although Wright's tortured financial explanations escaped hard questioning, the going was rougher when it came to his own activities. Responding to street talk and council questioning, Wright said he welcomed a "laying of the cards." One matter, his ownership of New Prague's Granada Theater, Wright said, was known to the council when he was hired. When Arnold Kosec asked Wright

SHELDON'S GIFT

about the truth of a story that he had sought a license for a theater in Hudson, Wisconsin, Wright said that he had done that only on behalf of an unnamed party. That answer prompted Kosec to bring up the Chief. When the council granted that license, Kosec said, five councilmen knew what was happening but the other four were completely in the dark. There remained, Kosec said, "something hazy" about the Chief's origins.[37]

Yet Wright had ardent defenders. When board member Arthur Hernlem, the city's postmaster, wondered aloud whether movies were declining and if a reduction in expenditures was warranted, another, Frank Ferrin, shouted "What do you want? We've got a manager here who is making money for you and he doesn't get the salary you get at the post office and yet he does five times the work!"[38] C.C. Bracher, the board president, added that, "we have every confidence in him [Wright] and in his ability." At the end, everyone, save perhaps Arthur Hernlem, appeared satisfied as the council unanimously voted confidence in the Auditorium and its "splendid" management.[39]

Satisfying the city council was one thing; Burnquist was another. Six weeks later the attorney general, despite misgivings and in the midst of a re-election campaign, sued the city, the Auditorium board, and former board members Dengler, Koehler, Curran, and Gerlach on Longcor's behalf. The suit sought a full accounting of all funds turned over to the city, reimbursement of the funds to the Auditorium, and Longcor's legal fees.[40]

Answering Burnquist's complaint, City Attorney Christianson asserted that monies turned over to the city were entirely from Metro profits, an argument that lacked veracity since the Auditorium did not separately account for the two theaters until 1932, well after the board made its largest contributions.[41] Anticipating a counter argument that the Auditorium-Metro "set up" was illegal from its beginning, Christianson said that no Auditorium funds were used to control or operate the Metro. Not only was the elimination of Metro competition legitimate, it made possible savings to the Auditorium. Moreover, at least $10,000 was repayment for deficits covered by the city and financial assistance after the 1918 fire. Additionally, he said, even if these arguments were in error, only $8,000, given in the previous six years, fell within the statute of limitations. Because of this, "any other payments prior to that period cannot be considered

Longcor's Complaint

having been outlawed under the law." Finally, Christianson asserted that a reserve fund of $100,000 was "sufficient to meet all contingencies in the operation and maintenance of said Auditorium, [that] any profits, funds or accumulations above said amount are subject to and may be used for any legitimate municipal purpose of said city."[42]

Although Burnquist doubtless wanted done with Red Wing, its Auditorium, its city council, and William J. Longcor, he rejected Christianson's response.[43] It was expected, as a result, that Burnquist's suit would soon be heard in state district court.[44] That was not to be. Months passed. Neither the district court nor the Minnesota Supreme Court heard it. Burnquist was re-elected and continued to chase down allegedly corrupt Farmer-Laborites. The United States entered World War II.

A year later, on December 7, 1942, the first Pearl Harbor anniversary, William J. Longcor walked a block and a half from his home on Twelfth Street to Watson's neighborhood grocery and fell dead. His obituary noted that he was seventy-five years old, a lifelong Methodist, and father of six, and that he had built many important buildings. No mention was made of his lawsuits or that he was a man of civic conviction who had risked much to pursue a principle and the law. Just three days later City Attorney William Christianson delivered a legal opinion to the Auditorium Board. Neither Longcor, Mohn, nor Burnquist were mentioned but the meaning was clear. The case had come to a quiet, negotiated end. "You ask my opinion as to what changes must be made in order to have compliance with that part of the Resolution accepting the Auditorium gift, which reads as follows . . ." Christianson wrote in preface. He then told the board to transfer their existing funds, from which all expenditures were made, from board control at the Goodhue County National Bank to a new fund, known as "Auditorium Fund" controlled by the city treasurer and from which, pending the establishment of fiscal procedures that Christianson recommended, all expenditures would henceforth be made.[45]

It was straightforward. The 1904 document said plainly that "all revenue derived from said property shall . . . be paid to the city treasurer, and shall by him be set apart and kept as a separate special fund." It also said that in "no case shall the said fund . . . be mingled with or transferred to any other fund . . . or used for any other purpose than the care, maintenance, and conduct of said Auditorium. . . ." Now,

Sheldon's Gift

years after the same order was given in 1919, years after Thomas Mohn offered the same opinion, and four and one-half years after Longcor filed suit, the board accepted the outcome.[46] With the start of a new year, it was promised, a new era of financial accountability began.

The city, however, made no pay back. Only the Auditorium's "present" account was turned over to the city. The "sinking" fund of more than $100,000 remained under board control. In September, the board designated member Ruben Cornell its "custodian" and authorized him to buy and sell bonds.[47] Neither the city council nor the newspaper mentioned the settlement. In an era when lawsuits were allowed an unnoted death, the city, the Auditorium board, and J.R.R. Burnquist were all assuredly relieved it was ended. The case was not mentioned for fifteen years. In 1958, the *Daily Republican Eagle* published a local history in conjunction with Minnesota's statehood centennial where it was said, incorrectly, that Burnquist issued "a ruling" against Longcor.

William Longcor is buried alongside his wife, Mary, in Red Wing's Oakwood Cemetery. *Longcor v. Red Wing*, however, has left a mark. Because of it, charitable Minnesotans whose gifts are not in trust gained a defender in the state attorney general who is charged with protecting philanthropic legacies. Whether and how effectively that official carries out that responsibility remains, sixty-five years later, an ongoing concern.

Note

[1] Minutes, T.B. Sheldon Auditorium Board, January 25, 1938; February 8, 1938.
[2] Minutes, T.B. Sheldon Auditorium Board, April 12, 1938.
[3] "Three Local Men to Operate Third Movie House Here," *Red Wing Daily Eagle*, August 23, 1938.
[4] *Longcor v. City of Red Wing et.al.* Goodhue County District Court, Civil Case Files (Case File No. 16563), Minnesota Historical Society. Also "Auditorium Board Attacked in Suit by Longcor," *Red Wing Daily Eagle*, August 29, 1938; T.B. Sheldon Auditorium Board, "Financial Reports Auditorium Board/Cash Receipts & Deposits 1918-1944," Red Wing, Minnesota , Minnesota Historical Society.
[5] Why the additional gifts were excluded is a matter of conjecture. The swimming pool was popular locally, and the swimming pool, it might have been argued, although the

trust deed said otherwise, was consistent with Sheldon's wish to provide for the entertainment of the citizens.

[6] *Longcor v. City of Red Wing et. al.*, Goodhue County District Court. Civil Case Files (File No. 16563), Minnesota Historical Society; "Court Decision Wanted in Auditorium Controversy," *Red Wing Daily Eagle*, September 9, 1938.

[7] *Longcor v. Ben Gerlach et. al.* Goodhue County District Court, Civil Case Files (Case File No. 16564) Minnesota Historical Society. Also see "Auditorium Board Attacked in Suit by Longcor," *Red Wing Daily Eagle*, August 29, 1938.

[8] Editorial, "The Auditorium Dilemma," *Red Wing Daily Eagle*, August 30, 1938. See also "City Taxpayers Are Aroused by Auditorium Suits," *Red Wing Daily Eagle*, August 30, 1938.

[9] Elmer W. Olson, "Aimless Amblings by Ambrose," *Red Wing Daily Eagle*, August 30, 1938.

[10] Ibid.

[11] Ibid.

[12] Minutes, Red Wing City Council, September 2, 1938; "Argue Third Theater; Council Does Nothing," *Red Wing Daily Republican*, September 3, 1938. Haustein's implication that Longcor was a tax scofflaw or too poor to be worthy of filing the suit was a cheap shot. The seventy-three-cent figure applied only to Minnesota personal property tax, a tax that preceded the current sales tax, not to income or real estate taxes. In reality, Longcor had paid considerable personal property taxes prior to the time he and his wife, in near retirement, sold their home and began to live with their daughter and son-in-law. N.P. Olson in the *Daily Eagle* repeated the charge.

[13] "Main Longcor-Auditorium Suits Not on Calendar," *Red Wing Daily Eagle*, September 29, 1938.

[14] Minutes, T.B. Sheldon Auditorium Board, November 16, 1938.

[15] "Remodeling Job at Auditorium Is Underway Today," *Red Wing Daily Eagle*, January 3, 1939.

[16] "Jesse James Rides Again, But It's a Peaceful Ride," *Red Wing Daily Republican*, February 20, 1939.

[17] In most jurisdictions the more plain spoken, "motion to dismiss for failure to state a cause of action" has replaced "demurrer."

[18] It was true; the city had received at least $54,000 in gifts from the Auditorium. There was no dispute as to the central fact of the case.

[19] "Longcor's Right to Sue Questioned in Auditorium Case," *Red Wing Daily Eagle*, September 15, 1938.

[20] "Longcor Case Goes to Court," *Red Wing Daily Republican*, January 30. 1939.

[21] The ruling was six to zero. Ailing Justice Royal A. Stone did not participate.

[22] Supreme Court of Minnesota, *Longcor v. City of Red Wing et. al.* No. 32262, January 12, 1940. 206 Minn. 627, 289 N.W. 570; "City Auditorium Wins in Theater Suit," *Red Wing Daily Republican*, January 12, 1940.

SHELDON'S GIFT

[23] State of Minnesota Session Laws, 45th Legislature, 1927, Chapter 180, H.F. 559, 272-273. The 1927 law read in part, "The attorney general shall represent the beneficiaries in all cases arising under this act and it shall be his duty to enforce such trusts by proper proceedings in the courts."

[24] Cyrus A. Field, "Proceedings in Memory of . . . Associate Justice Clifford L. Hilton . . . " Minnesota Reports Vol. 246, http://www.lawlibrary.state.mn.us/judges/memorials.

[25] Supreme Court of Minnesota, *Longcor v. City of Red Wing et. al.* No. 32262, January 12, 1940. 206 Minn. 627, 289 N.W. 570.

[26] Ibid.

[27] Ibid.

[28] "Red Wing Sued for "$54,000," *Red Wing Daily Republican*, May 31, 1940.

[29] Editorial, "The Auditorium and Mr. Sheldon's Will," *Red Wing Daily Republican*, January 25, 1940.

[30] "Longcor Demands State Act in Theater Case," *Red Wing Daily Republican*, March 12, 1940.

[31] "Council Gives Auditorium Board and Manager Vote of Confidence," *Red Wing Daily Republican*, April 18, 1940.

[32] "Council Asks for Copy of Theater Audit," *Red Wing Daily Republican*, May 8, 1940.

[33] "Auditorium Board, Manager, Praised by City Council," *Red Wing Daily Eagle*, April 18, 1940.

[34] "Council Gives Auditorium Board and Manager Vote of Confidence," *Red Wing Daily Republican*, April 18, 1940.

[35] Ibid.

[36] "Auditorium Board, Manager, Praised by City Council," *Red Wing Daily Eagle*, April 18, 1940.

[37] Ibid.

[38] Ibid.

[39] Minutes, T.B. Sheldon Auditorium Board, April 17, 1940.

[40] "Red Wing Sued for "$54,000," *Red Wing Daily Republican*, May 31, 1940.

[41] Minutes, T.B. Sheldon Auditorium Board, April 12, 1932.

[42] "File Answer to Auditorium Civil Action," *Red Wing Daily Republican*, June 25, 1940.

[43] "Attorney General Demurs to City Auditorium Reply," *Red Wing Daily Eagle*, July 9, 1940.

[44] "Red Wing Sued for "$54,000," *Red Wing Daily Republican*, May 31, 1940.

[45] Minutes, T.B. Sheldon Auditorium Board, December 22, 1942.

[46] Ibid.

[47] Minutes, T.B. Sheldon Auditorium Board, September 28, 1943.

Chapter Nine

The Best Years of Our Lives

"Why can't we have the best films in the swellest movie house in town just like we used to?"
~"Film Fan" (May 1942)

"This meeting has turned out to be a white-washing affair."
~Alderman Enoch "Nickie" Johnson (April 1943)

"I have asked him, and he denies it. I very much doubt the veracity of the story."
~Auditorium Board Member Arthur Hernlem (April 1943)

As the Great Depression faded and the 1940s began, moviegoers reveled in Hollywood's Golden Age. Although naysayers likely agreed with James Agee when he called movies "superb trash" and, in the main, "the same, only different,"[1] the films had become technically dazzling. The advent of three-color Technicolor in 1934 was the most noticeable change. Although expensive and used sparingly at first, it glamorized and enlivened not only blockbusters such as *The Wizard of Oz* and *Gone With the Wind* (both 1939) but a host of romantic and musical productions including Betty Grable's *Down Argentine Way* (1940) and *Moon Over Miami* (1941). Technicolor, however, wasn't the only advance. The decade also saw a host of other changes that included camera and editing techniques, film stock that vastly improved picture clarity, better sets, improved sound, and a more significant role for music that allowed it, as one historian wrote, to "mobilize the narrative."[2]

SHELDON'S GIFT

More than that, the release of some good films convinced many that a marked change in quality accompanied technical advances. Leading a subjective list of notable movies would be *Citizen Kane* (1941) and film versions of John Steinbeck's *Of Mice and Men* (1939) and *Grapes of Wrath* (1940). Others were *Mr. Smith Goes to Washington* (1939), *Destry Rides Again* (1939), and *Drums Along the Mohawk* (1939). At least one historian has suggested that quality improved as major studios, many of which suffered through bankruptcy early in the Depression, emerged from the control of stodgy bankers who weren't particularly good at making movies.[3] Yet despite technical and artistic successes, Hollywood studios weren't particularly profitable. Film historian Thomas Schatz suggests that although business generally improved, Hollywood assumed too early that the Depression was ended and made commitments to big, expensive pictures beyond what attendance and ticket income supported.[4]

Red Wing, in the decade that began with the Chief's opening in 1939, became a motion picture Eden. Where in 1936 there had been two aging theaters, now there were three state-of-the-art playhouses that, between them, presented virtually all of the 477 films produced domestically in 1940. At the Auditorium and Metro, for just thirty cents, patrons enjoyed Technicolor, high quality sound, and A-feature versions of Broadway hits that recalled Red Wing's halcyon days as a regular touring company stop. What's more, films, a time sensitive commodity that could go stale quickly as studio publicists generated excitement for forthcoming releases, appeared within six to eight weeks of major city openings.[5] At the Chief, meanwhile, there was an endless parade of fifteen-cent budget fare.

In 1940, the city council, despite grumbling and lack of evidence, gave the Auditorium board a vote of confidence for having set finances in good order. Indeed, despite continued board secrecy, there were signs of prosperity. A moderne marquee, which many declared for years to come was ugly and inappropriate, was installed at a cost of $1,600.[6] In 1940 and 1941, the entire staff, excluding Wright, who was under contract, were given five-dollar-per-month raises and a bonus amounting to a month's salary.[7]

Although business appeared good, within the Auditorium board all was not well. As Longcor's suit drifted into a third year, there were continuing repercussions resulting from earlier shenanigans. In 1937, pro-labor mayor John Kappel replaced

The Best Years of Our Lives

Walter Koehler with the board's first labor representative, Bernard Schilling, a Northern States Power Company employee and member of the Electrical Workers Union. In August, 1941, Schilling's term ended, and—to the surprise of many and against the yowls of the Red Wing Trades and Labor Council—Mayor William "Bill" Mossberg, a print shop owner, claiming that Schilling was uncooperative with the board and management, refused, over vociferous protests from aldermen Arnold Kosec and Enoch "Nickie" Johnson, to reappoint him.[8]

Mossberg's action and comments provoked an unprecedented public response from Schilling. In an open letter, Schilling claimed that he was not a difficult person but allowed that in his first years on the board there were conflicts (undoubtedly, though Shilling mentioned no names, with John Dengler, "Staff" Curran, and C.C. Bracher, all of whom had left the board by 1941). Schilling said that he had pushed openness and opposed both the film contract with the Chief and Wright's too-generous five-year contract. Had he been reappointed, Schilling said, he would have opposed both again. In his most telling criticism, Schilling said that at one time he demanded of the board in writing to know the "identity" of the Gopher Amusement Company but was ignored.[9]

Meanwhile, a statewide crisis that affected all independent exhibitors was brewing. Independent theater owners nationwide had long chaffed under what they regarded as unfair Hollywood trade practices, especially block booking. Although the Roosevelt administration at first took no interest, after 1937 the U.S. Justice Department pursued a case against Paramount Pictures and the other major producers to force them to divorce themselves from theater ownership and halt restrictive practices. In mid-1940, with the case ready for trial, the Justice Department signed a "consent decree" with five of the eight major producer-distributors (Columbia, Universal, and United Artists were not included because they did not own theaters). Under the arrangement, the Justice Department agreed that for the time being it would not pursue separation of film production and distribution from theater ownership. In return, the producer-distributors agreed to modify their block booking practices by selling films in blocks of just five rather than an entire season's output and to provide advance film screenings to independent exhibitors. The new understanding, which came too late to affect the 1940-1941 film season, took effect in September, 1941.[10]

Surprisingly, after agitating for change, the independent film exhibitors, organized as the Associated Film Distributors of America, protested the consent decree. To them, blocks of five meant that distributors would saddle them with four poor films for every good one and they would be worse off. In Minnesota, the local affiliate, the Allied Theater Owners of the Northwest, lobbied the Minnesota Legislature and succeeded in securing passage of a fair practices bill that required distributors to sell exclusively in blocks of their entire season output but allowing exhibitors to cancel up to twenty percent of the block.[11] Such a system, they argued, was fairer and less costly. The Minnesota law, at odds with the federal consent decree, put distributors in an untenable spot. Compliance with one law violated the other. Not surprisingly, they chose to comply with the federal mandate. In Minnesota, as the time for selling the 1941-1942 season approached, the five major distributors only sold films not covered by the decree—westerns, foreign-produced, and those released previously.[12]

In Red Wing, the looming crisis affected the Auditorium more than the other two theaters. The Metro was affected but received many films from Columbia and Universal, studios not party to the consent agreement. The Auditorium's key suppliers, Paramount, Twentieth Century Fox, MGM, and Warner Bros were all party to the agreement. The Chief received Auditorium rejects but with major studios reducing their B film output an increasing number of its films came from Republic, Monogram, and other independent producers. Westerns and major re-releases, which the Chief also ran, were not part of the agreement.

The situation eased in late fall (1941) when a New York federal judge released the producer-distributors from the consent decree for Minnesota sales.[13] The Minnesota law, however, called for all or nothing booking and the season was underway. For Wright, that meant contracting for more films for the year than were needed in addition to his commitments to less desirable independent, western, and foreign films. The crisis began to resolve itself in April 1942 when District Court Judge Albin Peterson ruled the Minnesota booking law unconstitutional. The producer-distributors prevailed. It was blocks of five after all. As a practice, however, block booking faded. Within a year, Warner Brothers gave it up altogether. For the major studios, block booking kept contract players and back lots busy. As the contract system broke down, however, and as studios cut back on B productions and focused on lucrative A features, block booking made less sense.[14]

As the crisis unfolded, the board encouraged Wright to do whatever necessary to keep the films coming.[15] In response, he booked, beyond the Auditorium's and the Chief's needs, low grade and re-release products. When the major studios began selling to independents again, Wright bought, due to Minnesota law, the entire output. As a result, as the 1941-1942 season ended, Wright found himself committed to too many films. To use those pictures, Wright declared a new summer fifteen-cent admission policy and began to advertise westerns, B's, reissues, and some truly poor independent films. Having advertised all films at fifteen cents, Wright couldn't change policy when a good film came along. More, the major distributors wouldn't allow new percentage films shown at fifteen-cent admission. In these situations, Wright sublet good films to the Chief, an action that produced a flood of letters to the *Daily Republican Eagle*. Although one writer praised the Auditorium for having lowered prices, "I'm all for it and so are a lot of others,"[16] most complained. "Wasn't it the understanding at the time the Chief was issued a license that it was to be a B-movie house giving the Auditorium only A pictures?" one writer griped. "Something is wrong in Denmark," another grumbled. "Let's have a new deal."[17] One asked, "Why can't we have the best films in the swellest movie house in town just like we used to?"[18] Complaints found their way to the city council where president Henry Tiedeman declared that, "This isn't our baby."[19] In late summer, Wright ended his low price policy and told the board he was "making progress" on new contracts.[20] By early 1943, negotiations were completed with all the major producers.[21]

A new harmony engulfed the board. Edward Edquist replaced the allegedly disruptive Bernie Schilling. Frank Ferrin, a cheerleader for Wright, resigned and was replaced by tire shop owner C.E. Tripp. The board directed Wright to negotiate a five-year renewal of the Auditorium's film sharing contract with the Chief. As 1942 ended, Wright, who lost his assistant to military service, was given a pay boost, in addition to a share of net receipts, from seventy-five to ninety dollars per week in recognition of the added time he said he was working.[22]

Unfortunately, the "era of good feelings" was short-lived. In January, 1943, C.E. Tripp, after serving just four months, resigned abruptly and was replaced by First National Bank president Leon Kaliher. At the same time, Wright, citing increased film rental and other costs, warned of diminishing profits. The only alternatives, Wright said, were to raise admission prices or sacrifice profit and "exhibit at approximately operating costs." The board took no action on Wright's suggestion, choosing instead to await the 1942 audit.[23]

In February, when auditor C.R. "Bob" Beattie, who had also performed the 1941 audit, submitted his report, holy Auditorium hell broke loose.[24] After a special session, the board sent Wright a registered letter telling him that after reviewing financial records from 1936 to 1942 and "the amounts paid to you in the form of weekly salaries, weekly drawings, share of profits, bonuses, other compensation, and expense money," that his services were "no longer desired." The letter, which demanded Wright's resignation by April 1, concluded, "In order to avoid any unpleasantness and to spare you any embarrassment in the matter, it was also decided that you would be given the privilege of resigning. We are also willing that you furnish the newspaper with whatever statement you desire regarding your resignation."[25]

Wright, however, told the board that he failed "to see any reason for my resignation as you requested." Instead, Wright invoked a clause in his contract that gave him the *exclusive* right to renew his contract for an additional five years! Although the board howled that it had no knowledge of Wright's exclusive power, its existence was later confirmed.[26] In the following days, City Attorney Christianson successfully negotiated a settlement in which Wright agreed to a short-term contract at seventy-five dollars per week to the end of 1943.[27] During the ensuing nine months, Wright and the board never spoke. All communication was written.

Within days, news of the latest Auditorium ruckus became "street talk." Alderman Nickie Johnson, no fan of Auditorium boards, called for and got a joint meeting of the board and city council to get to the "bottom" of things. At it, council president Tiedeman called for calm. "We don't want any hot discussions," he said. And it was—mostly—calm. New member Leon Kaliher spoke for the board. In 1936, he said, an initial five-year contract with Wright gave him a salary and a thirty-five percent share of net receipts, precisely the kind of contract that city attorney Charles P. Hall forbade for Neilsen in 1916. That contract allowed for renewal upon agreement of both parties. Just a year later, however, a new five-year contract replaced the old. In the latter version, which Kaliher said he didn't know about until he "dug it up," and city attorney W.C. Christianson said he was ignorant of, Wright was given sole authority to renew his contract for another five years.[28]

Fortunately, Kaliher said, the problem was resolved through negotiation. Moreover, Kaliher promised that future board meetings would be public, complete records would be kept, the city attorney would be consulted on legal matters, and manager contracts would be on an annual basis.[29] And, because the Auditorium had been losing money, "for some time," expenses would be trimmed.[30] Noting that the board had ignored previous promises of accountability, the *Daily Republican Eagle* nonetheless praised the board's action. With openness, the newspaper said, "there would be no grounds for rumors and false reports, and people would feel that they really were having a part in the conduct of their theater." The paper added, however, that openness had to be "compatible with operating a competing business." How conflicts between public accountability and competition could be resolved, the newspaper failed to say.[31]

Wright's exclusive contract option was outrageous, and its coming to light surely gave board members heartburn. Board members, however, said they were unaware of Wright's prerogative until after they fired him. Kaliher's assertion that Wright's contract was central to the matter was correct but sidestepped other important questions.

In 1942, it was true, Auditorium finances stumbled. Red Wing's movie houses were competitive and overbuilt. Including theaters in neighboring communities there was no dearth of opportunity to see a movie—good or bad. A larger complaint addressed diminishing film quality. As *Time* reported in June 1941, "Worse than seasonal, cinema's slump was attributed by producers to nearly everything (the draft, war worry, etc.). It's most likely cause: the paucity of good pictures recently coming out of Hollywood."[32] Bank Night giveaways, intended to lure mid-week patrons, drained profits everywhere.[33]

Overall, however, the Auditorium's finances weren't dire. The booking crisis was past. Robert Beattie performed a routine audit in 1941 and reported no irregularities. The board approved staff bonuses that same year. Most importantly, the value of the Auditorium's invested funds, the clearest and simplest measure of its fiscal health, remained at $120,000, just what it had been in 1940.[34]

Sheldon's Gift

Leon Kaliher hinted at the actual cause of Wright's dismissal when he told the city council, "There are many angles which make the entire matter hopelessly tangled."[35] Those "angles" undoubtedly related to Wright's other interests and relationships. Although Wright's ownership of New Prague's Granada was known, a likely problem was Wright's relationship with the Chief. Neither its owner, Walter Koehler, nor its manager, Orville Reich, had theater experience. Indeed, when Reich left for military service a replacement wasn't hired. That meant, unquestionably, that Wright managed the Chief. At the April 1943 board and council meeting, Alderman Arnold Kosec wanted to know whether there was an understanding whereby Wright managed the Chief. "We don't know," answered C.C. Bracher. Board member Arthur Hernlem added, "I have asked him, and he denies it. I very much doubt the veracity of the story."[36] What Hernlem and the other newer board members likely discovered was Wright's personal stake in the Chief. Indeed, Wright's 1937 "no-cut" contract, handed him by John Dengler, was surely intended to guarantee that Wright enjoyed a long tenure overseeing the Auditorium-Chief relationship. Although C.C. Bracher asserted that that relationship ". . . has been a benefit to the Auditorium"[37] it's more likely that film sharing favored the Chief by enabling it to sublet films under favorable terms. What is more, Wright profited from two theaters (the Chief and Granada) while relying heavily on an assistant manager to run the Auditorium.

For Leon Kaliher, the experience was too much. After agreeing in April to continue on the board "to do whatever I can for the interests of the people of Red Wing,"[38] he resigned in May. In the aftermath of Wright's dismissal, the board put a watchful eye to expenses. For a time the board went so far as to require that invoices be verified under oath, an action that suggests the possibility that Robert Beattie had uncovered irregular financial relationships with vendors. Advertising was reduced, Bank Night giveaways abolished, and Kiwanis and Chamber of Commerce memberships dropped.[39] Wright was told to cancel the Auditorium's contract with the Chief that the board had endorsed enthusiastically less than a year before.[40] When Wright asked the board for staff raises, it refused because of the "financial conditions of the business."[41] Eight resignations followed.[42] When Wright complained that the board's belief that it could get along with inexperienced help was based on "absurd" comparisons,[43] the

THE BEST YEARS OF OUR LIVES

board told Wright to advertise for replacements at existing wages. In what must have been disconcerting to Wright, new hires were made quickly.[44]

Wright may have been more troubled by the ease with which he was replaced. From three local applicants, the board chose Eddie Swanson, the Metro's popular manager, who accepted the position at just sixty dollars per week.[45] Afterwards, the *Daily Republican Eagle* clouded the entire episode when it wrote that the board was to be, "congratulated on finally emerging from a rather difficult situation due to various causes. . . ." In making a contract with Swanson, it said, "care had been taken to eliminate a number of angles which in the past have proven unworkable." None of this, the paper added, was Wright's fault since the problems grew from situations that preceded

Popular Metro and then Auditorium manager Eddie Swanson (c. 1943). (Photo: *Red Wing Daily Republican Eagle*. Courtesy of the *Red Wing Republican Eagle*)

him. At last, the paper concluded, cool heads prevailed. "At least there is no harm in hoping this may be the case."[46]

Before Wright's departure, the Auditorium's finances already improved. October 1943, one board member said, was the best "in many, many, months," a result largely due to the elimination of bank nights.[47] It was also true that the motion picture business improved. By 1943 wartime movie attendance rebounded. *Business Week* reported that Americans with "plenty of money and few things to spend it on flock to the picture theaters." The result, it said, was a "superstupendous-colossal" year in which weekly film attendance may have been as high as 100,000,000.[48]

In the next few years, the Auditorium's finances improved further. In 1944, the board spent $5,000 on redecorating and improvements.[49] In 1945 attendance rose sixteen percent over 1944 while non-film expenses rose less than two percent. The following year gross receipts increased twenty percent.⁵⁰ The value of invested funds, the best measure of success, rose to $132,000 in 1946 and $138,000 in 1947.⁵¹

Meanwhile, Wright's Red Wing movie career wasn't over. In December, 1946, Wright purchased Walter Koehler's Chief. For anyone who cared to look, Myra Wright, John's wife, the Red Wing Theater Company's corporate secretary, signed the title transfer.⁵² Within a week Wright, who now officed in Minneapolis just steps from Eddie Ruben's Welworth Theater headquarters on Hennepin Avenue, announced a partnership with Ruben, the Chief-Metro Theater Corporation. In Red Wing, management of the combined theaters was briefly assigned to Harold "Hoot" Bennett, George W. Johnson's son-in-law, and then, just months later, to Jerry Yanisch.⁵³

Most important was the change in programming. Upon merger of "Your Friendly Family Theatres," the Chief was home to westerns, re-runs, double features, and serials while the Metro ran its gentleman's agreement fare. Within weeks exhibition roles reversed. Big pictures, including Walt Disney's *Song of the South*, Cary Grant and Ingrid Bergman in *Notorious*, and Esther Williams's *This Time for Keeps*, ran at the Chief. Considering that George W. Johnson continued to own the Metro building, that the Metro was nearly thirty years the Chief's senior, and that A films were supplanting B's, the switch was apt.

───※───

As the Depression waned, local interest in community and professional theater, possibly inspired by the New Deal's Federal Theater Project, reasserted itself.⁵⁴ In 1940 Red Wing's College Women's Club (AAUW) persuaded the Auditorium board to contract with the Minnesota Stock Company for a series of seven plays (admission priced at just twelve dollars for all) and took it upon itself to sell season tickets.⁵⁵ The opening show, *First Lady*, played to a full house and garnered a favorable review that noted it was the first time in many years that Auditorium dressing room lights were on. Overall, the reviewer said, the evening was "encouraging for those who worked for the return of living stage to Red Wing."⁵⁶

The Best Years of Our Lives

Nevertheless, before the second play, the board, citing promises by the Minnesota Stock Company to present nationally known stars and what it said was the unacceptable quality of *First Lady*, cancelled the remaining performances.[57] Whether it was concern for quality or for finances (the AAUW club reported that season ticket sales were "good" and that combined with single admissions they were confident that the series would break even) isn't known.

In the same year, 1940, a community theater group, the Sheldon Players, presented a forgettable "human interest" play, *They All Want Something*,[58] and a legal thriller, *The Night of January 16*.[59] As everywhere, World War II in all its manifestations dampened community-inspired arts. By early 1945, however, with victory assured,[60] a demand for shared community experience and live performance began a postwar resurgence that in important respects has endured. That spring, thirty-nine-year-old Dr. Raymond Hedin, a Red Wing surgeon, who it was said had expressed dismay at earlier board behavior, was elected mayor. To Hedin, the idea that postwar government, communities, and individuals were empowered to work together to create a better community was unquestioned. As mayor, Hedin created a Citizens Postwar Advisory Committee to address local issues, including, prominently, housing for returning G.I.'s.

In July 1945 two members of the postwar committee, retailer George Boxrud and Presbyterian clergyman Clarence Langley, urged the Auditorium's board to offer cultural entertainment on a regular basis. They proposed six events, three musical and three lectures and forums on current affairs, all to be made available through University of Minnesota convocation "courses." Boxrud and Langley said that, rather than having to secure local sponsors for the events, they believed the Auditorium board was in a "better position" to sponsor and promote them.[61] To make the series affordable, the committee proposed setting admission at just fifty cents per event.[62] Although the board took the proposal "under advisement," with the mayor and community leaders behind the idea, this was no hat-in-hand request.

In August, manager Eddie Swanson reported that he consulted the Mayo Civic Auditorium in Rochester regarding its success in presenting similar programs and the University of Minnesota. Swanson proposed that, although individual tickets would be sold, series tickets be encouraged and that Red Wing women's clubs be asked to help sell them. The board endorsed Swanson's plan[63] and within weeks the artists and speakers were booked.[64]

As community spirit revived, demand for live performance, and enthusiasm for the arts rose. The board, in response, moved to protect the Auditorium's "main function," which it said was, "to supply high-class motion pictures consistently, and to this end protect its position as an exhibitor."[65] A new formal policy stated that no Saturday or Sunday rentals would be allowed, that rentals must be for non-sectarian, non-political purposes, and had to be expected to draw a whopping 600 persons or more. Events, moreover, were expected to be of the highest possible caliber and "non-controversial."[66] Bearing in mind the "caliber" of many films and the "caliber" of a "Jap" wrestler, or the political and controversial nature of its best speakers—William Jennings Bryan, Ignatius Donnelly, and "Fighting Bob" La Follette—the new policy was an astonishing turnabout. Because the growing numbers of requests for Auditorium use were not for religious or partisan events, the aim was to assure movie primacy. The new use policy drew no newspaper comment or community objection.

Although lectures were a part of the first two postwar seasons, including a 1946 discussion of the United Nations, by 1947 the programs (four or five each season) became entirely musical. Quality was remarkably high. In the first season, for example, the eccentric and challenging pianist and composer Percy Grainger appeared with violinist Leona Flood. A sampling of others includes one of the era's greatest violinists, Mischa Elman, Brazilian pianist Guromar Novales, flamenco guitarist Carlos Montoya, and soprano Suzanne Fisher.

Although the *Daily Republican Eagle* referred to the Artists Series as "highbrow," most performances were, in today's nomenclature, "middle brow." Then as today, even audiences for "serious" music preferred familiar classical or neo-classical work. What's more, performers willing to appear before small city audiences began to understand that acceptance often required that a certain part of a performance consist of folk and popular music. Suzanne Fisher, for instance, included *Frog Went a Courtin'* and *Mammy*.[67] Whatever the content, local enthusiasm for the Artists Courses was high and the early events sell-outs. In 1946, 784 season tickets were subscribed. On the evening of the first concert the box office sold an additional forty-eight tickets at $2.40 and fifty-eight balcony seats at fifty cents. The next year organizers sold 764 season tickets and most performances were again sellouts—an outstanding result for a city so small.[68]

The *Daily Republican Eagle* greeted the Artists Series with unbounded enthusiasm. An optimistic editorialist wrote that although many people did not like "highbrow" entertainment, the number who did was increasing because people had greater leisure time to cultivate such interests. "In a day and age when materialism threatens to flood out the qualities which differentiate human beings from mere animals with a high I.Q. rating," the writer held, "this is important."[69] In an unattributed and unrestrained review of *Rhythms of Spain*, the flamenco program featuring Carlos Montoya, the reviewer, who also hoped to see the modern dance of Martha Graham, jazz, and American folk dance, was rhapsodic. That zeal, moreover, was expressed in the context of *One World* idealism:

> For so long we Midwesterners have been forced to accept artistry by remote control, that it is as yet a little unbelievable that here in the intimate atmosphere of our own towns, we can see the living breathing artists of whom we have merely been able to read. Artists who have presented these same finely created offerings before famous audiences the world over . . . another indication of the oneness of the world and universality of artistry in any form.[70]

When the board, in a glow of postwar financial confidence that caused it, despite Longcor's suit, to consider some new scheme to spend "surplus" funds, the newspaper wholeheartedly approved. Echoing the long-held board view, the newspaper asserted that a $100,000 reserve fund was, "enough to guard against future extigencies [sic] that may arise," and that "there seems to be no sense in keeping a larger amount on hand." The paper noted, however, that general taxpayer relief was illegal. Nor could movie ticket prices be reduced because distributors set minimums and because undercutting by a tax-free entity would undermine competing businesses.[71] On the other hand, in keeping with the original spirit of the gift:

> . . . there is the matter of bringing higher class attractions to Red Wing than movies—attractions where not enough local patronage can be expected to meet the necessary expense. Why not a few ventures of this sort, with any loss incurred being covered by this so-called extra surplus fund?[72]

SHELDON'S GIFT

The newspaper failed to foresee that in a decade television, shopping, and spectator sports would overwhelm "uplifting" pursuits. It was also wrong to believe, as the board did, that a $100,000 "cushion" was as much as the Auditorium would ever need. What's more, the board ignored the suggestion that it could do more to support "high class" entertainment. As ticket sales for the 1947-1948 series began, board member Reuben Cornell, a Pittsburgh Plate Glass Company executive, saying that the board needed to know whether the Artists Series could be self-supporting, proposed, and the board passed, a resolution discouraging "high pressure" sales techniques.[73] The answer to Cornell's question, which all board members should have known, was that break even in the performing arts was difficult at best. Although the 1948 operatiing loss was small ($800),[74] there were major unrecoverable costs. In 1947, for example, the board purchased a new Steinway piano for a whopping $3,425![75] Moreover, the citizens who promoted the university series wanted performances accessible to all and as a result prices were kept low. In 1947, a five-concert series ticket cost just five dollars and individual concert balcony seats sold for only fifty cents.[76] Although ticket prices might have been raised, it isn't certain that seats could have been filled at higher prices or, consequently, that gross revenues would have increased. Undeniably, the board was discovering, though it did not admit it, the truth of what Lawrence Schmeckebier wrote in 1946 in the University of Minnesota-sponsored postwar study, *Art in Red Wing*:

> The more intangible values usually associated with the legitimate theater, music, and other so-called "fine" arts are not to be measured in terms of return on the investment and must therefore be subsidized by society, either through its government or its leading patrons. The pioneers of Red Wing recognized this responsibility, but in this case their successors have not accepted the heritage.[77]

While the board grumbled over small losses, Mayor Hedin, wanting to be sure that a concert series continued, appointed a committee of Harold Ullrich, business manager of Hedin's medical clinic and a committed proponent of the fine arts, local retailer Henry Swanson, and musician and music store owner Randall Webber. The committee's recommendation, understandably embraced by the board since it would incur no expenses, called for a "no loss," let-those-who-

The Best Years of Our Lives

Longtime Auditorium board member and arts supporter Harold Ullrich (c. 1960) (Courtesy of the Goodhue County Historical Society)

want-it-pay-for-it model. It wasn't philanthropy, to be sure, but it did place responsibility for sustainability on the city's cultural elite and its businesses. The model, promoted by the Community Concert Association, called for an annual volunteer season ticket drive. Sales were "sight unseen" as ticket subscribers were required to make their purchase without knowing what concerts or even how many would be offered. When the results of the subscription drive were known, concerts were booked. No ticket sales were permitted after the sales drive. There was no wait and see. There could be no losses. The Auditorium would receive its seventy-five dollars per night rent and the concerts would not impinge on the theater's movie business.[78] In November 1948, Ullrich happily reported that the first subscription sale was a resounding success. Led by Marge Vogel, 125 volunteers, an amazing number, sold 948 season tickets at six dollars for the series, a sell out. Four outstanding concerts were guaranteed.[79] The new plan was off on the right foot.

At the time Ullrich and his committee introduced Community Concerts to Red Wing, it was reported that the idea was new. The Community Concert Association, in fact, began in 1927 as the "organized audience plan." Despite the Depression, there were 335 local associations by 1940. In a flurry of postwar growth, that number expanded to over 1,000 communities by 1950. For a fee, it provided advertising materials and organizational help in selling subscriptions (memberships) and acted as a booking agent. As a model it worked well for communities with populations running from just 5,000 to over 100,000. In pure and modified forms it is alive to this day.[80] Some communities with established programs conduct subscription sales but also offer single ticket purchases. All communities have made a commitment to keeping prices affordable. Many have added annual and endowment fund drives. Over the years, the nature of the concerts has changed as well. The 1940s and 1950s were peak years for a middlebrow culture that believed it possible to better oneself through the Book-of-the-Month Club and by listening to "classical" music.[81] In recent decades, however, many communities have expanded programming to include generous helpings of jazz, blue grass, and country.[82]

In Red Wing, the Community Concert model, with one hiatus, survived for nearly forty years and for that the town is indebted to Raymond Hedin and Harold Ullrich. In another way, the Community Concert model with its emphasis on volunteers and expanded participation, however praiseworthy, was unfortunate. By shifting responsibility, the Auditorium Board relieved itself, even among members who unquestionably supported the fine arts, of leadership and an obligation for live and "uplifting" performance.

That the board was at best an unreliable supporter of the "fine" arts undoubtedly influenced the appointments that Dr. Ray Hedin made during his two terms as mayor. In December, 1945, C.C. Bracher died, and Hedin broke up the hitherto boys-only club by appointing the first woman member. She was Helen Pearce, a university graduate and director of the state unemployment office in Red Wing. When Mrs. Pearce resigned after suffering a stroke just two years later, Hedin appointed another woman, Eva Johnson, whose husband, "Nickie," was an alderman whose mistrust of the board was well known. From the dance bands Eva and "Nickie" led for many years, she knew the value of live performances. Then, in 1948, Hedin appointed Harold Ullrich, a true champion of the fine arts.[83]

Postwar enthusiasm for the arts was not confined to touring musicians. In the immediate postwar years a Male Civic Chorus and a Women's Glee Club were formed. The sixty-member male chorus, organized through the city's recreation department and directed by high school choral music teacher Carl "Cully" Sutherland, gave spring and fall concerts at the Auditorium from 1947 to 1954 and traveled to nearby communities. The chorus demonstrated the depth of community interest in both Minnesota's venerable choral music traditions and in postwar revival of community participation.[84]

The Best Years of Our Lives

Mary Gwen Owen Swanson (c. 1953). Swanson was married to Auditorium manager Eddie Swanson, was a professor of dramatic arts at Macalester College and was Red Wing's community and summer theater doyen. (Courtesy of the Macalester College archive)

"Can do" spirit was also a key to the postwar resurgence of community theater. In 1948 Ed Moore, on behalf of the Community Theater Guild, was granted Auditorium use for three plays.[85] Behind the Guild was an anonymous donor who insisted that Mary Gwen Owen Swanson direct the project. Swanson was Auditorium manager Eddie Swanson's wife and head of Macalester College's theater department. According to Swanson's later account, the sponsor, who also funded acting and music scholarships, peppered her with ideas transmitted through typed letters sent or delivered in sealed envelopes. In its first year, Swanson undertook four productions—a territorial centennial salute, a women's chorus concert, and two plays, *Naughty Marietta*, which played to an audience of 2,800 in three sold-out performances,[86] and *New Moon*. But dealing with the anonymous donor, whom Swanson couldn't identify and who funded the plays in cash through an intermediary, proved to be too much. After just a year, "she found it necessary to quit; and the anonymous sponsor would not provide financial backing with any other director in charge."[87]

Although the donor declined further support, community theater with Mary Gwen Owen Swanson's involvement survived. Swanson subsequently main-

159

tained a long association with such endeavors including bringing Macalester College players to Red Wing to present children's plays and working with the city's new radio station, KAAA, to offer local talent shows at the Auditorium that the radio station later re-broadcast.[88] Although community theater suffered fits and starts, it survived as summer theater. The Auditorium board, while sympathetic to community aspirations, griped about extensive requests to use its facilities from the public schools, community theater, the male chorus, a Kiwanis group known as the "Log Cabin Players," and the Junior Theater Guild. As community demand to use a facility created for its use accelerated, its board troubled itself with protecting its self-defined principal role, the commercial showing of Hollywood films.

In 1947 the Oscar for Best Picture of 1946 went to *The Best Years of Our Lives*, a story about returning G.I.'s who, as they adjusted to postwar America considered that in wartime they had lived already their best years. In postwar Red Wing, there was a flood of enthusiasm for viewing, listening to, and participating in theater, music, and dance. At the same time, three modern theaters offered timely showings of virtually all Hollywood films. It must have seemed to many that a new community was born. At the same time, although no one then knew it, that heady postwar culture was already eroding.

Notes

[1] Quoted in Thomas Cripps, Hollywood's *High Noon: Moviemaking and Society Before Television* (Baltimore: Johns Hopkins University Press, 1997), 2, 7.
[2] Paul Buhle and Dave Wagner, *Radical Hollywood: The Untold Story Behind America's Favorite Movies* (New York: The New Press, 2002), 161-62.
[3] Ibid., 10.
[4] Thomas Schatz, *Boom and Bust: American Cinema in the 1940's, History of American Cinema 6* (first paperback edition Berkeley: University of California Press, 1999), 11; Also see Lary May, *The Big Tomorrow: Hollywood and the Politics of the American Way* (Chicago: University of Chicago Press, 2000), 121. May argues that the movie industry misstated attendance figures for many years. Where the industry said there were eighty-five million people per week who attended the movies the more likely number, May says, based upon Gallup polls, was under sixty million.
[5] In major cities neighborhood show houses (nabs) complained of extended downtown runs. In some cases they shifted a popular film to a cooperating but competitor downtown theater. When the first run finally ended they started the clock ticking on the clearance

period—from six to eight weeks—before nabs could show the film on "second run." The "nabs" thus complained that many of their customers had already seen the film by the time they received it and that the film had gone stale. They wanted the distributors to start the clock ticking for clearance when the film run began not when it ended. Red Wing and other southern Minnesota cities were far enough from the downtown Twin Cities theaters that they received new films on a preferred basis, which meant generally a week or two before the "nabs."

[6] Minutes, T.B. Sheldon Auditorium Board, March 11, 1940; "New Canopy to be Built at Auditorium," *Red Wing Daily Republican*, March 12, 1940; "New Canopy Finished at Auditorium," *Red Wing Daily Republican*, September 25, 1940; "To Continue Improving of Auditorium," *Red Wing Daily Republican*, August 13, 1940.

[7] "Auditorium Help Given Bonuses," *Red Wing Daily Republican Eagle*, February 18, 1941. Also should cite Auditorium Board minutes for this. Both for 1940 and 1941—probably January both years.

[8] "Edward H. Edquist New Auditorium Board Member," *Red Wing Daily Republican Eagle*, August 2, 1941; Minutes, Red Wing City Council, August 1, 1941.

[9] "B.E. Schilling Makes Reply to Mossberg," *Red Wing Daily Republican Eagle*, August 6, 1941.

[10] The Consent Decree, District Court of the United States for the Southern District of New York in the matter of the *United States of America vs. Paramount Pictures, Inc. et. al.* (November 20, 1940)

[11] State of Minnesota, Session Laws, 52nd Session (1941) Chapter 460-H.F. 745, 836-839.

[12] See "Movie Dynamite?" *Business Week* (April 5, 1941), 30.

[13] "Movie Relief," *Business Week* (November 29, 1941), 44.

[14] *Paramount Pictures Inc. et. al v. James F. Lynch, Ramsey County Attorney, et. al*, (1941) Minnesota Attorney General Case Files, Minnesota Historical Society; "20th Set to Cut 'B' Output," *Variety* (August 12, 1942), 5.

[15] Minutes, T.B. Sheldon Auditorium Board, October 6, 1941.

[16] Letter to the Editor, *Red Wing Daily Republican Eagle*, June 5, 1942.

[17] Letter to the Editor, *Red Wing Daily Republican Eagle*, June 1, 1942.

[18] Letter to the Editor, *Red Wing Daily Republican Eagle*, May 28, 1942.

[19] "Council Takes No Action on Letter to Theater Board," *Red Wing Daily Republican Eagle*, June 6, 1942.

[20] Minutes, T.B. Sheldon Auditorium Board, August 10, 1942.

[21] Minutes, T.B. Sheldon Auditorium Board, January 11, 1943.

[22] Minutes, T.B. Sheldon Auditorium Board, August 10, 1942; Minutes, T.B. Sheldon Auditorium Board, December 22, 1942. The contract said that either party could terminate on sixty days notice; Minutes, T.B. Sheldon Auditorium Board, December 22, 1942.

[23] Minutes, T.B. Sheldon Auditorium Board, January 11, 1943.

[24] Minutes, T.B. Sheldon Auditorium Board, February 8, 1943.

[25] Minutes, T.B. Sheldon Auditorium Board, February 23, 1943.

[26] Minutes, T.B. Sheldon Auditorium Board, April 12, 1943.

[27]Minutes, T.B. Sheldon Auditorium Board, April 12, 1943.
[28]"Auditorium Board Adopts New Policy," *Red Wing Daily Republican Eagle*, April 13, 1943.
[29]These were precisely the measures Bernard Schilling proposed and for which he was ousted.
[30]"Auditorium Board Adopts New Policy," *Red Wing Daily Republican Eagle*, April 13, 1943.
[31]Editorial, "A Promise that Should be Kept," *Red Wing Daily Republican Eagle*, April 14, 1943.
[32]"Slump," *Time* (June 30, 1941), 65.
[33]Minutes, T.B. Sheldon Auditorium Board, March 8, 1939; for an excellent explanation of how bank night schemes worked, see H.O. Kusell, "Bank Night," *New Republic* 86 (May, 1936), reprinted in Gregory A. Waller (ed.), *Moviegoing in America: A Sourcebook in the History of Film Exhibition* (Malden, MA: Blackwell Publishers, 2002), 189-191. In the aftermath of Wright's summary dismissal the board abandoned Bank Night but it is improbable that Wright ardently supported giveaways.
[34]Minutes, T.B. Sheldon Auditorium Board, November 8, 1943. At the end of November, 1943, the maturity value of the invested bonds was $140,000 and the purchase price $120,000.
[35]"Auditorium Board Adopts New Policy," *Red Wing Daily Republican Eagle*, April 13, 1943.
[36]Ibid.
[37]Ibid. .
[38]"Auditorium Board Adopts New Policy," *Daily Republican Eagle*, April 14, 1943.
[39]Minutes, T.B. Sheldon Auditorium Board, June 14, 1943; April 28, 1943; April 21, 1943.
[40]Minutes, T.B. Sheldon Auditorium Board, July 13, 1943; August 9, 1943. The board was required to give sixty days notice of intent to cancel the contract on its anniversary date. That date had passed by the time the board decided it wanted out. A mutual agreement was negotiated.
[41]Minutes, T.B. Sheldon Auditorium Board, April 21, 1943.
[42]Minutes, T.B. Sheldon Auditorium Board, May 10, 1943; "Committee Named to Study Suggestion of Increase," *Red Wing Daily Republican Eagle*, May 11, 1943.
[43]Minutes, T.B. Sheldon Auditorium Board, May 10, 1943.
[44]"Auditorium Board Fills Vacancies," *Red Wing Daily Republican Eagle*, June 15, 1943.
[45]Minutes, T.B. Sheldon Auditorium Board, Minutes, September 13, 1943; September 28, 1943; "Auditorium Board Prepared For Switch in Management," *Red Wing Daily Republican Eagle*, December 14, 1943.
[46]"Swanson Good Choice," *Red Wing Daily Republican Eagle*, September 29, 1943
[47]Auditorium Theater Shows Profit for Month of October," *Red Wing Daily Republican Eagle*, November 9, 1943.
[48]"Big Movie Year," *Business Week* (February 13, 1943), 37; This figure is quite probably an overstatement.
[49]Minutes, T.B. Sheldon Auditorium Board, March 14, 1944.
[50]Minutes, T.B. Sheldon Auditorium Board, August 12, 1946; October 14, 1946.

The Best Years of Our Lives

[51] Minutes, T.B. Sheldon Auditorium Board, March 10, 1947; March 18, 1948; "Auditorium Has Increase in Net Profits During '46," *Red Wing Daily Republican Eagle*, March 11, 1947.

[52] Goodhue County Minnesota, Register of Deeds, Deed No. 141733, June 9, 1948, Book Z-8, 425. Although the sale was announced on December 31, 1946, the deed transfer was not recorded until June 1948, a full eighteen months later.

[53] "Metro and Chief Theaters Combine; Bennett to Manage," *Daily Republican Eagle*, January 3, 1947; http://users.acelink.net/mrrockydog/FTM/dat73.htm .

[54] Live theater struggled everywhere during the Great Depression. For a time the Women's Club of St. Paul tried to return it to the Shubert (later World and then Fitzgerald) Theater but the appeal of movies was too great and the effort failed. See Besse, *Show Houses*, 37.

[55] "Stage Plays Assured for the Auditorium," *Red Wing Daily Republican*, October 15, 1940; "College Women's Club Joins with Auditorium to Promote Stage Shows in Red Wing," *Red Wing Daily Eagle*, September 23, 1940. The College Women's Club was the local branch of the American Association of University Women (AAUW).

[56] "Footlights Flare Again as 'First Lady' Comes to City," *Red Wing Daily Republican*, October 24, 1940.

[57] "Stock Theatrical Series Cancelled by Auditorium," *Red Wing Daily Republican Eagle*, February 11, 1941; Minutes, T.B. Sheldon Auditorium Board, November 18, 1940; Minutes, T.B. Sheldon Auditorium Board, February 10, 1941. Season ticket holders received refunds.

[58] "'They All Want Something,' To Have Local Presentation," *Red Wing Daily Republican*, May 6, 1940.

[59] Advertisement, *Red Wing Daily Republican Eagle*, January 7, 1941.

[60] For a glimpse at how postwar attitudes shaped and were shaped by Hollywood, see Paul Buhle and Dave Wagner, *Radical Hollywood: The Untold Story Behind America's Favorite Movies* (New York: The New Press, 2002), passim

[61] Minutes, T.B. Sheldon Auditorium Board, July 7, 1945.

[62] "Auditorium Board Favors Culture Series at Theater," *Red Wing Daily Republican Eagle*, July 8, 1945.

[63] Minutes, T.B. Sheldon Auditorium Board, August 13, 1945; "Cultural Series Given Approval," *Red Wing Daily Republican Eagle*, August 14, 1945.

[64] Minutes, T.B. Sheldon Auditorium Board, October 8, 1945.

[65] Minutes, T.B. Sheldon Auditorium Board, September 10, 1945.

[66] Minutes, T.B. Sheldon Auditorium Board, September 10, 1945; "Theater Board Sets Rules for Building Rental," *Red Wing Daily Republican Eagle*, September 11, 1945.

[67] Fred Jonson, "Opera Singers Captivate Auditorium in Opening Art Series," *Red Wing Daily Republican Eagle*, October 16, 1946.

[68] Minutes, T.B. Sheldon Auditorium Board, December 9, 1946.

[69] Editorial, "Artist Series Aids," *Red Wing Daily Republican Eagle*, October 16, 1946. The word "materialism" in this context likely refers to the Marxist notion of historical

materialism or the idea that the basis of society is how people work, produce, to survive. It would be roughly seen as in opposition to "idealism" which here might be represented by the fine arts. As such, it represents an early cold war salvo. Ironically, the Russians maintained a relatively greater "highbrow" culture.

[70] "'Rhythms of Spain Captivate' Artist Course Audience," *Red Wing Daily Republican Eagle*, November 24, 1947.

[71] Editorial, "Concerning Auditorium Surplus," *Red Wing Daily Republican Eagle*, October 23, 1947.

[72] Editorial, "Concerning Auditorium Surplus," *Red Wing Daily Republican Eagle*, October 23, 1947. In a second editorial, "Powers of the Auditorium Board," *Daily Republican Eagle*, November 1, 1947, the newspaper pointed out that the terms of the Sheldon gift agreement explicitly permitted the Auditorium to charge lesser rents or give the Auditorium use free to community groups. The newspaper, in this case, was beating a solid drum, as it had done previously and would do again, on behalf of a wide variety of use for the Auditorium.

[73] Minutes, T.B. Sheldon Auditorium Board, May 10, 1947.

[74] Minutes, T.B. Sheldon Auditorium Board, March 8, 1948.

[75] Minutes, T.B. Sheldon Auditorium Board, May 10, 1947.

[76] Minutes, T.B. Sheldon Auditorium Board, October 13, 1947.

[77] Laurence E. Schmeckebier, *Art in Red Wing* (Minneapolis: University of Minnesota Press, 1946), 88.

[78] Minutes, T.B. Sheldon Auditorium Board, April 12, 1948.

[79] Minutes, T.B. Sheldon Auditorium Board, November 8, 1948; "Kick Off Dinner Starts Concert Series Campaign," *Red Wing Daily Republican Eagle*, October 26, 1948.

[80] See "History of the National Organization" at www.psconcerts.org/cchist.htm.

[81] See Susan Jacoby, *The Age of American Unreason* (New York: Pantheon Books, 2008), 103-107

[82] A website search of "community concerts" reveals many cities that continue this model. See for example, the Palm Springs, California organization's website at www.psconcerts.org.

[83] Minutes, T.B. Sheldon Auditorium Board, August 9, 1948.

[84] Anonymous Typescript, "A History of The Red Wing Civic Male Chorus" (unpublished, Red Wing, Minnesota, c. 1976) in possession of the author; Angell, *Red Wing, Minnesota: Saga of a River Town* (Minneapolis, Dillon Press, 1977), 358

[85] Minutes, T.B. Sheldon Auditorium Board, August 9, 1948.

[86] "Naughty Marietta Cast Set for 3-Day Presentation," *Red Wing Daily Republican Eagle*, November 13, 1948; "Naughty Marietta Finale Tonight," *Red Wing Daily Republican Eagle*, November 19, 1948.

[87] Mary Gwen Owen Swanson, "$80,000—What It Hath Wrought," *Red Wing Republican Eagle*, November 7, 1980; Angell, *Red Wing, Minnesota: Saga of a River Town* (Minneapolis, Dillon Press, 1977), 356.

[88] Minutes, T.B. Sheldon Auditorium Board, August 25, 1949.

Chapter Ten

The Lost Audience

". . . it is profitable for the theater to continue the showing of moving pictures"
~Auditorium Board (May 1955)

"If the failure of the Auditorium to make money was a matter of concern to the board . . . I assure you it was a matter of personal agony for Eddie."
~Mary Gwen Owen Swanson (January 1956)

In 1948 American movie houses began a stunning business decline. A few statistics reveal much. Between 1945 and 1948 the industry reported that as many as 90,000,000 Americans a week attended the movies. By 1950 weekly attendance dropped to 60,000,000 and in 1953 to just 46,000,000.[1] In nine years, attendance fell by half. Put another way, attendance declined by about ten percent a year for a decade.[2] In addition, although entrepreneurs built nearly 4,000 Drive-In theaters in the postwar years, four-wall theaters fell from over 20,000 at war's end to fewer than 15,000 in 1953. That more theaters didn't fail was likely because exhibitors raised admission prices over the period (from an average of thirty-five cents in 1945 to sixty cents in 1953). As a result, although annual box office receipts fell from $1.5 billion to $1.2 billion,[3] the decline was less drastic than the plunge in attendance.

The reason for this downturn is commonly attributed to television and suburbanization—both of which were important.[4] Industry data, however, shows, and Red Wing's experience confirms, that attendance began to fall in 1948 when only one in ten Americans had seen television. Nationally there were 350,000 televisions in 1948, but three-quarters of them were in the heavily populated eastern metropolises.[5] Although there were as many as 8,000,000 televisions in the United States by late 1950, only twenty percent of American households owned one.[6]

In Red Wing, with a large working class population, few "early adopters" had television before 1949.[7] The *Daily Republican Eagle* did not include television program listings until 1950. Christmas shopping advertisements for televisions first appeared the same year when a fourteen-inch Bendix table model sold for $259.95 at the Lee Zieman appliance store. It is true that there was pent-up wartime demand for consumer goods and Red Wing retailers rejoiced over their postwar Christmas sales. Still, average wages were $3,500 per year, and a consumer price index comparison with today suggests that basic televisions cost a lofty $1,500 to $2,000 in today's dollars.[8]

Though television accelerated the decline in movie attendance from 1950 onward there are other explanations for its beginnings. Some historians attribute some decline to film content in light of the emerging cold war, views that may explain a portion of the fall in business in large cities.[9] Such explanations, however, may be too complex to explain the declining attraction of movies in small cities. At one level, film going, once compelling, became commonplace. Americans enjoyed movies, but in the postwar years became, as one historian noted, "choosier."[10] Considering the baby "boom" that began shortly after war's end, the cost of a babysitter, and the rising price of admissions, it took a better picture to get Americans to leave home. Nevertheless, as historian Lary May points out, films of quality and interest were well attended.[11] Regardless, American movie attendance never again reached the relative levels of 1946 and 1947.

In Red Wing, demographics, and suburbanization indirectly, were factors. Stated simply, the population of Goodhue County was static between 1940 and 1965. Since Minnesota birthrates exceeded death rates, stasis is attributable to out-migration. That movement, to be sure, was accounted for largely by young adults of prime moviegoer age who sought education and jobs in larger communities.[12]

The Lost Audience

Film attendance also fell due to industry structural changes that affected Red Wing theaters directly. The first of these was falling film production and the second was a change in distribution arrangements after the Paramount antitrust case was settled by the U.S. Supreme Court in 1948.[13] In 1935, when the hubbub began over the Auditorium-Metro breakup, Hollywood released 525 films. By 1956 releases declined to just 272, a fall that continued into the 1960s when Hollywood releases averaged just 163 per year. There were, to be fair, a growing number of foreign-produced films available and in the mid-1950s these averaged nearly 200 per year.[14] Although theaters showed some foreign-produced films, they were not a sought-after commodity in small Midwestern cities. Thus, in towns such as Red Wing, exhibitors complained of a film shortage.

Diminishing Hollywood output, especially of B films, accelerated due to the *coup d'grace* block booking received from the 1948 Paramount decision. That decline of B films began ten years previously as studios, realizing that fixed costs were similar for all films and that A films commanded higher rental rates, rationalized production. Now, without required blocks, more theaters passed on B films, whose output declined further.[15] In major film markets such as Minneapolis and St. Paul, the Paramount case, including the divorce of production from exhibition, had minimal deleterious effect on downtown theaters where run dates of high grossing A films were extended. Neighborhood theaters, however, discovered that by the time a popular film reached them, a significant portion of their audience had already seen it. To compensate, neighborhood theaters turned increasingly to foreign and serious "art" films and to re-releases. Even so, those theaters suffered heavy casualties.

In smaller cities, the decline of film product had a different effect. Although theaters such as the Chief and Auditorium were "first-run" in their own markets,[16] they did not serve a sufficiently large population to justify extended runs. Nor did an audience exist for foreign or "art" pictures. What's more, the demand for low rental cost, good quality B films remained high. This was partly because rising rental rates for top features pinched exhibitors' budgets. Also, patrons, as one commentator said, often preferred "smaller" films. Seeking a night out on the town, many filmgoers did not want to see "problem films," preferring instead the likes of series comedies such as *Francis* (seven films, Universal

Pictures, 1950-1956) or *Ma and Pa Kettle* (seven films, Universal Pictures, 1949-1955). Moreover, in many small communities there remained a demand for bargain admission cowboy and gangster double features.[17] For many motion picture exhibitors, then, the Paramount case had the unintended consequence of further reducing output for the films they wanted.

Equally important, film bidding, a system potentially ruinous to weak competitors, replaced block booking, which independent theaters despised, incompetitive markets. In one-theater towns such as Lake City, just fifteen miles south of Red Wing, no bidding occurred. Distributors offered films at either a fixed price or percentage, and theater owners either accepted, rejected, or negotiated the fee.[18] But in competitive markets, when more than one theater wanted a particular film, theaters now bid for exhibition rights, a practice that led to higher costs.

In Red Wing, motion picture attendance declined. Already toward the end of 1949 Eddie Swanson and the Auditorium board discussed at length a trade journal article detailing the national slump and in the following months board discussions turned frequently to the quality and quantity of available films.[19] Operating losses mounted. In March 1951 a *Daily Republican Eagle* report on Auditorium finances revealed that the operating loss had increased from $1,021 the year before to $3,374. Invested funds, now covering losses, declined.[20] In the wake of the losses, the board, which committed itself to openness in 1943, dispatched Harold Ullrich and E.R. Quinn to ask the paper to withhold financial information in the future.[21]

Everyone hoped that business would pick up. It didn't. Between 1950 and 1953 the Auditorium's gross income fell from $47,700 to $40,000.[22] In late 1950, the Metro reduced show days to Friday through Sunday. On New Year's Eve 1950, the Metro presented a re-run of Abbott and Costello's *Naughty Nineties* (Universal, 1945). Just three days later, Chief-Metro manager Jerry Yanisch, citing a lack of business, announced that effective immediately the Metro would close through the winter months. It never re-opened.[23]

The Lost Audience

Still, not all was doom and gloom. With the demise of the Metro, there were now just two movie houses. Most importantly, thanks to the longstanding gentleman's agreement no bidding occurred. Under the circumstances, the Chief may have enjoyed a slight advantage because it had access to many lower cost pictures and to extraordinarily good ones as well. RKO, one of the Chief's exclusive producer-distributors, maintained a higher level of B output than other major studios. In addition, RKO distributed the popular and lucrative Walt Disney films that thus played the Chief exclusively. Red Wing also enjoyed a second gentleman's agreement on admission prices that allowed theaters to increase ticket prices, thus blunting the effects of postwar inflation[24] and patronage decline. In 1944 adult admissions increased to forty cents, in 1946 to fifty cents and in 1950 to sixty cents.[25] Admission price fixing was common. Theaters advertised "the best movies" or the "most comfortable seats" but never extended competition to price. A second response to declining attendance was to cut costs. As early as 1948, the Auditorium reduced newspaper advertising. At the same time Swanson contracted with the new, and only, local radio station, KAAA, to spend two dollars a day on ads.[26] With attendance falling, the board dispatched Swanson to ask newspaper publisher Albert Marshall for free placement of "reviews," later called "Eddie Ad Libs," in exchange for increased paid advertising. As business swooned, Swanson also pursued publicity through "heralds, window cards, mailing lists and radio talks."[27] In 1949 the board reduced usher service and saved $25 a month by ending what had become something of an institution—Sunday afternoon organ recitals preceding movies.[28]

While cost cutting was important, the board didn't hesitate to spend its invested funds on the new, audience-grabbing technologies of 3-D and Cinemascope. They were not alone in pinning high hopes on these wonders as glowing reports from within the industry led theater owners to conclude that although expensive, they offered salvation. At the Auditorium, manager Eddie Swanson reported on the "third dimension," in March 1953.[29] At $4,000 for a new screen and projection equipment, 3-D, which required the use of special glasses, was relatively low cost and the board concluded it "owed" it to Red Wing. Importantly, the board hoped that by raising adult admission for 3-D pictures to eighty-five cents, including viewing glasses, the system would prove profitable.[30]

SHELDON'S GIFT

Although the Auditorium believed it "owed" 3-D to residents, the Chief brought it to them first. On June 2, the Chief presented *Man in the Dark*, a 3-D thriller.[31] The following day, the Auditorium announced that it would begin 3-D the next week with Warner Bros. *House of Wax*, a film whose tag line was "Beauty and Terror Meet in Your Seat."[32] The "third-dimension" however, was a flop. The Auditorium booked a western, *Arena*, for a four-day run in August, and in September the Chief screened *The Charge at Feather River*. By October, when the Chief presented *The Moonlighter*, audience enthusiasm for 3-D had wilted. In early 1954, there was a brief revival, or "second wave" of 3-D. Among some memorable and popular films was an MGM production of Cole Porter's *Kiss Me Kate*, *Creature from the Black Lagoon*, and Alfred Hitchcock's *Dial M for Murder*. Nevertheless, by the spring of 1954, 3-D was over. Better 3-D films such as *Kiss Me Kate* were usually shown "flat" when they reached the theaters.

There were many reasons for 3-D's failure. People disliked the special cardboard glasses. Side viewing often resulted in a distorted image. Because two projectors were needed, a reel-change intermission was usually necessary. When film broke, projectors had to be synchronized or the 3-D illusion was lost and patrons complained of headache. Most importantly, a greater key to attracting audiences was not the illusion of depth but the perceived quality of the content.

When 3-D premiered at the Auditorium in late summer 1953, the board was already considering Cinemascope,[33] a more expensive technology. It was not "third dimension." Nevertheless, because of its wide screen format,[34] stereophonic sound, and "you see it without glasses!" advantage, it was irresistible to theater owners. Owned by Twentieth Century Fox, Daryl F. Zanuck counted on it to pull in new and "lost" audiences. To coerce theaters to purchase projection equipment, Twentieth Century Fox announced that it would produce all of its films in Cinemascope.[35]

Both the Auditorium and Chief had little choice but to invest in the new technology. That winter the Auditorium asked the Frosch Theater Supply Company to present a Cinemascope proposal. On the day Maitland Frosch came to Red Wing to meet with the Auditorium's board, Harry Greene, Eddie Ruben's general manager, called the Chief and spoke to John Wright and local manager James Fraser. Greene told Fraser to go to the Auditorium, intercept Frosch, and to

The Lost Audience

bring him to the Chief where he was to telephone Greene. Fraser did as told. On the telephone call, Greene reminded Frosch that Welworth (Wright's partner) was a very good customer and told him to delay Cinemascope installation at the Auditorium until after the Chief had it. If the Chief got the system first, Greene said, he could pressure Twentieth Century Fox to award its blockbuster Cinemascope film of Lloyd C. Douglas' *The Robe* to it rather than to the Auditorium where it would have played under the split agreement. And that is just what happened.[36]

In February 1954, the Auditorium accepted a $12,000 Cinemascope bid from Frosch. But when Eddie Swanson tried to book *The Robe,* Fox told him, although the film was already booked for the Chief, that the picture was in such high demand that a print was not available. Instead, Swanson booked a newer feature, *How to Marry a Millionaire*.[37] As Cinemascope was about to be installed at the Auditorium, the *Daily Republican Eagle* noted that the Auditorium would soon present it. Three weeks later, the board was doubtless drop-jawed when the Chief trumpeted a seven-day Cinemascope run of *The Robe!*[39] The Auditorium was second again. At one level it was a simple tale of minor business coercion and upstaging. That upstaging, however, breached the gentleman's agreement, a fact noted by Wright's manager, Jim Fraser.

In postwar film history, 1954 was an optimistic "blockbuster" year. Cinemascope, however, probably had less to do with it than a string of popular films that began with Columbia's *From Here to Eternity*.[40] It continued with *The Caine Mutiny, On the Waterfront, Rear Window, Three Coins in the Fountain, Seven Brides for Seven Brothers, The Glenn Miller Story, Sabrina, The Barefoot Contessa, A Star is Born*, and probably the best of the 3-D films, but one that did not need that illusion for success, *Dial M for Murder*.[41] One commentator, Freeman Lincoln, saw hope not only in the new technologies and a good crop of films but in television saturation. Americans, he wrote in 1955, had had enough of television with its, "poor vaudeville, 1930s western re-runs, and bad commercials. What's more, they like to get out of the house."[42]

Nineteen fifty-five again saw the release of a few first-rate films including *We're No Angels, Oklahoma, Picnic, Marty,* and *Mr. Roberts.* There was even a smattering of "problem" films purporting to speak to younger filmgoers that

Sheldon's Gift

included *Blackboard Jungle* and *Rebel Without a Cause*. The feel-good films of 1955 were Benny Goodman and Nat King Cole biopics. At about the same time Hollywood released a spate of B pictures that ostensibly spoke to teens. In 1956 a new genre, rock 'n' roll films, began with Elvis Presley's *Love Me Tender*, Bill

Chief advertisement - 1954. The Chief scooped the Auditorium for the Twentieth Century Fox Cinemascope *The Robe*. Note also that the Chief is offering a good selection of A and the remaining B films. The face is of manager James Fraser. (Photo: *Red Wing Daily Republican Eagle*. Courtesy: *Red Wing Republican Eagle*)

172

The Lost Audience

Haley's *Rock Around the Clock* and a raft of lesser films including *Rock Pretty Baby, Rock, Rock, Rock*, and *Rockin' the Blues*. Although youth movies weren't new, these films brought the culture and music of the 1950s to the movies. They were, in an important sense, an "edgier" version of Ricky Nelson's idyllic TV life on *Ozzie and Harriet*. Still, though "edgier," they stopped short of addressing seriously teen crime, alcohol and drug abuse, and sexual promiscuity.

Despite the "big-film" output in 1954 and 1955, 3-D and Cinemascope, teen-films, cost cutting, and price increases, it wasn't enough. Although the Auditorium's receipts increased by $2,000 in 1954, expenses rose and the operating loss was $800 greater than in 1953. To make matters worse, the costs for 3-D and Cinemascope and covering the operating deficit reduced investment principal from $128,000 to $113,000.[43] On top of it all, there were extraordinary repairs. Throughout the postwar period, the board's minutes reveal how costly such items were. In 1952, for example, the board accepted a bid of $5,270 for new carpeting. That amount was four percent of accumulated reserves at a time when that fund earned interest of only two to three percent annually. In 1953 the community room and furnace needed major repair.[44] It was always something, and it was frequently major. Finances headed in the wrong direction.

By the end of the first quarter in 1955 another poor year loomed. To make matters worse, in April the board learned that a Drive-In theater was under construction just outside the city. It was a shame, board minutes noted, that "no control could be exercised regulating the licensing of same."[45] On July 28 the Red Wing Drive-In, owned by Lowell and Gordon Speiss, opened with a Cinemascope showing of *Broken Lance*. Although it always played teen, horror, and sci-fi films, its 1955 re-release showings of *The French Line* and *How to Marry a Millionaire*[46] demonstrated that it intended to compete for adult business.

In the face of new competition, the Auditorium considered, as it had done for several years, another source of income—a candy counter. By the 1950s it is possible that Red Wing's Auditorium, protecting good "taste" and lovely surroundings, was the only movie house in America without a concession stand. As postwar patronage declined, the board discussed installing a candy counter but vowed not to permit popcorn in the "austere atmosphere of the dignified Auditorium."[47] The *Daily Republican Eagle* ridiculed that stand in "Theater Stand Minus Popcorn Like Ham

Sheldon's Gift

and Eggs Sans Ham."[48] Two years later the board considered installing a soft-drink vending machine and asked Eddie Swanson to ask other theaters what income could be expected. Swanson reported that other theaters weren't helpful because all ran full concession counters. What income to expect from soft drink vending alone they couldn't say. Over the next two years, as finances deteriorated, the board began selling on-screen advertising and installed a small concession stand but banned drinks in the auditorium proper and all sales at live performances.[49] In the period from 1951 through 1955, its total operating losses were approximately $45,000.[50]

A measure of the board's financial anxiety was its response to Robert Beattie's 1954 audit. When that report was received board member Ora Jones, Jr., asked Eddie Swanson to prepare a budget that did not include motion pictures.[51] In October, Beattie, who Swanson turned to for assistance, told the board that it could survive on an operating budget of $12,100. Estimated income of $4,600[52] from investments and $1,000 to $2,000 from stage shows and rentals left an annual loss of approximately $5,500 to $6,500. Facing another losing year the board knew that unless film quality and quantity improved, television lost some of its appeal, or concession sales brought substantial income, continuing movies was only delaying bankruptcy. Although the board considered Beattie's report seriously, it decided, "as yet it is profitable for the theater to continue the showing of moving pictures." Jones believed that the dire financial estimates should be shared with the City Council. But no such report, by Jones or other board members was ever made.[53] Board member S.B. Foot, who a year earlier insisted on preparation of a five-year financial plan, a report that was not delivered, moved that . . . [the showing of movies] be "continued indefinitely."[54]

If financial troubles were not enough, at Christmas 1955, manager Eddie Swanson, age sixty-seven, died. Although Swanson was ill with cancer for several years, he kept his health concerns to himself and his family. His wife, Mary Gwen Owen Swanson, thanked the board for supporting Eddie and pointed out proudly that *Box Office* named him Showman of the Month. She also talked about Eddie's efforts to make the Auditorium profitable. "There is great desolation," she said, "in being caught up in a revolution and in feeling that no matter what one does . . . or where one turns there is no way out . . . until the chaos runs its course."[55]

The Lost Audience

Eddie Swanson, to say the least, was a beloved person and all the local notables attended his funeral at Christ Episcopal Church, a stone's throw across East Avenue from the Auditorium.[56] As it would turn out, however, after his family, Eddie Swanson was possibly most missed by Chief owner John Wright.

Notes

[1] Cobbett S. Steinberg, *Film Facts* (New York: Facts on File, Inc., 1980), 46-47.
[2] Lary May, *The Big Tomorrow: Hollywood and the Politics of the American Way* (Chicago: University of Chicago Press, 2000), 223.
[3] Cobbett S. Steinberg, *Film Facts* (New York: Facts on File, Inc., 1980), 39, 41, 44, 48.
[4] Ibid., 39.
[5] For an excellent introduction to early television history including production and sales statistics, see "Television History-The First 75 Years," http://www.tvhistory.tv.
[6] Lary May, *The Big Tomorrow: Hollywood and the Politics of the American Way* (Chicago: University of Chicago Press, 2000), 224.
[7] In 1949 The Tomfohr Implement Company, Red Wing dealer for Admiral Television, invited residents to view their product in action at a local bar.
[8] Samuel H. Williamson, "Five Ways to Compute the Relative Value of a U.S. Dollar Amount, 1790-2005," www.MeasuringWorth.com. Price comparisons are difficult and can be based on a number of calculations. I have used the most conservative measure, the consumer price index (CPI).
[9] Lary May, *The Big Tomorrow: Hollywood and the Politics of the American Way* (Chicago: University of Chicago Press, 2000), 224.
[10] Thomas Cripps, *Hollywood's High Noon: Moviemaking and Society Before Television* (Baltimore: The Johns Hopkins University Press, 1997), 66.
[11] Lary May, *The Big Tomorrow: Hollywood and the Politics of the American Way* (Chicago: University of Chicago Press, 2000), 224.
[12] Lowry Nelson and George Donohue, *Social Change in Goodhue County, 1940-1965*, Bulletin 482 (Minneapolis: University of Minnesota, Agricultural Experiment Station, 1966), 7, 17-18.
[13] *United States v. Paramount Pictures Inc.* 334 US 131 (1948). For a discussion of the decree see Thomas Schatz, *Boom and Bust: American Cinema in the 1940s*, Vol. 6 *History of the American Cinema*, ed by Charles Harpole (Berkeley: University of California Press, 1999), 323-328.
[14] Cobbett S. Steinberg, *Film Facts* (New York: Facts on File, Inc., 1980), 42-43.
[15] Michael Conant, "The Impact of the Paramount Decrees," Reprinted in Tino Balio (ed.),

The American Film Industry (Madison.: University of Wisconsin Press, 1976), 346-370.

[16] The time delay (clearance) between a film opening in a downtown metropolitan theater and in a neighborhood theater was six to eight weeks, with small cities typically receiving a preference of two weeks before the "nabs." But while those pictures were second run in a metropolitan neighborhood theater they were first run in small cities.

[17] Freeman Lincoln, "The Comeback of the Movies," *Fortune*, 1955, reprinted in Balio, (ed.), *The American Film Industry* (Madison: University of Wisconsin Press, 1976), 380.

[18] Interview with Lawrence Bentson, August 5, 2006.

[19] Minutes, T.B. Sheldon Auditorium Board, November 14, 1949; December 12, 1949.

[20] "$3,374 Loss in Theater Operation," *Red Wing Daily Republican Eagle*, March 13, 1951.

[21] Minutes, T.B. Sheldon Auditorium Board, May 14, 1951. Representatives of a unit of city government, one that citizens were ultimately responsible to maintain through taxes, asked the city's newspaper to withhold important public information. It is clear evidence that the board viewed its responsibility as operation of a competitive commercial enterprise rather than of a public institution. In another instance board members blamed shortfalls on free Auditorium use by the public schools. Although mid-week free use influenced financial shortfalls marginally, it is remarkable that the board blamed the very reason for the Auditorium's existence.

[22] At it's height in the late 1920s gross income ranged from $50,000 to $60,000.

[23] Yanisch also managed the Chief. "Red Wing Briefs," *Red Wing Daily Republican Eagle*, January 3, 1951; "Metro Theater Closed," *Red Wing Daily Republican Eagle*, June 3, 1951.

[24] In 1946 inflation was 8.37%, rose to 14.59% in 1947, and was still 7.87% in 1948 before declining sharply in 1950 and 1951. See John J. McCusker, "What Was the Inflation Rate Then?" *Economic History Services*, http://eh.net/hmit/inflationr.php.

[25] Minutes, T.B. Sheldon Auditorium Board, March 14, 1944; October 14, 1946; November 13, 1950.

[26] Minutes, T.B. Sheldon Auditorium Board, January 10, 1948.

[27] Minutes, T.B. Sheldon Auditorium Board, March 13, 1950; April 10, 1950; July 9, 1951; January 14, 1952; February 9, 1953.

[28] Minutes, T.B. Sheldon Auditorium Board, July 9, 1951; May 9, 1949.

[29] Minutes, T.B. Sheldon Auditorium Board, March 9, 1953.

[30] Minutes, T.B. Sheldon Auditorium Board, August 10, 1953; April 20, 1953.

[31] Advertisement, *Red Wing Daily Republican Eagle* (May 28, 1953); Advertisement, *Red Wing Daily Republican Eagle*, June 2, 1953.

[32] The film was a remake of *Mystery of the Wax Museum* (Warner Bros., 1933), a remarkably good two-color Technicolor film.

[33] Minutes, T.B. Sheldon Auditorium Board, August 10, 1953.

The Lost Audience

[34] This was the size for the Auditorium. After Cinemascope was introduced, many theaters that did not have full width screens or where the show house was too narrow to install one, cropped the Cinemascope image to fit. As a result, Cinemascope and competing wide-screen formats were soon available at virtually all theaters.

[35] Freeman Lincoln, "The Comeback of the Movies," *Fortune* (February, 1955) reprinted in Tino Balio (ed.), *The American Film Industry* (Madison, Wisconsin: University of Wisconsin Press, 1976), 374.

[36] James Fraser Testimony, Supplemental Partial Transcript of Proceedings, *John Wright and Associates Inc, plaintiff, v. Harold R. Ullrich et. al., Defendants*, Civ. No. 3-59-169, United States District Court for the District of Minnesota Third Division, 203 F. Supp. (1962) 1070-1074.

[37] Minutes, T.B. Sheldon Auditorium Board, February 16, 1954; April 17, 1954.

[38] "Cinemascope to Be Installed at Auditorium," *Red Wing Daily Republican Eagle*, February 17, 1954.

[39] Advertisement, *Red Wing Daily Republican Eagle*, March 15, 1954.

[40] Presented at the Chief in October 19, 1953, and reprised there after winning eight Oscars.

[41] Freeman Lincoln, "The Comeback of the Movies," *Fortune*, (February 1955) reprinted in Tino Balio (ed.), The American Film Industry (Madison, Wisconsin: University of Wisconsin Press, 1976), 374.

[42] Ibid.

[43] *John Wright & Associates, Inc. v. City of Red Wing and Others*, No. 37,501, Supreme Court of Minnesota 254 Minn. 1; 93 N.W.2d 660; 1958. LEXIS 705, November 28, 1958.

[44] "Minutes," T.B. Sheldon Auditorium Board, November 28, 1952; April 13, 1953.

[45] "Minutes," T.B. Sheldon Auditorium Board, April 14, 1955.

[46] Advertisements, *Red Wing Daily Republican Eagle*, April 14, 1955; July 19, 1955; July 28, 1955; August 24, 1955; August 3, 1955.

[47] Minutes, T.B. Sheldon Auditorium Board, April 9, 1951.

[48] "Theater Stand Minus Popcorn Like Ham and Eggs Sans Ham," *Red Wing Daily Republican Eagle*, May 15, 1951.

[49] Minutes, T.B. Sheldon Auditorium Board, December 14, 1953; October 10, 1955; November 12, 1956; February 8, 1954; June 16, 1955.

[50] Findings of Fact, *John Wright and Associates Inc, plaintiff, v. Harold R. Ullrich et. al., Defendants*, Civ. No. 3-59-169, United States District Court for the District of Minnesota Third Division, 203 F. Supp. (1962).

[51] Minutes, T.B. Sheldon Auditorium Board, May 23, 1955.

[52] The board did not consider how it might derive additional income from its investments, which were committed entirely to government bonds. Unfortunately, more aggressive investments were unlikely to have produced a markedly different result. Although equities did well between 1956 and the early 1960s, postwar stocks up through 1955 moved sideways.

[53] Ora G. Jones, Jr., Cross Examination, Supplemental Partial Transcript of Proceedings,

John Wright and Associates Inc, plaintiff, v. Harold R. Ullrich et. al., Defendants, Civ. No. 3-59-169, United States District Court for the District of Minnesota Third Division, 203 F. Supp. (1962), 219-221.

[54] Minutes, T.B. Sheldon Auditorium Board, January 15, 1954; October 10, 1955.

[55] "Eddie Swanson, Show Man 50 Years, Dies," *Red Wing Daily Republican Eagle*, December 27, 1955; Minutes, T.B. Sheldon Auditorium Board, January 9, 1956.

[56] "Final Tribute Paid to Eddie Swanson," *Red Wing Daily Republican Eagle*, December 29, 1955.

Chapter Eleven

Wright Made Wrong

"This is a Bombshell" ~Mayor Harry Rardin (November 1958)

". . . a subterfuge . . . a Philadelphia lawyer's loophole . . . I have other words for this kind of trickery, and so do you." ~G.W. Townsend (March 1959)

". . . surely no one would ask the court to restrain competition which has been characterized as the heart, brain, soul, and life-giving fluid of our economy." ~Judge John C. Cahill (January 1960)

As Auditorium finances deteriorated, the Chief's circumstances were initially less dire. Wright's and Ruben's decision to close the Metro in 1951 gave the Chief access to the dwindling supply of B films, including some rather good ones, as well as high-quality A's through the gentleman's agreement. Despite real estate taxes of $2,500 a year, the Chief benefited from low overhead costs, strong candy and popcorn sales, the particularly good pictures of 1954 and 1955, and, because of its ongoing association with Welworth Theaters, access to Tom Burke's Theater Associates booking service.

What's more, Wright replaced manager Jerry Yanisch, who had "gone sour on him" with twenty-five-year-old James Fraser. Fraser, already experienced, began theater work as a high schooler and at twenty-one managed the Lode Theater in Houghton, Michigan. Then, when drafted into the Army, he supervised a dozen theaters. In late 1954 Fraser answered Wright's "blind" advertisement for a manager and was hired. Fraser, who said he found the Chief a "100 percent mess" cleaned it and substantially increased its advertising, efforts that he later described as having improved business by "leaps and bounds."[1]

This is not to say that all was well for the Chief. For small city exhibitors, who presented as many as 130 films per year, sufficient quantity was a problem. Already an Auditorium issue, by the mid-1950s film shortages also affected the Chief,[2] which bought many films from Republic and RKO. In 1950 Republic released forty films annually, but just eighteen when it ceased production in 1957. RKO under Howard Hughes's quixotic leadership also saw its output decline until it too ceased production in 1957. A side effect of RKO's demise was that Walt Disney films, which RKO distributed, created its own distribution company, Buena Vista, as RKO collapsed.[3]

When Eddie Swanson died, the Auditorium sought a new manager. Harold Ullrich encouraged James Fraser to apply and he landed the job in February 1956. Wright fumed because he lost a good manager and because Fraser took knowledge about his business to a competitor.[4] The new Red Wing Drive-In was also a competitor. Owner Gordon Speiss, who was not party to film splitting, began to bid, especially against the Chief, mainly for teen pictures. Although Wright insisted the Drive In's impact was minor,[5] Fraser later said, "They clobbered us good."[6] In early 1956, with the loss of Fraser, Drive In competition, and the continuing slide in business, Wright tried to sell the Chief. He asked $130,000, a sum that a theater broker said was fair and would have yielded a good capital gain. But no buyer was found.[7]

At the Auditorium, the board hoped to return to profitability. Fraser, its new manager, accepted that aim enthusiastically. As Fraser settled in, he griped regularly about "product" shortage. For Fraser, an ardent Catholic who wanted the Auditorium's films to reflect, as closely as possible, the tastes of the then-powerful Legion of Decency, it was not only a matter of A films; it was a matter of "family" films. In his quest for them, Fraser precipitated what became an eight-year protracted legal battle. As Wright and Fraser both described it, Fraser told Wright that the demise of RKO and Disney's creation of Buena Vista, its own distribution company, was cause to modify the gentleman's agreement. To Fraser, Buena Vista was a new player of the same standing as Warner Bros. and MGM.

WRIGHT MADE WRONG

The Auditorium and the Chief, he said, should split Disney pictures fifty-fifty. To him, it was a fair proposition. Moreover, Disney released just a half dozen pictures a year, and Wright himself had violated the split agreement when he grabbed *The Robe*. If Wright refused, Fraser told him, he would ask for the right to bid for Buena Vista films, a request that the company would readily approve.[8]

Wright, who despised bidding, was outraged and refused to release any Disney pictures. To him, Fraser's demand signaled the end of the cooperation that made it possible to mitigate the distributors' power. Specifically, Disney films were sure winners that generated huge concession sales. It was also a matter of the potential loss of many more films if bidding permeated the Auditorium-Chief relationship. Not only was bidding costly, distributers sometimes considered factors such as seating capacity. Because the Chief was smaller, it would be at a disadvantage. Fraser made good on his word, and Buena Vista granted him bidding rights. Wright, angry and sticking to a principle, for a time refused to bid. As a result, Disney films were awarded to the Auditorium.[9]

How much the Auditorium board understood of the bidding conflict isn't clear. The board said later that it told Fraser to do nothing illegal or unethical. Fraser admitted that he never asked for permission to bid for Disney Films and didn't discuss his conversation with Wright or subsequent actions with the board.[10] To be sure, there was nothing illegal or, strictly speaking, unethical about Fraser's actions. Still, the Auditorium's sudden procurement of coveted Disney pictures must have been noticed. Nor did the board question Fraser when he reported that the Drive In's Speiss wanted to split some first-run films and threatened bidding if his request was denied. Fraser refused to share films and told Speiss confidently to bid if he wanted to. When told of that exchange, the board, after operating under split arrangements for twenty years, may have wondered what Fraser was leading them into.[11]

For several months, Wright, seething, did nothing. Then, on February 2, 1957, he wrote to Mayor Harry Rardin, a fellow small businessman with whom he believed he had a cordial relationship, telling him about his problems, warning of his intention to file suit, and providing a copy of his proposed complaint asking that the Auditorium be enjoined from engaging in the motion picture business.[12] Four days later, they met at Rardin's dress shop[13] where Rardin told Wright he knew nothing of a controversy and suggested a meeting of the board and city council to "see what we could iron out." But Wright, Rardin said, told him it was "too late for that."[14] Rardin did, however, take the matter to the city council.[15] But the council, after questioning Fraser but no board members, took no action, preferring instead to "await further developments."[16] Rardin didn't subsequently try to bring the parties together. Wright, although he denied telling Rardin that it was "too late" for negotiation and wanted Rardin's help to end the Auditorium's "abusive" practices, took no action to mediate the dispute.[17] Nor did the board. Instead, at its February meeting, a lobby remodeling plan but not Wright's complaint, was discussed.[18] Although everyone knew that legal action would be costly and potentially protracted, no one tried to head it off.

On February 19, Wright filed suit in state district court in Red Wing.[19] Although the key issue was bidding, that practice, detestable to Wright, wasn't illegal. Instead, Wright focused, as Longcor did, on Sheldon's will, which specified that his gift was to be used for a "public" purpose. Operation of a movie house, Wright said, failed to meet that criteria. Wright also charged that by selling concessions, income from which was essential to a movie house's survival,[20] the Auditorium was engaged in an ordinary business, an act that violated Sheldon's intent and exceeded any reasonable test of permissible municipal activity. Finally, Wright charged that the Auditorium held an unfair competitive advantage because, if it chose to, could always outbid the Chief because it had the economic power of government, and tax advantages, behind it.[21]

In answer, the city asserted that the Auditorium was independent, not a city department, and that because it had been conducting its movie business for so long and in so doing kept the Auditorium from becoming a taxpayer burden any issues raised by Wright were irrelevant. Moreover, in showing motion pictures the city was fulfilling Sheldon's wish to entertain citizens; its form was immaterial. End of story.[22]

In November, following a brief May bench trial, District Judge W.A. Schultz handed down a decision. It was neither complicated nor surprising. If

WRIGHT MADE WRONG

there was a complaint to be made, Shultz ruled, it should have been done earlier. The Auditorium's practices were grandfathered behavior. Besides, it was enough that the Auditorium was available and put to occasional public use. For Schultz, "there was no genuine issue to be tried."[23] For the Auditorium board and City Attorney Charles Richardson there were huzzahs all around.[24]

In January, Wright appealed, and that fall the Minnesota Supreme Court heard the case of *John Wright & Associates v. City of Red Wing and Others*. On November 28, 1958, the court delivered its opinion. For Wright it could not have been better. Schultz was reversed unanimously. In the absence of express legislative authority, Justice William P. Murphy wrote, a city could not engage in ordinary private business activity nor was a public purpose served by the city's operation of a motion picture theater. In what seemed a direct barb at Mayor Rardin, a motion picture house, the court said, was no different from a clothing store.[25]

To the "grandfathered" argument that easily swayed Judge Shultz, Murphy wrote that "the passage of time alone cannot give validity to an activity

T.B. Sheldon Memorial Auditorium 1958. The unpopular marquee was set atop the 1936 canopy in 1940. (Courtesy of the Minnesota Historical Society)

183

... [which] was unauthorized and illegal from its inception ... [and where] discontinuance will not result in unfair or oppressive consequences to the municipality," Indeed, Murphy noted that the Auditorium had lost money for years. Ending its movie business would benefit, not harm, taxpayers. Murphy also rejected a city argument that Wright had no standing to complain, a successful defense when applied to Longcor. In this case, said Murphy, Wright suffered a personal loss. Longcor hadn't. Longcor was irrelevant. Because Wright suffered losses, he was entitled to an injunction halting the city's movie business. Murphy then remanded the case to Judge Schultz to order the Auditorium to cease exhibition of motion pictures as quickly as practicable.[26]

Local reaction was stunned disbelief. Mayor Rardin said, "This is a bombshell. We have been caught unprepared. Not much thought had been given to the fact that the Supreme Court might rule the way it did. There are many facets now facing us and they pose real problems." Although city officials considered asking for a rehearing or for legislative authority, few were hopeful. Other options were to sell the theater to a private operator, lease it to a private party, or operate it solely for events not in "conflict with private enterprise."[27] Most assumed that the Auditorium's motion picture days had ended. The *Daily Republican Eagle* asked whether Sheldon's gift would,

> ... stand empty and deserted—a gaunt monument to hopes that Red Wing people would always be enthusiastic supporters of the dramatic and musical arts? Or will some way be found to keep the place open and available for attractions of a high cultural and civic character?[28]

Whatever the Auditorium's future, the editorialist noted,

> Nobody wants an ill-digested conclusion on the part of those charged with responsibility. The matter should be well-weighed. But it does seem that good use can, and should, be made of an institution that has brought so much credit to our fair community.[29]

Well put.

WRIGHT MADE WRONG

In January 1959, the Minnesota Supreme Court denied a city petition for re-argument.[30] Wright's attorneys demanded that Judge Shultz enjoin the Auditorium. And he did.[31] But in an attached memorandum, Shultz noted that the question of whether the Auditorium might lease its facility to a third party was not before the courts. Because of this, Shultz wrote, "it is the understanding of the court that the defendants are not to be enjoined from doing something that they have not done."[32]

Meanwhile, a one-sided public relations war demonizing Wright began on the pages of the *Daily Republican Eagle* when a letter-writer identified only as "Disgusted Citizen" accused Wright of having come up with a "shrewd, legal way" to grab all of the theater business.[33] Shortly thereafter, Mary Gwen Owen Swanson, Eddie's widow, wailed about the "miscarriage of justice" and called for a "massed cry" of protest. "What manner of man or group of men would perpetrate such a situation," Swanson wondered, and why, she implored, "is it that anything of potential given to the people always turns out to be coveted by the greedy eyes of would-be Empire-Builders?" Who, she asked, meaning Jack Wright, would engage in a treacherous conspiracy to bring down the "poor, poor Auditorium . . . [ellipses Swanson] this lovely theater, a gift of such grace and beauty and a place of such pleasure to the people of the community!" It was strong stuff. As for solutions, Swanson was dead set against selling the theater or shuttering it. Nor was she keen on leasing it, an idea that she suggested might have been Wright's motive all along—that he would lease the Auditorium and thus "control" the city's theater business. Still, Swanson knew that competition wasn't the way to survive. "Movies," she wrote, "are not sold like bananas, you know, at a specifically marked price. . . . They are bargained for and the only way an operator of a movie house can be sure to be in a position to make a profit is to control the movie product in a town, to be able to say to the movie company, 'we offer so much for the produce, take it or leave it.'"[34] Swanson was correct. Monopoly was one way to say to a distributor "take it or leave it." The other way, the system that reared Ruben, Swanson, and Wright, was cooperation.

Others weighed in. Mrs. Arnold Kaehler wrote that she wondered if the public didn't care that one man was trying to thwart the citizens by taking "away" the Auditorium. As a result of this "tragic" situation, she said, she would see no more movies in Red Wing.[35] "Taxpayer" wrote that Wright, "had few friends in Red Wing but now, in view of the sentiment of the people, he has NO friends."[36] The Business and Professional Women's Club "vigorously" protested Wright's actions.[37] Some of the sharpest criticism came from Leroy "Muntz" Munson, a businessman who called Wright "selfish and dollar hungry" and wondered why he hadn't tried to close the Auditorium when he was "riding the 'Gravy Train' as its manager." Wright, Munson thought, should have trouble living with himself because Red Wing had treated him well. Now he betrayed it.[38] That Wright had a legitimate grievance and was trying to survive in an industry in trouble was given no credence. Nor was Wright acknowledged for voicing a mythology held dear in America—that the small businessman was the backbone of the economy and that a level playing field was the essence of freedom.

The model that guided most Red Wingites was expressed by a letter writer who wanted the people to "get up in arms."[39] The framework was not understanding but war. In that model Wright became analogous to a Godless commie. It was he who had "stirred the hornets nest." Whatever happened to him was his own fault. Wright had tried to "hornswagel" the public so "he has the only right to the pot of gold at the foot of the rainbow."[40] The *Daily Republican Eagle*, less militant than its readers but no less understanding of Wright, hoped that for the sake of all incensed citizens a way could be found to "circumvent" the decision.[41] "Perhaps some angle may be uncovered whereby this dark picture can be brightened; perhaps a rift will be found in the clouds that now shroud it."[42]

The "angle," was already found. On January 23, the board announced that it had entered into a $500-per-month lease with James Fraser who would continue to operate the Auditorium as a movie house. In the lease, the board retained rights to veto "objectionable" entertainments and to weekday public use just twelve days per year with additional time available for a rental fee paid to Fraser. Major repairs, undefined, were the board's responsibility.[43] Board President Harold Ullrich emphasized that Fraser was a "completely private operator. He's on his own to sink or swim in his own business."[44]

For his part, Fraser assured locals that he would present "the same high caliber . . . entertainment as in the past."[45] As if to underscore that claim, the Red Wing Art Association, as part of "Art Week in Red Wing," sponsored a mid-week

WRIGHT MADE WRONG

Auditorium showing of Lawrence Oliver's 1944 film, *Henry V*.[46] That event was touted as proof that because "art is in the movies" citizens should "leave no stone unturned to preserve the character of this unique community asset."[47] Unfortunately, that film was the only Art Week event at the Auditorium. On that weekend the Auditorium's own booking was *Tarzan's Fight for Life*, a film that invited cinema aficionados to take in "The island of killer crocodiles!—The dread 'spread-eagle' torture!—The hypnotized strangler!—Spine-chilling native blood rites!—and Tarzan's beautiful mate attacked!"[48]

Seemingly straightforward, Fraser's lease raised questions. As a public facility bids might have been expected. The lease sum was no more than the board's underbudgeted and unfunded annual depreciation. Considering the sums spent on maintenance the $6,000 fee was unlikely to cover more than major repairs, if that. Indeed, the building was then appraised at about $300,000. A twenty-five-year depreciation schedule suggests a $15,000 a year set aside—more than twice Fraser's lease.

The lease should have, but didn't, raise real and personal property tax questions since Minnesota statute provided that when a municipal property was used for for-profit purposes it reverted to the tax rolls. The Chief paid $2,500 annual real property taxes. Finally, the board determined that the dressing rooms, community room, and other areas was public space not leased to Fraser. For that reason the board paid one-third of utility costs. It seemed reasonable, but wasn't. "Public" space, for the most part, couldn't be used when Fraser showed movies. It was all or none. In fact, since the Auditorium was reserved for "public" use just twelve days a year, Fraser might have been expected to foot the bill for ninety percent, not sixty percent, of utility costs. For Fraser, the lease was a "sweetheart" deal that allowed movies to continue while the board spent its way to ruin. Fraser was a young businessman on his own, but one with nothing at risk.

About town there were hurrahs. On January 29, twenty-six merchants bought a two-page newspaper advertisement wishing Fraser well. "It is essential to the city of Red Wing to have the Auditorium, not only for the entertainment it provides for its own citizens, but for the economic health of our community . . ." the sponsors wrote in their open letter to Fraser.[49] In the following weeks, support widened. The local Lion's Club sold discount coupon books good for Auditorium movie tickets. The drive's goal, organizers said, was to "provide James Fraser . . . sufficient working capital with which to provide the city with top movie attractions."[50] Sales drives often support schools and charities of course but raising capital for a private businessperson "on his own" was another matter altogether. A month later young Jim Fraser was handed a Junior Chamber of Commerce Distinguished Service Award for his "lasting contribution to community welfare."[51]

Wright cried foul. His attorneys petitioned the Minnesota Supreme Court for a *writ of mandamus*, an order to trial judge Schultz to comply immediately with the Supreme Court's decision. Schultz's memorandum leaving the door to a lease open, Wright's petition said, "wholly [ignored] the issues of the case which this court has resolved in favor of the claims of [Wright]."[52] In oral argument, Wright's attorney, G.W. Townsend, charged that Fraser's lease was ". . . a subterfuge . . . a Philadelphia lawyer's loophole . . . I have other words for this kind of trickery, and so do you." The question, Townsend charged, was "has the lower court attempted to subvert and pervert the order of this Court? And it certainly has!" The lease was irrelevant. When the legislature allowed the city to accept Sheldon's gift it specified that the Auditorium was "exclusively" for a "public purpose." "The operation of a private business," Townsend said, "was never contemplated . . . nor authorized . . . ."[53]

For Red Wing, city attorney Charles Richardson argued that Judge Schultz did not err. The Sheldon deed, he said, explicitly allowed leasing, an argument that Richardson previously acknowledged was weak. He added, however, that Judge Schultz followed the Supreme Court's decision correctly because the question of leasing wasn't previously before the court.[54]

As they awaited a decision, the city, mindful of a Supreme Court mention that Auditorium use as a motion picture theater lacked legislative authorization, asked its state representatives to introduce bills sanctioning the lease and the showing of motion pictures. Whether successful or not, the newspaper said,

Wright Made Wrong

> . . . it is comforting to know that the great majority of citizens who are incensed at the action which threatens to take from them an institution they have cherished for half a century has a champion in the legislature ready and willing to take any action possible to prevent such an occurrence.[55]

A bill was introduced on March 13, 1959,[56] and its first committee hearing didn't go well. Minneapolis representative F. Gordon Wright, John Wright's brother, denounced it and raised the uncomfortable question of real and personal property taxes.[57] The lease, Gordon Wright said, "is just an escape from the Supreme Court decision and I have no doubt that the forthcoming ruling of the Supreme Court will uphold my position."[58] Although Wright's opposition dealt a blow, the bill remained alive.[59] Buttonholing ensued. In the final vote, the legislation, including a requirement that Red Wing call a special election to approve or reject Fraser's lease, but silent on the matter of taxation, passed both houses by lopsided margins.[60]

While awaiting a Supreme Court ruling on his petition for a *writ of mandamus*, Wright took action to counter the lease, the legislation, and bad publicity. Although prior to Fraser's lease both theaters faced bidding challenges from the Red Wing Drive-In, both the Auditorium and the Chief honored the gentleman's agreement with the exception of Disney films. When the Auditorium signed Fraser's lease, Wright wrote to the Auditorium's film distributors—Paramount, Twentieth Century Fox, United Artists, Warner Bros., and MGM. He told them that as a result of his unanimous Minnesota Supreme Court victory Fraser was operating an illegal theater and that they should quit selling to him. Some took Wright at his word. Others agreed to sell to Fraser but only under competitive bidding. As a result, Fraser, facing a serious film shortage, demanded competitive bidding from the Chief's suppliers, principally Universal and Columbia. In retaliation, Wright demanded bidding rights from all of Fraser's film distributors. A full-scale, expensive bidding war ensued. Ironically, Wright, to whom bidding was odious, brought it on.[61]

In February, Wright distributed widely the *Chief News*, a newspaper-like broadside that hit on all of Wright's key issues. Headlines included: "Auditorium Board Misused Trust: Oppressive Tactics, Illegal Acts of Board and Manager Bring On Fatal Lawsuit," and "Read What Mr. Sheldon Really Said." The *News* included an abbreviated Auditorium budget from 1951 to 1956 demonstrating how the board's reserves were shrinking and how its motion picture business depended on candy and popcorn sales. It also included a list of the Chief's better coming attractions. Some, including *Porgy and Bess, Ben Hur,* and *North by Northwest,* demonstrated that the Chief also exhibited a broad range of A features.[62]

The *Chief News* included the state Supreme Court's opinion as well as the text of Wright's letter to Mayor Rardin. It was all there, including a claim that the *Daily Republican Eagle* failed to fairly represent Wright's side of the story by refusing to print a copy of Wright's letter to Rardin and the text of the Supreme Court's opinion. Wright wrote that as a result the newspaper had, ". . . contributed greatly to the success of this most unwarranted campaign of vilification and abuse." On the other hand, Wright said, the paper had "devoted columns and columns to letters written, in ignorance of the true facts, by people intentionally misled and misinformed and who might conceivably be of quite another shade of opinion had they been in possession of all these facts."[63]

Likely only a handful of Red Wingites waded through all 10,000 words. Though it explained a great deal, the *Chief News* didn't explain the realities of bidding, the gentleman's agreement, or detail how Wright was damaged. Nor did Wright attack Fraser's lease terms, which might have been helpful, undoubtedly because he held that the lease itself was a subterfuge. The *Chief News* might have been better prepared but it wouldn't have changed anyone's mind. "Facts" didn't matter.

The day after the *Chief News* appeared, the *Daily Republican Eagle*, in an editorial entitled "We Are Accused," played victim to Wright's "unreasonable" attack. The "who us?" editorial explained that the newspaper didn't publish either Justice Murphy's decision or Wright's letter to Rardin for "simple" reasons. The court decision, ". . . couched in legal language not easily understood by non-lawyers, would have filled four . . . columns. And the publication of these documents without explanations as to their meanings would have been pointless." As for Wright's lengthy letter to Rardin, the paper felt that it was better to have Wright explain it himself. Although the paper, it said, invited Wright to respond, he hadn't done it, something that was "hard to reconcile" with his charge of unfair treatment. As for the newspaper supporting the Auditorium, "We have made no bones about the fact that we feel . . . John Wright is rendering a disservice to the community in bringing legal action. . . ."[64]

WRIGHT MADE WRONG

The newspaper's view that the public was unable to understand Justice Murphy's opinion is questionable. Phrases such as "the Auditorium is in a position where it can and does have undue advantage over the plaintiff" and . . . "The plaintiff is thereby damaged and injured, which damage and injury is real and serious"[65] didn't require a law degree to understand. Nor did it make sense for the paper to claim that it could not afford to give so much column space as Wright demanded to Auditorium issues. That argument might have made sense had it not been for many days of page-one coverage devoted to the suit, its editorials, several "Aimless Amblings by Ambrose"[66] columns, and the many reader harangues.

The newspaper may have thought it peculiar that Wright refused to argue his case in a letter but it made sense. Wright had a unanimous court on his side. Why plead one's own case when others and the facts spoke for themselves. It was not surprising that sentiment ran strongly against Wright when the newspaper never presented Wright's side of the issue.

As the referendum neared, Wright distributed leaflets urging a "no" vote. Compared to the forces aligned against him, however, Wright may as well have stayed abed. In the days before the referendum, the *Daily Republican Eagle* ran sample ballots, which called simply for a yes or no vote on the question, but offered no details on the lease that voters were being asked to approve. A volunteer committee, "Friends of the Auditorium," headed by "Muntz" Munson bought a full-page ad urging a yes vote.[67] The AFL-CIO also urged a "yes" vote to "save" the Auditorium. The Chamber of Commerce, although it did not otherwise advocate voting, took no position but urged everyone to vote.[68] No business, labor, or civic group fostered discussion of the lease.

On the weekend before the election, a *Daily Republican Eagle* editorial reminded voters that stage plays were a thing of the past, that movies were a logical extension of what the Auditorium always presented, and that a taxpayer burden would result if the Auditorium's movie business ended. Although the sniffy writer declared that "we have little use ourselves" for movies, he was certain that the Auditorium offered many excellent films.[69] Populism from above. It was Jens K. Grondahl restated—movies are for the "unmoneyed" class. The paper also printed that day a letter from Dr. N.L. Werner who said a "yes" vote would enable citizens to gain control of their Auditorium and an opportunity for "licking this bunch forever." How leasing a facility that had never asked citizens what they wanted from their opera house would result in public control Werner didn't say.[70]

Although some feared the outcome, anxiety was unwarranted.[71] In one of the most lopsided elections in Minnesota history fifty-three percent of eligible voters turned out to vote 2,762 to 47 in favor of a lease whose terms were not public. Trust ran high. In one precinct, the vote was unanimous.[72] The forty-seven percent who didn't vote may not have cared about the Auditorium but they didn't care about John Wright either.

A few days after the election the Minnesota Supreme Court ruled, four to three, in a decision written by Justice Frank Gallagher, that without "any express directions the trial court was free to proceed in any manner not inconsistent with the opinion." The court didn't consider a lease previously and couldn't do so now. Challenging the validity of a lease required a new proceeding.[73] For Wright, it was bad news. Still there was reason to believe he would prevail. Although four of seven justices agreed that Wright wouldn't get his writ, only three signed on to Gallagher's opinion. The fourth, Justice Murphy, who wrote the unanimous opinion favoring Wright the previous November, wrote a separate, concurring opinion.[74]

Justice Martin Nelson, noting that Wright based his suit on two premises, wrote the minority (three justices) opinion. One premise was that common commercial ventures were beyond the scope and authority of the city. It was, in the Latin, *ultra vires*. The second was that Sheldon's will directed his gift for "exclusively" beneficent and public purposes. Because both premises were before the court, Nelson wrote, the purpose for which the building was leased could not be for an ordinary for-profit movie theater "whether it is operated directly by the board or leased by the board and operated therein by a lessee of the board."[75]

Nelson also addressed the city's argument that the Sheldon enabling document allowed the board to "let or lease" the property and that case law in *Anderson vs. City of Montevideo* permitted a municipality to lease property it no longer used.[76] The city also argued that what was meant by the term "let or lease" in the enabling documents was beyond the court's authority to determine because, as in Longcor, enforcement of charitable gift terms rested with the state's attorney general. To Nelson, Longcor was irrelevant. Wright could sue where Longcor couldn't, Nelson said. Longcor sought to right a general wrong that the attorney general could correct. Wright's suit, however, was a "private action." Indeed, it would be inappropriate for the attorney general to aid a private party in such a matter. To sum up, Nelson reaffirmed that "Any and all authority to lease and let was before the court when the matter was heard and decided," and that operation of a motion picture theater was a competitive business not authorized by either the Sheldon documents or statute.[77]

The third opinion, Justice William P. Murphy's, concurred that Wright was not entitled to his writ. Murphy held that his earlier opinion [in Wright] was confined to a finding that the city could not engage in a private business, a finding that did not "disturb" *Anderson v. City of Montevideo*. The lease could not have been before the court, Murphy said, because Wright had no more standing than Longcor. "Our decision [in Wright]," Murphy wrote, "has given him the only relief to which he is entitled—namely, to be free from the direct competition of a business conducted by the city." The court's decision, said Murphy, "was not intended to leave the city with a large auditorium on its hands which it could not rent out to others."[78]

Despite the setback, Wright had to have been hopeful. It seemed reasonable to rely on the three dissenting votes. If just one of the three who joined with Gallagher opposed the lease, Wright would prevail four to three. Wright pressed on.[79] In August he filed a new suit in Goodhue County District Court asking for a permanent injunction overturning Fraser's lease.[80] Judge John C. Cahill of Waseca heard the case in late October.[81] Although arguments plowed old ground, accountant C.R. Beattie testified that the lease would save the Auditorium $2,150 per year in overhead. That, combined with the $6,000 lease payment would result in an annual gain of $8,150, a happy consequence that the *Daily Republican Eagle* headlined, "Auditorium Profit Cited by Leasing Municipal Theater,"[82] It wasn't mentioned that $8,150 would have to cover the Auditorium's share of normal expenses and all major repairs. If previous costs were any gauge, it wasn't enough.

SHELDON'S GIFT

On January 7, 1960, Cahill found for the city and its lease. If Wright suffered a loss, it was due to nothing more than competition. Without defining fair competition, Cahill added that, "surely no one would ask the court to restrain competition which has been characterized as the heart, brain, soul and life-giving fluid of our economy."[83] As expected, Wright appealed to the Minnesota Supreme Court. What's more, whether to bolster his case or because business was simply rotten, Wright closed the Chief on June 1.

On November 18, 1960, in an opinion that must have stunned Wright, the Minnesota Supreme Court upheld Cahill unanimously.[84] Wright won unanimously, lost narrowly, and now lost unanimously. The justices who appeared to be with him abandoned him. Although Justice Frank Gallagher spoke for the court, the opinion reflected Justice Murphy's views and relied heavily on *Anderson v. Montevideo*.[85] Nor, because the theater lacked a specific public purpose, was built as a theater, and was used in a manner consistent with that purpose did the lease violate Sheldon's terms. Further, the court said that even if the city exceeded its authority, Wright could not "sue on his own behalf to compel compliance with a condition impressed upon a gift for a charitable purpose." That was a matter for the attorney general. Longcor. Citing *Tennessee Electric Power Co. v. Tennessee Valley Authority* and *Alabama Power Co. v. Ickes*, the court added, "damages because of competition by a municipal or governmental agency, operating an otherwise lawful business, do not support a cause of action or a right to sue."[86] Wright was wrong. Was it over? No.

Notes

[1] James Fraser Testimony, Supplemental Partial Transcript of Proceedings, *John Wright and Associates, a Corporation, Plaintiff, v. Harold R. Ullrich et. al*, Defendants, Civ. No. 3-59-169, United States District Court for the District of Minnesota Third Division, 203 F. Supp. 744, 1962718.

[2] James Fraser Deposition, *John Wright and Associates Inc, plaintiff, v. Harold R. Ullrich et. al., Defendants*, Civ. No. 3-59-169, United States District Court for the District of Minnesota Third Division, 203 F. Supp. 744, 1962.

[3] Findings of Fact, *John Wright and Associates Inc, plaintiff, v. Harold R. Ullrich et. al.*,

Defendants, Civ. No. 3-59-169, United States District Court for the District of Minnesota Third Division, 203 F. Supp. 744, 1962.

[4] James Fraser Testimony, Supplemental Partial Transcript of Proceedings, *John Wright and Associates Inc, plaintiff, v. Harold R. Ullrich et. al., Defendants*, Civ. No. 3-59-169, United States District Court for the District of Minnesota Third Division, 203 F. Supp. 744, 1962.

[5] "Wright Tells of 20 Years in Red Wing Theater Business," *Red Wing Daily Republican Eagle*, September 26, 1961.

[6] "Theater Managers Testify Wright Said Chief Outgrossed Auditorium," *Red Wing Daily Republican Eagle*, October 21, 1961; James Fraser Testimony, Supplemental Partial Transcript of Proceedings, *John Wright and Associates Inc, plaintiff, v. Harold R. Ullrich et. al., Defendants*, Civ. No. 3-59-169, United States District Court for the District of Minnesota Third Division, 203 F. Supp. 744, 1962.

[7] "Wright Investigators Tell of Questioning Red Wing Residents on Theater Situation," *Red Wing Daily Republican Eagle*, October 18, 1961.

[8] John Wright Deposition, James Fraser Testimony, Supplemental Partial Transcript of Proceedings, *John Wright and Associates Inc, plaintiff, v. Harold R. Ullrich et. al., Defendants*, Civ. No. 3-59-169, United States District Court for the District of Minnesota Third Division, 203 F. Supp. 744, 1962.

[9] See "Disney Films Started Theater Feud Here," *Red Wing Daily Republican Eagle*, September 27, 1961. In March, 1958 the Chief was awarded the new Disney release *Old Yeller*.

[10] James Fraser Testimony, *John Wright and Associates Inc., Plaintiff v. Harold R. Ullrich et. al., Defendants*, Civ. No. 3-59-169, United States District Court for the District of Minnesota, Third Division, 203 F. supp. 744, 1962. , 1102-1103.

[11] Ibid.

[12] Letter, John Wright to Harry Rardin (February 2, 1957), Reprinted in "Read the Facts," *The Chief News*, February 24, 1959.

[13] Minutes, Red Wing City Council, February 7, 1957.

[14] Harry Rardin Testimony, *John Wright and Associates Inc., Plaintiff v. Harold R. Ullrich et. al., Defendants*, Civ. No. 3-59-169, United States District Court for the District of Minnesota, Third Division, 203 F. supp. 744, 1962, 7-9.

[15] Minutes, Red Wing City Council, February 7, 1957; "Legality of Auditorium as Film Playhouse Questioned," *Red Wing Daily Republican Eagle*, February 3, 1957.

[16] "Legality of Auditorium as Film Playhouse Questioned," *Red Wing Daily Republican Eagle*, February 7, 1957.

[17] John Wright Testimony, *John Wright and Associates Inc., Plaintiff v. Harold R. Ullrich et. al., Defendants*, Civ. No. 3-59-169, United States District Court for the District of Minnesota, Third Division, 203 F. supp. 744, 1962 ,749-752. Also see "Rardin: Wright Spurned 'Peace' Bid," *Red Wing Daily Republican Eagle*, September 8, 1961.

[18] "Plan Remodeling at Auditorium," *Red Wing Daily Republican Eagle*, February 12, 1957; Minutes, T.B. Sheldon Memorial Auditorium, February 11, 1957.

Sheldon's Gift

[19] Wright was represented by the Fryberger, Townsend and Ewing law firm.
[20] In 1956, the first full year of offering concessions, the Auditorium grossed $7,481.50 or fourteen percent of its income, from them. That income was largely responsible for reducing the operating loss from $5,000 in 1955 to $1,000 in 1956. See *John Wright & Associates, Inc. v. City of Red Wing and Others*, No. 37501, Supreme Court of Minnesota, 254 Minn. 1; 93N.W.2d 660; 1958 Minn. LEXIS 705 (November 28, 1958).
[21] "Auditorium Operation Violates Terms of Will," *Red Wing Daily Republican Eagle*, March 20, 1957.
[22] "City Answers Wright Complaint," *Red Wing Daily Republican Eagle*, May 14, 1957.
[23] "City Wins Theater Court Suit," *Red Wing Daily Republican Eagle*, November 16, 1957.
[24] Minutes, T.B. Sheldon Auditorium Board, December 9, 1957.
[25] *John Wright & Associates, Inc. v. City of Red Wing and Others*, No. 37501, Supreme Court of Minnesota, 254 Minn. 1; 93N.W.2d 660; 1958 Minn. LEXIS 705 (November 28, 1958).
[26] Ibid.
[27] "Auditorium Ordered to Quit Movie Business," *Red Wing Daily Republican Eagle*, November 28, 1958. Although the 1904 agreement explicitly allowed leasing, it was thought, at least on November 28, 1958, that "it was doubtful that such a lease could provide for continued operation of the theater as a movie playhouse."
[28] Editorial, "Past, Present, and Future," *Red Wing Daily Republican Eagle*, December 1, 1958.
[29] Ibid.
[30] "Auditorium Re-argument Is Denied," *Red Wing Daily Republican Eagle*, January 10, 1959.
[31] "Auditorium Hearing Scheduled Friday," *Red Wing Daily Republican Eagle*, January 13, 1959.
[32] "Court Sets February 16 for Last Movie at Auditorium," *Red Wing Daily Republican Eagle*, January 20, 1959.
[33] Letter to the Editor. "Unfortunate," *Red Wing Daily Republican Eagle*, December 3, 1958. At this time, the newspaper, as did many others, withheld the names of letter-writers upon the writer's request. The writer was required, however, to identify him or herself to the paper.
[34] Mary Gwen Owen Swanson, Letter to the Editor, "Questions Motives in Auditorium Case," *Red Wing Daily Republican Eagle*, December 27, 1958.
[35] Letter to the Editor, "Doesn't Public Care About the Auditorium?" *Red Wing Daily Republican Eagle*, January 17, 1959.
[36] Letter to the Editor, "Public Does Care About Auditorium," *Red Wing Daily Republican Eagle*, January 24, 1959.
[37] Letter to the Editor, "Business Women of City Protest Theater Closing," *Red Wing Daily Republican Eagle*, January 24, 1959.

[38] Letter to the Editor, "Writer Asks: How About It, John?" *Red Wing Daily Republican Eagle*, January 24, 1959.
[39] Letter to the Editor, "He Wants People to Get Up in Arms Over Auditorium," *Red Wing Daily Republican Eagle*, January 31, 1959.
[40] Ibid.
[41] Editorial, "The Picture Looks Dark," *Red Wing Daily Republican Eagle*, January 13, 1959.
[42] Ibid.
[43] "Auditorium Will Continue Movies," *Red Wing Daily Republican Eagle*, January 24, 1959.
[44] Ibid.
[45] Ibid.
[46] "Art Week Events," *Red Wing Daily Republican Eagle*, January 24, 1959.
[47] Editorial, "Art for Today," *Red Wing Daily Republican Eagle*, January 24, 1959.
[48] Advertisement, *Red Wing Daily Republican Eagle*, January 23, 1959.
[49] Advertisement, *Red Wing Daily Republican Eagle*, January 29, 1959.
[50] "Lions Stage Drive to Aid Auditorium in Ticket Sales," *Red Wing Daily Republican Eagle*, February 13, 1959.
[51] "Jim Fraser Presented Jaycee Distinguished Service Award," *Red Wing Daily Republican Eagle*, March 11, 1959.
[52] "State High Court Asked to Rule on Legality of Auditorium Lease," *Red Wing Daily Republican Eagle*, January 27, 1959.
[53] "Has City Right to Lease Auditorium?" *Red Wing Daily Republican Eagle*, March 4, 1959.
[54] Ibid.
[55] Editorial, "Rift in Auditorium Gloom," *Red Wing Daily Republican Eagle*, February 6, 1959.
[56] "Bill to Legalize Auditorium Lease Is Introduced," *Red Wing Daily Republican Eagle*, March 13, 1959.
[57] "Auditorium Bill May Be Aired on Friday," *Red Wing Daily Republican Eagle*, March 19, 1959.
[58] "Auditorium Theater Bill Hits Opposition at Public Hearing," *Red Wing Daily Republican Eagle*, March 20, 1959.
[59] "Auditorium Lease Bill Is Rejected 5-3 at House Committee Hearing," *Red Wing Daily Republican Eagle*, March 24, 1959.
[60] "City May Vote on Lease of Auditorium Theater Here," *Red Wing Daily Republican Eagle*, April 3, 1959; State of Minnesota, An Act Authorizing the City of Red Wing to Lease the T.B. Sheldon Memorial Auditorium, Chapter 544, H.F. 1205, April 24, 1959, 854-855; "Auditorium Lease Bill Passes Senate 45-4; Governor's O.K. Seen," *Red Wing Daily Republican Eagle*, April 20, 1959; "Governor Signs Bill for Leasing of Auditorium," *Red Wing Daily Republican Eagle*, April 25, 1959
[61] John Wright Deposition and Testimony, James Fraser Deposition and Testimony, Partial

Supplemental Transcript of Proceedings, *John Wright and Associates Inc., Plaintiff v. Harold R.Ullrich et. al., Defendants*, Civ. No. 3-59-169, United States District Court for the District of Minnesota, Third Division, 203 F. supp. 744, 1962 ,749-752.

[62] The *Chief News*, February 24, 1959.

[63] Ibid.

[64] Editorial, "We Are Accused," *Red Wing Daily Republican Eagle*, February 26, 1959.

[65] *John Wright & Associates, Inc. v. City of Red Wing and Others*, Supreme Court of Minnesota, 254 Minn. I; 93 N.W.2d 660; 1958 Minn. LEXIS 705, November 28, 1958.

[66] In a column about the unexpected death of a neighbor, E.W. Olson paid tribute to her citizenship. "She couldn't see how anyone could want to hurt the Auditorium or its public life; that institution had come to be an old friend to her, even as it has to so many other Red Wingites." Wright was mugged in a memorial. See Elmer W. Olson, "Aimless Amblings by Ambrose, *Daily Republican Eagle*, April 7, 1959.

[67] Advertisement, "Save Our Auditorium," *Red Wing Daily Republican Eagle*, June 6, 1959; "5,312 Are Eligible to Vote Monday," *Red Wing Daily Republican Eagle*, June 6, 1959.

[68] Editorial, "On to the Polls," *Red Wing Daily Republican Eagle*, June 6, 1959.

[69] Ibid.

[70] Letter to the Editor, *Red Wing Daily Republican Eagle*, June 6, 1959.

[71] "Light Vote Cast in Special Election Here," *Red Wing Daily Republican Eagle*, June 8, 1959.

[72] "Voters Say Emphatic 'Yes' to Leasing of Auditorium Theater," *Red Wing Daily Republican Eagle*, June 9, 1959.

[73] *John Wright and Associates, Inc. v. City of Red Wing and Others* (No. 37,760) Supreme Court of Minnesota (256 Minn. 101; 97 N.W.2d 432;1959 Minn. LEXIS 625) (June 19, 1959).

[74] Ibid.

[75] Ibid.

[76] *Anderson v. City of Montevideo* (1917), 137 Minn. 179, 162. N.W. 1073.

[77] *John Wright and Associates, Inc. v. City of Red Wing and Others* (No. 37,760) Supreme Court of Minnesota (256 Minn. 101; 97 N.W.2d 432;1959 Minn. LEXIS 625) (June 19, 1959). For a fair summary see "State Court Refuses to Void Theater Lease," *Red Wing Daily Republican Eagle*, June 19, 1959.

[78] Ibid.

[79] "Next Move in Theater Case Up to Wright," *Red Wing Daily Republican Eagle*, August 5, 1960.

[80] "Fraser Made Party to Wright Suit against Theater," *Red Wing Daily Republican Eagle*, August 2, 1959.

[81] "Next Move in Theater Case Up to Wright," *Red Wing Daily Republican Eagle*, August 5, 1960.

[82] "Auditorium Profit Cited by Leasing Municipal Theater," *Red Wing Daily Republican*

Eagle, October 29, 1959.

[83] "Orders Filing of Briefs in Theater Leasing Action," *Red Wing Daily Republican Eagle*, November 6, 1959; "Judge Rules for Auditorium Theater," *Red Wing Daily Republican Eagle*, January 7, 1960

[84] Jack Ladner, "Auditorium Theater Lease Ruled Valid by State Court," *Red Wing Daily Republican Eagle*, November 18, 1960.

[85] *Anderson v. City of Montevideo* (1917), 137 Minn. 179, 162. N.W.1073.

[86] *John Wright and Associates Inc. v. City of Red Wing and Others*, No. 38,138 Supreme Court of Minnesota, 259 Minn. 111; 106 N.W.2d 205; 1960. Minn. LEXIS 658 (November 18, 1960).

Chapter Twelve

Conspiracy

"I think they [the distributors] are selling to a bastard operation, which has no legal right to exist, and forcing us to compete with them." ~John Wright (October 1959)

". . . if the people running the Auditorium had to put up their own money and carry the ball themselves, and seek a profit they would operate the theater in an awfully lot different manner than they do." ~John Wright (October 1959)

"If the Auditorium was good enough for Wright then, it's good enough for him now." ~Patron, The Spot (October 1961)

In September 1959, before the legality of Fraser's lease was decided in state courts, Wright filed a federal antitrust suit either as a hedge against an unfavorable state outcome, because federal courts allowed damage recovery, or both. It had nothing to do with Sheldon's intent or municipal authority. This was about "conspiracy in restraint of trade"[1] and aggrieved competitors. Section 2 of the 1890 Sherman Antitrust Act reads:

> Every person who shall monopolize, or attempt to monopolize, or combine or conspire with any other person or persons, to monopolize any part of the trade or commerce among the several States, or with foreign nations, shall be deemed guilty of a misdemeanor, and, on conviction thereof; shall be punished by fine not exceeding five thousand dollars, or by imprisonment not exceeding one year, or by both said punishments, in the discretion of the court.[2]

Conspiracy

The act also said, and this was the crux of it, that injured parties "shall recover three fold the damages by him sustained, and the costs of suit, including a reasonable attorney's fee."[3]

A conspiracy required conspirators, and to Wright there was a raft of them: the Auditorium board; the City of Red Wing; the *Daily Republican Eagle*; Philip Duff, the newspaper's managing editor and owner; James Fraser; and three film companies—Paramount, Twentieth Century Fox, and United Artists. Through their actions, Wright's complaint charged, conspirators "obtained a monopolistic power ... which on a purely bona fide competitive basis, neither said Auditorium nor said alleged lessee could have achieved." According to Wright, those conspirators "knowingly engaged in concerted and parallel action designed to [eliminate] ... the plaintiff as an effective competitor."[4] The specific charges fell into two broad categories. One was the action taken to create Fraser's lease, pass enabling legislation, and help Fraser succeed. The second was action that disparaged Wright publicly and organized a boycott of his business.[5] As a corollary, Wright charged that the Auditorium and the newspaper created the misperception that unless the Auditorium prevailed it would become a public tax burden. That implied, Wright's suit said, "that [the] Auditorium is operated as a motion picture theater at a profit, whereas for more than six years past, it had operated ... at a substantial loss." Wright was correct. The board knew for years that it was headed for insolvency.[6]

A key contention was Wright's allegation that Fraser did not operate in a businesslike manner because he was subsidized by his unrealistically low rent lease. Because of that, Wright charged, Fraser made irrationally high bids that Wright could not match. In an instance that particularly angered Wright, Fraser bid fifty percent of gross receipts for Disney's *Tonka* and, according to Wright, lost money for the Auditorium.[7] Wright also claimed that the defendants gave Fraser free newspaper advertising, loans, and backed a campaign to sell, "by use of pressure and persuasion by influential residents" advance tickets to the Auditorium whose purpose was to provide Fraser with working capital.[8] To Wright, "... if the people running the Auditorium had to put up their own money and carry the ball themselves, and seek a profit, they would operate the theater in an awfully lot different manner than they do."[9]

Sheldon's Gift

In deposition, Wright railed against the film distributors for having dealt with Fraser's "illegal" operation and for "unfair, inequitable and unreasonable" bidding. The distributors, Wright added, "stand there and sandbag each exhibitor for everything they can get. They break them both financially." "It's been," Wright charged, "the ruination of this business, and many people in it." But when the distributors' attorney, Mandt Torrison, asked if it wasn't true that there was "no point or purpose on the part of the distributors of motion pictures to reduce their prospective clients?" Wright managed only, "I wouldn't think so, no. The contrary would be true, probably."[10] Following the exchange, the film distributors, Paramount, Twentieth Century Fox, and United Artists moved successfully for a summary dismissal.[11]

Wright's federal case wasn't heard for eighteen months. Meanwhile, Wright closed the Chief and lost his Minnesota Supreme Court appeal. In July 1961, Judge Dennis Donovan held a pre-trial conference where Wright claimed damages of $165,000. Applying the Sherman Act treble damages criteria, that made his claim worth a sizeable $495,000. When the bench trial began on August 20, attention focused first on Fraser's bidding for Disney releases[12] and the muddy claims on both sides relative to Disney's importance. It was clear, however, that Fraser did nothing illegal.[13]

As the trial progressed, Wright hoped to prove conspiratorial actions by the newspaper, the board, and townspeople who he charged had organized a Chief boycott, written untrue letters and news stories, and failed to report the Auditorium's financial problems. As Wright called witnesses, however, testimony often reduced itself to simple contradiction. Mayor Harry Rardin, for example, said that he asked if a joint meeting of the board and city council might help resolve the issues but that Wright told him it was "too late."[14] Wright denied it. What's more, reasonable explanations abounded. Philip Duff's managing editor, Fred Jonson, said that he typically accepted his reporters' stories as written and wasn't told by Duff how to represent the case. Jonson came across as professional and experienced—a good man doing his job.[15] Nor could Wright make much of the relationships between the alleged conspirators. The defendants did "hobnob," at Kiwanis and Lions Club luncheons.[16] So what? In small cities people knew one another, especially within the professional and business elite.

Conspiracy

Elmer W. Olson, who wrote "Aimless Amblings by Ambrose" and who Wright referred to as a "so-called" columnist was a frequent and harsh Wright critic.[17] But Olson testified that he was merely a free-lance writer whose column was just local "gossip." As to where he got his information, Olson said vaguely his views were his own and that information came from memory and from "around and about." At that Judge Donovan remarked to Wright attorney Dwain Ewing, "You perhaps gather he's proving the title [Aimless Amblings]."[18]

Ewing had no more success when he asked Philip Duff, the newspaper's former managing editor and new owner about letters to the editor, advertising, and his associations. Wright contended that many letters to the editor, "purporting to have been received from local citizens"[19] and signed "Fed Up Taxpayer" or "Disgusted Citizen" were bogus. But Duff countered, correctly, that some letters vilifying Wright or encouraging parents to "demand that their children refrain from viewing motion pictures at the Chief Theater"[20] were printed over author signatures. He also explained that the paper's longstanding policy required that that letters be signed but permitted them to be published with a pseudonym.[21] Wright also claimed that the newspaper gave Fraser free advertising, a charge he couldn't prove,[22] and that he was given poor ad placement. The latter charge was demolished when defense attorney Milton Holst produced thirty-eight newspapers and asked Wright in each case if the Chief's ad placement was fair and Wright admitted it was.[23] Nor could Wright explain why the newspaper would want to lose the Chief's $3,000 per year in advertising revenues[24]

The degree to which Red Wing opinion was molded by its newspaper or was reflected in it is important. Whichever came first, the chicken or the egg, there was no question that the *Daily Republican Eagle*'s letters reflected public opinion. When Wright's lawyers sent "undercover" investigators to Red Wing, they interviewed at least twenty-five people. At the Spot, a Bush Street bar, investigator George Mikesh posed as a potential Chief buyer and testified that patrons disparaged Wright. "If the Auditorium was good enough for Wright then (when he was its manager)," one said, "it's good enough for him now."[25] Although that view was widely held, it didn't concede that Wright only complained when he believed the Auditorium acted unfairly.

Sheldon's Gift

Duff and his newspaper were said to have been complicit in a broad city-wide effort involving union members, the Chamber of Commerce, women's groups and the local Kiwanis and Lions clubs in calling for a Chief boycott.[26] That someone attempted to organize such a boycott is certain but the instigators were elusive. Three women employees of the LaGrange Shoe Company testified that a boycott petition circulated through their department, but none admitted knowing where it originated. One, Mrs. Ben Rigelman, signed, she said, because, "I didn't like to see the Auditorium being closed down." The others ignored the petition and claimed that very few people signed. Indicative of the amnesia that gripped some locals, Bill Morse, manager of the Chamber of Commerce, testified that he heard rumors of a boycott but couldn't recall details.[27] Not surprisingly, board members, who were frequently vague or forgetful, didn't hesitate when asked if they had ever suggested to ". . . anybody that people should forego attending the Chief theater. . . ?" Each answered in a loud, firm "NO."[28]

In another line of attack Wright alleged that the Auditorium withheld financial information and that had townspeople known of the Auditorium's dire finances they would have felt differently about the Chief. Perhaps. When Ewing asked Harold Ullrich how Ora Jones' report on the Auditorium's dreary finances was conveyed, Ullrich matter of factly said that the board's minutes were public information.[29] That wasn't a forthright answer since the board had decided not to discuss its finances with the city and had asked the newspaper to withhold financial information.[30] Tellingly, newspaper accounts of the trial largely ignored the Auditorium's finances.

Wright's strongest arguments focused on the terms of Fraser's lease and whether board members, businessmen, bankers, and others unfairly assisted Fraser. A principal feature of Fraser's lease, for example, apportioned costs between motion pictures and live events. But when accountant C. Robert Beattie was asked whether his accounting separated motion picture and other costs, Beattie said no.[31] As it was, the division of costs seems to have been motivated by a strong desire to help Fraser succeed, just as Wright charged. All of this led Ewing to observe that the city and Auditorium had long maintained an anti-competitive policy against private theaters.[32] Nothing was truer.

When Ewing asked how the board hit upon a $500 per month rental, Ullrich said that it informally took into account, he thought, but could not be

Conspiracy

sure, depreciation, maintenance, insurance, and janitor costs. Lease income, he believed, would leave the Auditorium within $1,200 of breaking even—a deficit that could be offset by rentals. If not rigorous it sounded reasonable. To it, board member S.B. Foot added that unlike a corporate board, the Auditorium's wasn't required to give shareholders a return on their investment.[33] That was correct, but only to the extent that the Auditorium broke even or the city covered its deficits if and when its funds were exhausted. A larger question, not directly raised, was what obligation the board had to determine and execute a market rate lease, a key to fair competition.

Although Wright's case was credible in some respects, it was weak in explaining his own circumstances. Wright, for example, claimed that the Chief enjoyed many profitable years before his troubles with Fraser began in mid-1956. But under cross examination by Charles Richardson, Wright's story faltered. In 1953, Richardson demonstrated, Wright lost $2,300 from motion picture operations and only because of on-screen advertising and concessions eked out a profit of $455. Richardson also pointed out that Wright failed to include tax and insurance costs of more than $200 per month. A forthright accounting, Richardson charged, would have shown a $2,000 loss.[34]

The Chief's best years were 1954 and 1955 when the industry perked up and when James Fraser was manager.[35] When Fraser quit, Wright experienced a dreadful run of short-term managers. He fired one for molesting young boys and dismissed another for incompetence. One was convicted of embezzlement.[36] In his cross-examination, Richardson asked Wright if it wasn't often true that "poor management is what spoils business, isn't that a fact?" Wright answered, "Yes, I would say poor management would, yes—could."[37]

Wright also admitted that business was lost to general conditions--reduced film offerings, competition from the Red Wing Drive-In, the rapidly rising cost of good "product," and television's impact on the audience for "B" or "action" films. But even though Wright's views were widely accepted in the industry, matters weren't clear-cut. When Benjamin Berger, a prominent theater owner, testified on Wright's behalf, he spoke about why Disney films were important to the Chief. Berger said that television had harmed B but not A picture houses. B pictures, he said, were television. Why, he asked, would anyone pay to see what

205

could be had free? Under cross-examination, however, Berger admitted to closing theaters in Duluth and Superior, Wisconsin, and that his theaters in Hastings and St. Peter were doing poorly. Neither of the latter theaters were subject to competitive bidding and all showed A features.[38]

Overall, Charles Richardson prepared the city's witnesses well. On the other side, Wright and those who testified on his behalf were less well coached. The trial, expected to take three weeks, lasted eight. The record was voluminous. There were 325 exhibits, and the court's minutes alone consisted of 226 pages. Judge Donovan heard final oral arguments in St. Paul on January 9 and 10, 1962. With nighttime temperatures at fifteen below zero, Dwain Ewing, Wright's attorney, likely felt that his case had received a reception as frigid as the weather. Still, Ewing might have hammered at whether the board gave Fraser a sweetheart lease that allowed Fraser to sidestep the reality that constrained Wright. Instead, Ewing, inexplicably, reargued the question of Fraser's lease as a subterfuge, a question already decided by the Minnesota courts and irrelevant in the federal trade case.[39]

On the other side, Richardson ignored Fraser's lease and offered plausible explanations to each of Wright's charges. It boiled down, he said, to a simple issue: Was the Chief's demise due to the actions of the Board, Fraser and the newspaper or to other factors including competition from the Drive-In, the general decline in business, and Wright's management problems? In Richardson's summation, the board was nothing more than a body of dedicated citizens trying to do their best under difficult circumstances.[40]

Judge Donovan took it all under advisement and ruled ten weeks later. To begin, Donovan restated the "gist" of Wright's complaint—that the defendants "knowingly engaged in concerted and parallel action designed to promote the operation of [the Auditorium] as the only 'first run' motion picture theater in [Red Wing] and to accomplish this objective eliminated the plaintiff as an effective competitor." They were charged with having done this, in Donovan's summary, by misusing their advantageous competitive position (including tax exemption), discouraging people from patronizing the Chief, and "disseminating false and misleading information concerning plaintiff for the purpose of arousing public sentiment against it and inciting a boycott of the Chief."[41]

Although Donovan tried to find a directly applicable case, none, he concluded, spoke specifically to Wright. To find his decision, Donovan probed widely for precedent. He cited *American Tobacco Co. v. United States* (1946)—"it is the existence of the power to exclude competitors . . . Together with the intent to exercise such power, which is condemned. . . ." And, drawing upon *United States v. Griffith* (1948), Donovan wrote that one "of two theaters in a city such as Red Wing must not use monopoly power to crush or damage a competitor." "If the end sought is monopoly," Donovan added, citing *Theater Enterprises v. Paramount Film Distributors Corp* (1954) "it is of no consequence that the means were lawful or unlawful. No formal agreement is necessary to establish a conspiracy and business behavior is admissible as circumstantial evidence from which an illegal agreement may be inferred."[42] For Wright, so far so good.

But it was not to be. In other cases, *Whitwell v. Continental Tobacco Co.* (1903), *Terminal Warehouse Co. v. Pennsylvania Railway Co.* (1936), *Eastern States Retail Lumber Dealers Association v. United States* (1914) and in *Johnson v. J.H. Yost Lumber Co.* (1941), Donovan settled on his decision. Acts that only "incidentally or indirectly" restricted competition and where the principal purpose was to advance legitimate trade, weren't proscribed. Parallel actions alone were not proof of conspiracy. It would be unreasonable to conclude otherwise, he wrote, since the vigorous conduct of business was not illegal.[43]

To prove restraint of trade, Donovan said, a defendant's conduct "must rise above the realm of mere suspicion." And that's where Wright's case failed. Donovan found that the evidence did not reveal "any substantial basis from which to infer the existence . . . of a fraudulent or illegal agreement or conspiracy . . . or the existence of any intent on the part of defendants to exercise monopoly. . . ." Consequently, Wright's problems were likely the result of a "nationwide decline in the motion picture industry [do to] television." Although Wright had "cast suspicion upon the acts of defendants, the Court is not convinced that the required burden of substantial evidence is present to such an extent . . . to warrant a finding that said antitrust laws have been violated."[44] Suspicions abounded. But there was no substantiation. No damages. No $165,000 times three.

Sheldon's Gift

Jack Wright was handed a small consolation. In his opinion, Donovan scolded the board, the newspaper, the city, and its townsfolk for their insensitivity to Wright's problems:

> The defendants, together with many other citizens, in their enthusiasm for the Auditorium may have exercised occasional injustice and bad judgment in dealing with plaintiff and its problems. After all, plaintiff's president had been one of the City's exemplary citizens and, as such, certainly was entitled, throughout the crisis he faced at the Chief, to perhaps a greater exercise of tact and understanding on the part of the City and its leaders. It appears from the evidence that some citizens were too willing to prejudge the plaintiff in the role of obstructionist without having fully informed themselves of the vexatious problems which at that particular time beset it.[45]

This, the *Daily Republican Eagle* said, was a "mild rebuke,"[46] a reprimand consigned promptly to the nearest wastebasket.

Although Donovan's rebuke was correct, he mistakenly characterized Wright as an "exemplary citizen." To townspeople, Wright wasn't a citizen at all but an "outsider." In 1960 John and Myra Wright hadn't lived in Red Wing for almost seventeen years. Unlike Eddie Swanson, and then Jim Fraser, Wright was never a small city "good old boy." The Kiwanis and Lions weren't Jack's forte. Fraser had jumped in and made himself at home. He joined the service clubs, sold Kiwanis peanuts on street corners, and dressed in clownish garb for "Krazy Daze" sales. Not Wright. Jack was in Red Wing for twenty-five years but was never of it. Nor was Wright's Chief an exemplary business. Its origins were mysterious and despite its original purpose as an appendage of the Auditorium most citizens saw it as a threat to "their" Auditorium. What's more, the Chief was a B movie house. Even though it became an A exhibitor, it intermingled "sage brush sagas" and other B fare and never conquered its reputation. Although B pictures and poverty row studios were dead or dying when Wright's lawsuits began, Red Wing movie goers could not help but link the Chief to Gene Autry, serials, the Bowery Boys, and the slapdash output of RKO under Howard Hughes. When Wright charged that the defendants engaged in "concerted action designed to promote the operation of [the Auditorium] as the only 'first-run' motion picture theater in Red Wing," he was correct—to a point. But they didn't seek that status; they assumed

Conspiracy

they were simply protecting what was rightfully theirs. It is a business truism that it is relatively easy to downgrade one's product yet retain public luster for some time afterwards but nearly impossible to upgrade a reputation no matter how improved the product. The Chief couldn't conquer its history.

—✦—

W right didn't quit. Appealing to the Eighth Circuit Court in St. Louis his attorneys claimed that Judge Donovan erred when he said Wright didn't prove the defendants' "specific intent" to monopolize. In *United States v. Griffith* (1948), Wright's attorneys declared, Justice William O. Douglas wrote, "It is sufficient that a restraint of trade or monopoly results as the consequence of a defendant's conduct or business arrangements. Specific intent in the sense in which the common law used the term is necessary only where the acts fall short of the results condemned by the Act."[47]

But Justice Pat Mehaffy, also citing *Griffith* and Second Circuit Court Justice Learned Hand's opinion in *United States v. Aluminum Company of America* [ALCOA] (1945), found that Wright had wrongly assumed, "proof of intent was unnecessary because [he] labored under the erroneous premise the trial court was obliged to find an inherently unlawful monopoly existed. . . ." To Mehaffy, Fraser's monopoly resulted from several factors including normal competition. Such monopoly, Mehaffy wrote, was not unlawful but "accidental."[48]

Wright also claimed that although it was unnecessary to prove specific intent to monopolize that he had done so nevertheless. That intent manifested itself, his lawyers claimed, in the media and through "excessive" bidding practices. But the court was unconvinced. Fraser's bidding, the court found, resulted from Wright's threats to the film distributors. Although the court acknowledged that bidding may have increased the costs of film exhibition, the practice was legal.[49] To clinch it, Judge Mehaffy presupposed that if Wright's claims were valid, the Auditorium should have experienced an increase in gross receipts when the Chief closed. Instead, its gross receipts fell from $51,300 in 1959 to $49,300 in 1960. Mehaffy concluded, therefore, as Judge Donovan did, that Wright's problems were due to poor managers, competition from television, and other problems and misfortunes. Fraser's monopoly was indeed "accidental." As Judge Hand wrote in ALCOA, "The successful competitor, having been urged to compete, must not be turned upon when he wins."[50]

The appellate decision was handed down on March 2, 1964.[51] It was the end of the line. The Chief had closed, and Fraser, who by then also owned the Red Wing Drive-In, enjoyed a monopoly, accidental or not, on Red Wing's theater business. It had been over seven years since Fraser demanded a share of Disney films. Fraser had leased the Auditorium for five years already. How was it working out?

Notes

[1] Morton Keller, *Regulating a New Economy: Public Policy and Economic Change in America, 1900-1933* (Cambridge: Harvard University Press, 1990), 80-81. The U.S. Supreme Court ruled in 1915 that the movies were a medium of entertainment "substantially engaged in interstate commerce and thus subject to the antitrust laws." In Wright's case it was also true that Wright's business, which drew substantially from Wisconsin residents, was also engaged in interstate commerce for that reason.

[2] The Sherman Antitrust Act (Sherman Act,) July 2, 1890, ch. 647, 26 Stat. 209, 15 U.S.C.§ 1–7.

[3] Ibid. The treble damages clause is also found in The Clayton Antitrust Act of 1914, October 15, 1914, ch. 323, 38 Stat. 730, codified at 15 U.S.C. § 12–27, 29 U.S.C. § 52–53.

[4] John Wright Deposition, *John Wright and Associates Inc., Plaintiff v. Harold R. Ullrich et. al., Defendants*, Civ. No. 3-59-169, United States District Court for the District of Minnesota, Third Division, 203 F. supp. 744, 1962.

[5] "Republican Eagle Made Party to Suits by Wright," *Red Wing Daily Republican Eagle*, September 10, 1959.

[6] Minutes, T.B. Sheldon Memorial Auditorium, May 14, 1951.

[7] John Wright Testimony, Supplemental Partial Transcript of Proceedings, *John Wright and Associates Inc., Plaintiff v. Harold R.Ullrich et. al., Defendants*, Civ. No. 3-59-169, United States District Court for the District of Minnesota, Third Division, 203 F. supp. 744, 1962, 809-810. Wright was correct. Thirty percent of gross receipts was common and forty percent was paid for excellent pictures. Fraser's bid was very high.

[8] John Wright Deposition, *John Wright and Associates Inc., Plaintiff v. Harold R.Ullrich et. al., Defendants*, Civ. No. 3-59-169, United States District Court for the District of Minnesota, Third Division, 203 F. supp. 744, 1962.

[9] Ibid.

Conspiracy

[10] Ibid.

[11] Mandt Torrison Affidavit, February 10, 1960, *John Wright & Associates Inc. v. Harold R. Ullrich et. al. Defendants*, Civ. No. 3-59-169, United States District Court for the District of Minnesota, Third Division, 203 F. supp. 744, 1962.

[12] "Wright Suit Opens in Federal Court," *Red Wing Daily Republican Eagle*, August 20, 1961; "Disney Films Started Theater Feud Here," *Red Wing Daily Republican Eagle*, September 27, 1961.

[13] James Fraser Testimony, Supplemental Partial Transcript of Proceedings, *John Wright and Associates, Inc. Plaintiff, v. Harold R. Ullrich et. al., Defendants*, Civ. No. 3-59-169 United States District Court for the District of Minnesota Third Division, 203 F. Supp. 744; 1962 Film distributors have made the case that it is not bidding but film splitting that is is an illegal restraint of trade. Such a case, however, would be difficult to prove since such agreements, as between the Chief and the Auditorium, are informal pacts. Second, pact or no, it is not possible to force any exhibitor to bid on any film he or she does not wish to show.

[14] Harry Rardin Testimony. Supplemental Partial Transcript of Proceedings, *John Wright and Associates v. Harold R. Ullrich et. al,*. Civ. No. 3-59-169, United States District Court for the District of Minnesota, Third Division, 203 F. supp. 744, 1962 U.S. Dist. (March 28, 1962); "Rardin: Wright Spurned 'Peace' Bid," *Red Wing Daily Republican Eagle*, September 8, 1961.

[15] "Marshall and Jonson Testify in $165,000 Wright-Auditorium-RE Suit," *Red Wing Daily Republican Eagle*, September 22, 1961.

[16] Ullrich and Duff were ardent Democrats who worked together in 1958 to promote the U.S. Senate candidacy of Red Wingite Eugenie Andersen.

[17] John Wright Deposition, *John Wright and Associates v. Harold R. Ullrich et. al.*,Civ. No. 3-59-169, United States District Court for the District of Minnesota, Third Division, 203 F. supp. 744, 1962 U.S. Dist. (March 28, 1962), 53.

[18] "R-E Columnist Testifies at Wright Conspiracy Trial," *Red Wing Daily Republican Eagle*, September 21, 1961.

[19] John Wright Deposition, *John Wright and Associates v. Harold R. Ullrich et. al.*, Civ. No. 3-59-169, United States District Court for the District of Minnesota, Third Division, 203 F. supp. 744, 1962 U.S. Dist. (March 28, 1962), 42.

[20] Ibid., 50-51.

[21] "News Stories of Wright Case 'Fair and Factual,'" *Red Wing Daily Republican Eagle*, September 6, 1961. Duff also explained, with less credibility, that all letters were destroyed after two or three weeks.

[22] John Wright Deposition, *John Wright and Associates v. Harold R. Ullrich et. al.*, Civ. No. 3-59-169, United States District Court for the District of Minnesota, Third Division, 203 F. supp. 744, 1962 U.S. Dist. (March 28, 1962), 51.

[23] "Boycott Petition Against Chief Theater Is Given Scant Backing," *Red Wing Daily Republican Eagle*, October 6, 1961.

[24] "DRE Wright Case Reporting was "Fair and Factual" Court Is Told," *Red Wing Daily*

Republican Eagle, January 11, 1962.

[25] "Wright Investigators Tell of Questioning Red Wing Residents on Theater Situation," *Red Wing Daily Republican Eagle*, October 18, 1961.

[26] Ibid., 41-43

[27] "Boycott Petition Against Chief Theater Is Given Scant Backing," *Red Wing Daily Republican Eagle*, October 6, 1961.

[28] "Five Defendants Deny Ever Telling Anyone to Stay Away from the Chief," *Red Wing Daily Republican Eagle*, October 25, 1961.

[29] *John Wright and Associates, Inc. Plaintiff, v. Harold R. Ullrich et. al., Defendants*, Civ. No. 3-59-169, United States District Court for the District of Minnesota Third Division, 203 F. Supp. 744; 1962, 124.

[30] Minutes, T.B. Sheldon Auditorium Board, May 14, 1951.

[31] C.R. Beattie Testimony. Supplemental Partial Transcript of Proceedings, *John Wright and Associates, Inc., Plaintiff, v. Harold R. Ullrich et. al., Defendants*, Civ. No. 3-59-169, United States District Court for the District of Minnesota Third Division, 203 F. Supp. 744, 1962, 1224-1229.

[32] "Ewing Charges City Council Had Designs Against Chief," *Red Wing Daily Republican Eagle*, October 4, 1961.

[33] "Laughter Breaks Decorum at Wright Suit Hearing," *Red Wing Daily Republican Eagle*, September 7, 1961.

[34] John Wright Testimony, Supplemental Partial Transcript of Proceedings, *John Wright and Associates, a Corporation, Plaintiff, v. Harold R. Ullrich et. al, Defendants*, Civ. No. 3-59-169, United States District Court for the District of Minnesota Third Division, 203 F. Supp. 744, 1962, 698-704.

[35] Ibid., 812-815.

[36] Findings of Fact, *John Wright and Associates, a Corporation, Plaintiff, v. Harold R. Ullrich et. al, Defendants*, Civ. No. 3-59-169, United States District Court for the District of Minnesota Third Division, 203 F. Supp. 744, 1962.

[37] John Wright Testimony, Supplemental Partial Transcript of Proceedings, *John Wright and Associates, a Corporation, Plaintiff, v. Harold R. Ullrich et. al, Defendants*, Civ. No. 3-59-169, United States District Court for the District of Minnesota Third Division, 203 F. Supp. 744, 1962, 718.

[38] Benjamin Berger Testimony, Partial Transcript of Proceedings, II, *John Wright and Associates Inc, plaintiff, v. Harold R. Ullrich et. al., Defendants*, Civ. No. 3-59-169, United States District Court for the District of Minnesota Third Division, 203 F. Supp. 744, 1962, 416-439. See also "Wright Investigators Tell of Questioning Red Wing Residents on Theater Situation," *Red Wing Daily Republican Eagle*, October 18, 1961; "Wright Case Draws to End," *Red Wing Daily Republican Eagle*, October 19, 1961.

[39] "Arguments Given in Wright Theater Suit," *Red Wing Daily Republican Eagle*, January 10, 1962.

[40] Ibid.

Conspiracy

[41] *John Wright and Associates, Inc., Plaintiff, v. Harold R. Ullrich, et. al., Defendants*, Civ. No. 3-59-169, United States District Court for the District of Minnesota, Third Division, 203 F. Supp. 744; U.S. Dist. (March 28, 1962).
[42] Ibid.
[43] Ibid.
[44] Ibid.
[45] Ibid.
[46] "Court Clears Wright Case Defendants," *Red Wing Daily Republican Eagle*, March 28, 1962.
[47] Clerk of U.S. Court of Appeals for the Eighth Circuit, Records and Briefs, September Term, 1963. *John Wright and Associates, Inc., Appellant, v. Harold R. Ullrich et. al*, Appellees, No. 17193, 328 F.2d 474; 1964.
[48] *John Wright and Associates, Inc. Appellant, v. Harold R. Ullrich et. al, Appellees*, No. 17193 United States Court of Appeals Eighth Circuit,328 F.2d 474; 1964 (March 2, 1964).
[49] Ibid. The court here cited *Royster Drive-In Theaters, Inc. v. American Broadcasting, Inc.* (2nd Cir. 1959)
[50] Ibid.
[51] "Wright's Appeal Rejected," *Red Wing Daily Republican Eagle*, March 4, 1964.

Chapter Thirteen

Ruin and Restoration

"Walt Disney pictures don't draw." ~James Fraser (November 1976)

"If it's too historical it can get dull." ~Rowe Million (November 1980)

"Nowhere in the country, maybe in the world are the arts a self-sustaining enterprise. The theater will continue to need the support of community-spirited Red Wing residents."
~Steve Schmidt (October 1986)

For many years Mary Lee Wahlin wrote "Town and Country," a *Daily Republican Eagle* column that appeared alongside household hints, dress patterns, and school cafeteria menus. Although she usually addressed "women's" interests, Wahlin, who resided outside Red Wing, nevertheless urged citizens to approve Fraser's lease. The Auditorium, she wrote, was a source of area pride and Red Wing voters actually "have the responsibility of not only voting for themselves but for the hundreds of us who cannot vote but feel the same way."[1]

Wahlin's comment touched a core issue that local whining about possibly higher taxes obscured. The Minnesota Supreme Court was wrong when it likened motion picture theaters to other main street businesses. Movie houses were community symbols, windows to a cosmopolitan world and a place for shared secular culture that promoted an illusion of classlessness. For the Auditorium it wasn't always so. In the beginning, with lofty ticket prices, talk of belonging to all the people was hyperbole. Movies, however, were homogenizing. No wonder, the chips down, citizens defended the Auditorium. To Wahlin's credit, she was among a handful who acknowledged Wright's legitimate complaint. "Perhaps it was unfair for the city to be in a competitive business . . . without the same obstacles to overcome as a private business," she wrote. At the same time, however, Wahlin assumed, unquestioningly, that Fraser's lease made it a "different story" by leveling the field.[2]

As Jim Fraser began his lease, he must have been optimistic. He was, though still a young man of thirty-five, for the first time running his own business. Even better, he received extraordinarily favorable terms and hadn't ventured capital. Community backing must also have encouraged him. It was hard to tell, of course, whether it was love of the Auditorium, hatred of taxes, or a lynch-mob loathing of Jack Wright that visited upon him so much good will. It was also impossible to know whether good will would translate into ticket sales. Still, motion picture attendance seemed to have leveled off.[3] Perhaps the worst of television's assault had passed and an audience for good A "product" remained. It was a reasonable assumption.

At the same time, Fraser's enthusiasm had to have been tempered by competitive reality. Small cities preferred American films starring familiar Hollywood faces. Those films were increasingly in short supply. In 1959 producers released only 187 U.S. made films, far fewer than the nearly 400 annual domestic movies in the previous decade.[4] Assuming that the Auditorium and the Chief each changed films twice weekly those two theaters alone could consume all domestic production. That meant that both theaters on occasion resorted to foreign films, enough so that Fraser once fielded board complaints as to why the Auditorium presented so many of them.[5]

Competition for good films was keen. It became intense when Wright warned film distributors not to sell to the Auditorium. As a result, the gentleman's agreement failed and competitive bidding became common. Overall, Fraser won the best films. During a period of just five months in 1959, Fraser later agreed, the Auditorium outbid the Chief for seventeen films, a number large enough to lend support to Wright's charge that Fraser's behavior was "unbusinesslike." During the same period, however, Fraser lost five films to selective bidding by the Red Wing Drive-In. Because of bidding, film shortage, attendance decline, and Wright's suit, Fraser's first months as an independent businessman were trying.[6]

215

Sheldon's Gift

By midyear 1960, Fraser's prospects seemed to improve. In June, Wright closed his Chief leaving Fraser with the town's sole four-wall theater. Yet by November 1962, three and a half years into his lease, Fraser was six months in arrears, in debt to distributors, and blaming his delinquencies on film rental costs.[7] Whether business was simply poor or his other commitments took precedence Fraser didn't say and the board didn't ask. Those other interests were considerable. In 1959, with the ink on his Auditorium lease barely dry, Fraser leased the municipal Plum Theater in Plum City, Wisconsin, and operated it on weekends even though the theater was unequipped for either wide-screen projection or stereophonic sound.[8] In 1961 Fraser purchased the Red Wing Drive-In from Gordon Speiss. Although terms and financing weren't disclosed[9] that purchase gave Fraser a stake in a business that he thought was leading a movie-goer resurgence[10] and a monopoly on Red Wing's film trade. In 1964 Fraser purchased a theater in Waseca and also managed and had business interests in a Rochester movie house.[11]

Although Fraser halved his delinquency by mid-1963, his persistent debt was a board concern. Fraser's business turned worse in 1965 when John Wright sold his Chief to Mr. and Mrs. Willis Menge who previously operated theaters in North Dakota. The Menges renamed their movie house the Red Wing Theater and undertook extensive refurbishing including new seats, carpet, lobby and concession stand.[12] No renovations or a Zenith "handcrafted" television door prize, however, overcame the stench of the Christmas grand re-opening film, *Pinocchio in Outer Space*, an "all-new, full-length cartoon feature in COLOR!"[13] Nor was the Menge's timing fortuitous. In 1966 weekly movie attendance fell from forty-four to thirty-eight million and the following year plummeted to barely eighteen million.[14]

To make matters worse, Fraser failed to negotiate a film-sharing agreement with the Menges and ruinous bidding returned. Within a year Fraser, explaining why his lease payments were four months overdue, blamed "tremendous" losses on bidding.[15] Although Fraser pleaded hard times, he nevertheless, in May 1967, purchased the Red Wing Theater—which he promptly renamed the Chief, the name familiar to everyone above the age of three. Although financial arrangements aren't known, one suspects that after just two years the Menges had suffered a financial shellacking and eagerly accepted any offer.

Ruin and Restoration

Although Fraser's finances improved for a time and the board stopped complaining, by early 1968 Fraser was $2,800 in arrears and his now-corporate check for $1,000 bounced. At the end of the year Fraser, citing high maintenance expenses and claiming that he drew no Auditorium salary, (he did admit to an annual profit of between $1,500 and $4,000) asked for a new three-year lease at the same $500 per month he had paid for a decade. The board squawked but demanded no financial details other than Fraser's assertion that his only interests at the time were in the Auditorium, the Drive-In and the Chief and finally offered a one-year extension.[16]

Jim Fraser's troubles paled against the board's. Predictions for success under Fraser's lease were woefully wrong. Not only did the board grapple with Fraser's arrears, expenses piled up. In 1959 it was exterior repainting. Next was $7,000 for seat reupholstering.[17] In 1961 the board estimated that its invested funds would be depleted in fifteen years if necessary repairs were made.[18] Member and banker Ora Jones, Jr., wanted to share such vital information with the city council in order to make long-range plans. But City Attorney Charles Richardson advised withholding the information until after the Wright case concluded.[19] The board never made that report. Nor did it plan. In 1963 it was the exterior canopy and in 1965 converting the coal furnace to natural gas. Some repairs seemingly had nothing to do with the Auditorium's responsibilities. When Fraser presented a $700 bill for projector repairs the board balked but paid.[20] Indeed, with community use limited to just a dozen days of the year, the board footed big bills for picture house wear and tear. In a letter to the board in 1969 local physician Dr. George Hawley complained about the restrooms, lounge, carpets, leaking canopy, and the need for exterior sandblasting. Even Fraser complained.[21]

For the board it must have been discouraging. As the decade wore on, members resigned or declined reappointment. S.B. Foot and E.R. Quinn were gone before Wright's case ended. Ora Jones, Jr., left in 1966. Harold Ullrich, who served twenty-seven years, seventeen as president, stayed until 1968. New members inherited mounting costs. Oscar Wintervold, the volunteer in charge of the Auditorium's stage for decades, called for new curtains, spotlights, electrical work and a new stage floor. The latter need was apparent to all when the Lola Montes Flamenco troupe appeared at a community concert and dust flew through the theater. Wintervold estimated stage needs alone at over $20,000, a huge sum considering how few live performances were presented.[22]

To make matters worse, late in 1968 the Goodhue county assessor raised the issue that had been the mute elephant in the corner throughout the Wright cases—taxes.[23] Over the next two years discussions between the city attorney and the county led nowhere and in early 1970 the county assessed a personal property tax of $3458.24. The board, which was responsible for taxes under Fraser's lease, contested the assessment, pleading that it couldn't continue as a movie theater if taxes were levied.[24] That was true and was one key to Wright's case. Once again the board was back in court, this time arguing that it should escape taxation because its situation was akin to Bloomington's tax exempt Metropolitan Stadium, a view that prevailed.[25] A bullet was dodged.

Meanwhile, major repairs, for stage improvements, drapes, paint, and myriad other items all costing $35,000 couldn't be deferred. No community fundraising was attempted. In April 1971 there was a reopening gala. The entertainment was a community theater production of George Bernard Shaw's *Pygmalion* directed by Robert Prigge, one of many local theater enthusiasts. The laudatory printed program paid homage to Sheldon, swept over history, and honored Red Wing's community theater traditions. It did not mention that recent expenditures took the board a giant step closer to bankruptcy.[26]

The plainest measure of the Auditorium's finances continued to be the value of its investments. In the immediate postwar years those funds totaled about $130,000. By mid 1971 the value sank to just $51,000. Over the next three years repair costs, including a $5000 bill from James Fraser for projector maintenance, mounted. In 1974 investment value bottomed at $12,000.[27]

Despite financial troubles, there were bright spots. Community theater, revived in 1948, faded during the early 1950s but was reborn in 1958 when a young persons' social organization, the Penthouse Club, created the Red Wing Summer Playhouse, an organization that became the longest lived of any Red Wing community theater group. Eddie Swanson's widow and Macalester College drama professor Mary Gwen

Ruin and Restoration

Owen Swanson directed its first offering, *The Solid Gold Cadillac*. Although the Auditorium board supported community drama, the only financial assistance it offered was a reduction in rental fees to no more than $100 per night.[28]

After failing in the late 1950s,[29] community concerts revived. In 1964, the Red Wing Community Concert Association organized under the new leadership of Mrs. Milton Hosking and Richard Skewes. Following closely its previous model and assisted by booking agent Columbia Artists Management, the Association conducted early fall membership drives with one or two artists already booked and limited attendance to members. After the drive the association booked an additional program or two depending upon its success. With membership subscriptions of 700 or more, that formula allowed the Association to function for another twenty years. In addition, performances expanded to include jazz, folk music, and ballet. The quality was good and in the 1960s included the Don Shirley Trio, the Ruth Page Chicago Opera Ballet Company, and the William Carter Dana Ensemble.[30] One or two "highbrow" entertainments annually, however, was as much as the local market could seemingly bear and those performances sometimes included popular and show music. The best-attended programs were now the likes of George Shearing, ragtime pianist Max Morath, and the Serendippity Singers.[31]

Meanwhile, the Red Wing citizens who created Community Concerts in the 1940s supported the new organization but turned their attention to the Twin Cities for more challenging entertainments. In the 1960s Harold Ullrich, Janet Musty, Elizabeth Hedin and others promoted ticket sales for the Metropolitan Opera's annual spring appearances at the University's Northrup Auditorium and formed a local opera study group. When the Tyrone Guthrie Theater opened in Minneapolis in 1963 an overlapping group of Red Wingites promoted ticket sales.[32]

Save for a dozen week-night events each year, the Auditorium remained a movie house—one that did not always present the "finest" films. When the Menges owned the Red Wing [Chief] Theater, they occasionally presented serious films including, in 1967, the Royal Ballet's *Romeo and Juliet* starring Margo Fonteyn and Rudolph Nureyev. Nor did the Auditorium present all of the best films after

Sheldon's Gift

Fraser purchased the Chief. In 1970 Auditorium board member Evalyn Foot asked Fraser why so many good films played the Chief. Fraser told her that increasingly the best films were available only on contracts requiring a several day showing. Because of this, Fraser explained, he could more profitably show better films at the Chief due to its lower operating costs.[33] Fraser's truthful explanation foreshadowed the death of single screen theaters and the advent of multiplexes.

A second reason Fraser showed many of the most popular films at the Chief resulted from the breakdown of Hollywood's moral code in effect since 1934. Gradually, beginning in the 1950s, producers, and especially independent and foreign producers, ignored code restrictions on violence, nudity, and adult themes.[34] A failed attempt to revise the code and two Supreme Court decisions[25] led, in 1968, to the voluntary Motion Picture Association of America (MPAA) rating system that in modified form remains in effect. Changing mores and the initiation of the MPAA code resulted in many of best films being rated R and X (now NC-17).[36] Indeed, award-winning movies *Midnight Cowboy* (1969) and *Clockwork Orange* (1971) were both rated X. Because of such films' popularity and because of Auditorium sensibilities to periodic bluenose complaints, Fraser usually presented money making adult fare, ranging from the X-rated *Story of O* (1975), *Inserts* (1977), a "Degenerate Film with Dignity," and *The Cheerleaders* (1973) to sophisticated blockbuster R films including *Ordinary People* (1980) at the Chief. "I've got to make my money somewhere or just fold up my tent," Fraser said. The difference was dramatic. *The Snow Bunnies* (R Rated, 1972), Fraser noted, drew 602 patrons while *Robin and Marion* (PG 1976) drew half that. Ironically, the pictures that began the Auditorium's protracted troubles with John Wright were no longer prime box office. "Walt Disney pictures don't draw," Fraser said. Still, Fraser was mindful of community acceptance as he tried to balance adult fare and "family" films.[37] Fraser undoubtedly had his problems. At the same time, the board didn't question if Fraser's ownership of the Chief and Drive In created a conflict of interest. What is more, after fifteen years of a lease touted as financial salvation the Auditorium was flat broke, its lessee in arrears, and unable to claim even that it consistently presented the most popular films.[38]

Ruin and Restoration

At its financial nadir, the board snagged a life buoy. As if manna, money suddenly became available from an unlikely source, city revenues. What is more, its source allowed citizens to feel generous without having to spend a nickel. Coinciding with financial rock bottom, the Northern States Power Company (now Excel Energy) opened nuclear power plants at Prairie Island. Although located several miles from the city, Red Wing annexed the site. The tax benefit was immediate. Within two years Northern States Power Company provided forty percent of Goodhue County's tax revenue and a whopping seventy percent of city property and school taxes.[39] With the city flush, and with an arts friendly mayor in Ed Powderly, the Auditorium's board asked for and got $14,500 to "help out." Although city subsidies became regular they did not cause a financial about-face. The board's 1976 bare bones budget, which included nothing for depreciation or transformative programming, was $19,800. Its only income was Fraser's lease (yet $6000) and a city appropriation of $13,800.[40]

Auditorium lessee James Fraser (c. 1976). (Courtesy of the *Red Wing Daily Republican Eagle*)

Led by newer members, the board asked for more than twelve days per year use. But Fraser's lease was an obstacle. When member Rowe Million, the high school's drama coach, called for reduced rate rental for local non-profit groups, the board learned that it would have to pay Fraser $225 per weekend evening and seventy-five dollars per weeknight, amounts that neither the board nor local groups could afford.[41] Still, change was afoot. The Red Wing Historic Sites Committee became an insistent voice. Under Mrs. Milton Holst's leadership the committee

Sheldon's Gift

pushed for a return to the original façade and fought unsuccessfully to halt the erection of a new and unquestionably unattractive signboard. They lost that skirmish because the Auditorium was yet too much a motion picture theater; but they gained a significant victory when the Minnesota Historical Society placed the building on the Historic Site Register.[42]

William "Bill" Sweasy, president of the Red Wing Shoe Company, the town's largest employer, was another voice for change. Sweasy, whose company undertook significant historic renovations aimed at downtown revival, became involved in the Auditorium's dire affairs in the early 1970s when he raised money for restoration of the Auditorium's Kilgen organ. In September 1975, Sweasy proposed eliminating dependence on Fraser's lease by employing a full time booking agent for plays, orchestras, and traveling shows. While some board members were skeptical, others were enthusiastic. Mary Ann Ferrin, for example, thought that success was possible and said that a good agent, "with guts," could get good shows.[43]

Although there wasn't then enough money to hire a theatrical manager, James Fraser began booking modest increases in the number of live performances. There were also new ideas. City Administrator Jack Arnold talked of securing federal funds for a theater administrator and blocking out certain periods for movies and others for live performances and plays. Jim Touchi and Bruce Hoium proposed a nine-week summer arts festival and Gary Gisselman and Mike Steele offered to rent the theater for six months of the year as a professional playhouse. None of those proposals began and each may have suffered from insurmountable problems. For the most part, however, the board fretted that even if successful such programs would adversely affect Fraser's movie business.[44] Holding with movies, the lease, and a few live presentations was safer. The Auditorium had been a movie house so long it became impossible for many to imagine it as anything else.

Money also mattered. City subsidies resulted in Fraser's rent accounting for less than twenty-five percent of the budget. Still, as the decade closed, Fraser's lease seemed indispensable. Despite remodeling in 1970-1971, maintenance and repair costs rose precipitously. Oscar Wintervold told the board that a new electrical system, stage lighting, and other work would cost $25,000. An exterior painting project uncovered the need for brick tuck-pointing at a cost estimated at $200,000.[45]

Ruin and Restoration

There was also a mounting understanding that Lawrence Schmeckbier was correct in 1946—the fine arts demand subsidy. In 1977, Carrie Conklin of the Red Wing Historic Preservation Committee noted that board members and the mayor had "expressed their feeling that they too would like to see more live production, but that experience has shown that the arts must be subsidized as it is very difficult for live productions to come out financially through ticket sales only."[46] A year later board member Curtis Gruhl, an elementary teacher who became a key figure in the Auditorium's future, added that the board needed to know what kind of commitment the community and the city council would make. Without those commitments, he said, progress wasn't possible.[47]

As the 1980s began, it was clear that single screen movie houses, especially grand palaces with extraordinary expenses, were financial dead ducks.[48] But the commitments Gruhl said were necessary for change weren't forthcoming either. Still, Gruhl and others pushed, with some success, for more live performance and greater community use. In 1980, for example, a play written locally by Rita Healy and directed by Rowe Million, *To the Tune of Eighty Thousand*, a song and dance story of the Auditorium, boasted a cast of seventy. "If it's too historical it can get dull," director Million noted.[49] From the outside, Carrie Conklin encouraged the board to get serious about historic preservation. As Conklin and Gruhl knew, the two issues were linked. Historic buildings could be saved—but without a reuse plan money was unlikely to be forthcoming.

A turnabout began in 1982 when the board was inspired by restoration of Oshkosh, Wisconsin's privately owned Grand Opera House, which, like the Auditorium, was a movie house for years. The effort to restore and rehabilitate the Grand as a vibrant live performance venue was a fifteen year undertaking that eventually resulted in municipal ownership, governance by a non-profit board, and a great deal of community financial support.[50] Two Milwaukee consultants who spearheaded the Grand and other restorations encouraged the board. The Auditorium, they said, was in "light years" better condition than most theaters being restored. That it had been in continuous use mattered a great deal. So too did the fact that the community concert series continued and that Fraser was booking occasional live entertainment. As conversations continued, it seemed that it might be possible, especially if an audience could be drawn from surrounding communities and the Twin Cities, to offer classical concerts, bluegrass, rock, jazz, opera, dance, and Las Vegas type entertainers, as well as traveling and local theatrical productions.[51]

Funding such an ambitious project required, the Milwaukee consultants said, a combination of city bonds, government and foundation grants, city contributions, and individual and corporate support. What Red Wing lacked, they added, was a citizens committee (in Oshkosh there had been a committee of over a hundred drawn from a wide cross section of the community). Such a committee would generate ideas, enthusiasm and money. To Curt Gruhl, who recommended the establishment of a committee of thirty to forty people, not all of them Red Wing citizens, it was the right place to begin. For a body that for seventy-five years was uninterested in sharing its business with anyone, Gruhl's suggestion was itself ambitious. By the end of 1982, Gruhl had put together a small citizens group that included Elizabeth Hedin, Bill Sweasy, and Marilyn Albrecht.[52] While all were key to success, it wasn't broad community representation.

The following year Gruhl and Bill Sweasy kept the project moving forward. They contacted Rochester's Mayo Civic Auditorium, Albert Lea's Capp Emmons Theater,[53] and the Phipps Center in Hudson, Wisconsin for information and ideas. Meanwhile, Summer Playhouse director Todd Wronski investigated live theaters in Stillwater, Spring Green, Wisconsin, and Woodstock, Illinois.[54] Although the board held a public exploratory hearing little was accomplished. Jan and James Fraser, with Jan increasingly taking on a major role as James's health deteriorated, justifiably pointed out that they had booked a number of live events that included "big band" orchestras, a Kilgen Organ concert, barbershop quartet singing, and local nature filmmaker Richard Behrens. Although the Frasers held that commercial films and live entertainment could exist together, they couldn't. The board wanted local groups to use the Auditorium on weekends. But coordinating live performances with films that needed to be booked well in advance and often required a Friday, Saturday, Sunday run proved impossible.[55]

Early in 1984, board president Jim Teele, at the urging of Carrie Conklin, appointed a task force that included Gruhl, Marilyn Albrecht, Mary

RUIN AND RESTORATION

Anne Ferrin and five community members. A non-board member, Rhoda Newlin, became chairperson and arts consultant Daniel Pierotti advised them.[56] It was a step forward but not broad community participation.

In January 1985 the board hired Sovick, Mathre, Sathrum, and Quanbeck of Northfield, Minnesota, for an architectural feasibility study. A preliminary budget, set at $3,000,000, included $250,000 to begin a new endowment. It was proposed that half the funds come from a local fundraising campaign and half from a city bond issue. Lest citizens thought that three million dollars was extravagant, Gruhl, who was then board president, pointed out that the Auditorium needed $750,000 just to meet current building codes. Nor did three-million dollars include programming costs that Gruhl and others hoped would result in eighty events per year and draw half the audience from the Twin Cities.[57]

On July 1, a task force report based on communities and circumstances similar to Red Wing's echoed Gruhl's call for restoration mated to aggressive programming. Second, it recommended seating for just 471, a size said to reflect a realistic estimate of anticipated audiences. Most important, a city subsidy would have to continue, in the task force's view, after the restoration. Put positively, the subsidy would be for a "growing" arts facility. Private philanthropy, for the restoration and in the future was also crucial. The question was whether citizens were up to the task.[58]

The City Council received the Task Force recommendation enthusiastically.[lix] A fundraising committee, The Friends of the Auditorium, was organized. In November, a city referendum overwhelmingly approved a $1.5-million bond issue 1899 to 377.[60] A fundraising campaign began immediately under the leadership of Scott Jones, son of former board president Ora Jones, Jr., and Spence Broughton, president of the Citizens Fund Insurance Company. Thanks to their leadership, gifts, and support from other wealthy citizens and enterprises, the $1.5-million goal (a match to the $1.5-million bond authorization) was exceeded in early 1986.[61] With money committed, the Frasers' lease wasn't renewed. A commercial motion picture, the 1935 RKO Fred Astaire and Ginger Rogers classic, *Top Hat*, was shown for the last time on May 9, 1986, an occasion that honored the Frasers for their thirty-year Auditorium "run."[62]

As construction bids were let, the board busied itself with hiring a full time manager. From three finalists it chose Steven Schmidt, a Midwesterner and arts programs professional who had spent the previous four and a half years in El Paso, Texas directing its Art Resources Department and managing some 250 events a year.[63] In accepting the position, Schmidt, who was impressed by the Auditorium's space, the community's financial support, and by the altruism that leaders like William Sweasy brought to the project,[64] said that he was eager to help bring about "the renaissance of Red Wing." The Auditorium's role, as Schmidt saw it, was to sponsor outreach and residency programs, children's shows in cooperation with the schools, traveling art exhibitions and a whole host of other arts functions. On-stage performances, he said, would be "comprehensive" and include country and western music, humor, classical music, modern dance and more.[65]

As restoration began, near-tragedy struck. On the morning of January 13, 1987, local dignitaries congregated in the Auditorium lobby for a "Lobby Busting" kickoff. When manager Steve Schmidt opened doors to the auditorium to allow donors and officials a last look inside, he was greeted by smoke and fire rising along the proscenium arch. Stunned, Schmidt hustled his baffled guests out the front doors. As he crossed Third Street, Schmidt heard the explosion and felt the concussion that raised the roof and blew open chained-shut doors. Flames shot from everywhere. The fire, attributed to a worker using a torch to cut through ductwork, caused $750,000 in damages and a six month work delay. No one was injured and no one thought of abandoning the restoration. Indeed, unlike the fire of 1918, insurance was adequate and the tragedy made possible additional, previously unplanned, renovations.[66]

Steven Schmidt, first director of the remodeled "Sheldon" (1986) (Courtesy the *Red Wing Republican Eagle*)

With restoration underway, the board, increased to seven members[67] and

Ruin and Restoration

with Mary Ann Ferrin[68] as president, grappled with fundraising and program planning. The initial capital fundraising went exceedingly well. Now the challenge was raising sufficient funds annually to enhance the endowment and supplement the operating budget. "Nowhere in the country, maybe in the world," Schmidt said, "are the arts a self-sustaining enterprise." Ticket revenue, he added, was always insufficient and therefore, "The theater will continue to need the support of community-spirited Red Wing residents."[69] From Schmidt it was recognition that public arts programming rested on a four-legged financial stool of city funds, ticket sales, a substantial endowment, and annual philanthropy.

A fundraising effort was undertaken by a new volunteer group, the Friends of the Auditorium, that would primarily solicit individuals to attend galas. In the Friends first year, its goal was to gross $30,000. Its first gala resulted in huzzahs all around when it netted $40,000. Board participation proved more difficult. In January 1988, when Schmidt spoke with the board it was the first time that members, mayoral appointees, were asked to accept a personal responsibility. In April, the board committed to raise $45,000 from local companies in support of the annual budget. Despite Schmidt's urgings, the board declined face-to-face solicitation and then evaded developing a list of prospects. In May, citing a need for more planning and claiming its goal was "unrealistic" members promised weakly to "plant the seeds for future donations" and shifted fundraising responsibility from the business community to the Friends.[70]

Meanwhile, as construction moved toward completion, a grand reopening was planned for September 1988. As the Special Edition of the *Republican Eagle* pointed out, the Auditorium, now called simply the Sheldon, was again a "Shining Jewel." Intricate plaster and woodwork highlighted a masterfully re-created inner lobby. Gold gilt, the re-creation of murals on walls and ceiling, and the restoration, sans supporting poles, of the horseshoe balcony made for a stunning theater proper. In addition, Roy and Merle Meyer gave generously to create a multi-purpose venue for recitals, art exhibits, and lectures in space that was once the upper and rear balconies.[71]

The grand reopening, an affair that manager Schmidt said "will overflow with "God, mother, and apple pie," was held in September.[72] The joyful and well-attended events featured a parade, park concert, and a concert by popular pianist

Marvin Hamlisch.[73] Jim Fraser, who suffered a stroke some years before, did not live to see it. He died, a "movie man" through and through, at age fifty-nine, a year after the Auditorium's last picture show.

Infused with grand opening optimism, the board set a 1989 budget of $450,000. Of that amount, they expected to derive $128,000 from ticket sales and $100,000 from an increased annual city allocation. The remainder would come from endowment income ($17,000) and private gifts ($205,000).[74] As for programming, Schmidt repeated that he intended to ". . . provide a broad range of accessible, quality events--including jazz, folk, gospel, and chamber music." Schmidt was well aware of market forces. Appropriate programming, he once said, is "what the market will support. You don't program for yourself, you program for your ticket-buyers."[75] At the same time, Schmidt planned a wide variety of programs, some of which the market undoubtedly couldn't support. "We need to look at the entire fiscal year," he said. His hope was that the Sheldon could meld becoming a presenting house for imported entertainment, a producing house for local events, and a rental house. "I was hired to try an experiment," Schmidt said. "If it doesn't work, I'll make recommendations so it will work within the resources."[76]

It was all ambitious, heady, and optimistic. The board, unfortunately, didn't fully share Schmidt's broad vision for growing programming sustained through active community fundraising.[77] And, although Schmidt had vocal supporters, they weren't on the board.[78] Just before year end the board, which gave Schmidt a raise the previous year, handed him a miserly personnel review and told him to write "planned and measurable" goals. Understandably, Schmidt, disheartened, resigned.[79]

As Schmidt departed, the board searched for a new manager, lured many applicants, and selected Sean Dowse, who had been manager of Minneapolis' Cricket Theater.[80] As the transition to a new manager took place the board prevailed on Scott Jones and Spence Broughton to again lead a fundraising campaign that by the end of 1989 reported surpassing its $200,000 goal, an amount the leaders said was possible annually.[81] First year performances booked by Schmidt were impressive and included an opera, Puccini's *Madame Butterfly*, an *Up with People* choral concert, a Heart of the Beast Puppet Theater residency, the Laurentian String Quartet, a soprano soloist, the Berlin Chamber Orchestra, recitals, organ concerts, folk music, lectures, and community theater.

Ruin and Restoration

Fifteen years after the Auditorium's finances hit rock bottom, arts fever in Red Wing ran higher than it had since the immediate post World War II years. In the end, a broad consensus involving a funding scheme that tied taxpayers and the elite together in an uneasy alliance to promote and sustain a performing arts venue became a reality and a rejuvenated source of community pride.

Notes

[1] Mary Lee Wahlin, "Town and Country," *Red Wing Daily Republican Eagle*, April 25, 1959.
[2] Ibid.
[3] Cobbett S. Steinberg, *Film Facts* (New York: Facts on File Inc.1980), 46.
[4] Ibid., 43.
[5] Minutes, T.B. Sheldon Auditorium Board, February 16, 1968. The board was displeased because Fraser showed many foreign films. Many, such as Peter Sellers, *The Mouse that Roared*, had an international cast and were largely filmed in England. Others, including the acclaimed Brazilian film, *Black Orpheus*, never played Red Wing.
[6] "Auditorium Profit Cited by Leasing Municipal Theater," *Red Wing Daily Republican Eagle*, October 29, 1959; James Fraser Testimony, Supplemental Partial Transcript of Proceedings, *John Wright and Associates, a Corporation, Plaintiff, v. Harold R. Ullrich et. al., Defendant*, Civ. No. 3-59-169 United States District Court for the District of Minnesota Third Division.
[7] Minutes, T.B. Sheldon Auditorium Board, November 26, 1962.
[8] James Fraser, (column),"Waxing Nostalgic at Christmastime," *Red Wing Republican Eagle*, December 11, 1980.
[9] "Fraser Purchases Drive-In Theater," *Red Wing Daily Republican Eagle*, April 1, 1961.
[10] "Fraser Addresses Business Women," *Red Wing Daily Republican Eagle*, November 18, 1958.
[11] "Waseca Theater Purchased by Fraser of Red Wing," *Red Wing Daily Republican Eagle*, September 17, 1964.
[12] "Chief Theater to Re-Open," *Red Wing Daily Republican Eagle*, October 16, 1965.
[13] Advertisement, *Red Wing Daily Republican Eagle*, December 24, 1965.
[14] Cobbett S. Steinberg, *Film Facts* (New York: Facts on File Inc., 1980), 43, 46.
[15] Minutes, T.B. Sheldon Auditorium Board, November 22, 1965; October 10, 1966.
[16] Minutes, T.B. Sheldon Auditorium Board, January 2, 1968, April 22, 1968; October 14, 1968; November 13, 1968 and December 9, 1968.
[17] Minutes, T.B. Sheldon Auditorium Board, September 14, 1959; April 12, 1961; January 13, 1964. The main floor was reupholstered in 1964 but the balcony would wait for another five years.

Sheldon's Gift

[18] Minutes, T.B. Sheldon Auditorium Board, May 22, 1961.
[19] Minutes, T.B. Sheldon Auditorium Board, June 19, 1961.
[20] Minutes, T.B. Sheldon Auditorium Board, September 16, 1963; August 20, 1965; May 2, 1965.
[21] Minutes, T.B. Sheldon Auditorium Board, September 8, 1969; November 13, 1968.
[22] Minutes, T.B. Sheldon Auditorium Board, April 13, 1970.
[23] Minutes, T.B. Sheldon Auditorium Board, November 3, 1968.
[24] Minutes, T.B. Sheldon Auditorium Board, February 9, 1970; February 16, 1970.
[25] Minutes, T.B. Sheldon Auditorium Board, October 13, 1970; January 11, 1971.
[26] Souvenir Program, *Pygmalion* (Red Wing: np, nd. [1971]).
[27] Minutes, T.B. Sheldon Auditorium Board, June 11, 1965; May 17, 1971; October 11, 1971; November 13, 1972; September 9, 1974.
[28] Minutes, T.B. Sheldon Auditorium Board, March 10, 1958.
[29] "Community Concert Association Folds Up," *Red Wing Daily Republican Eagle*, October 1, 1957.
[30] "Red Wing Concert Group to Open Office," *Red Wing Daily Republican Eagle*, September 28, 1964; "Community Concert Sets Renewal Week," *Red Wing Daily Republican Eagle*, October 4, 1966; "Concert Series Drive is Started," *Red Wing Daily Republican Eagle*, September 19, 1967; Dave Schliep (review), "Michael Maude Dancers Offer Color, Variation," *Red Wing Daily Republican Eagle*, January 24, 1968; "Community Concert Series Begins Here Tuesday," *Red Wing Republican Eagle*, December 13, 1980;
[31] "Concert a Sellout," *Red Wing Daily Republican Eagle*, October 2, 1974); "Community Concert Wednesday," *Red Wing Republican Eagle*, February 23, 1981. Also see Community Concert Association Folder, Goodhue County Historical Society (unnumbered), which includes programs and the Columbia Artists Management booklet, Outline of Community Concert Association: Plan of Organization.
[32] Mabel McMullin, "Between Us," (column) *Red Wing Daily Republican Eagle*, November 24, 1961; "Opera Tickets Go on Sale Here," *Red Wing Daily Republican Eagle*, April 8, 1964; "Guthrie Theater Invites Red Wingites," *Red Wing Daily Republican Eagle*, March 26, 1963..
[33] Minutes, T.B. Sheldon Auditorium Board, September 21, 1970. With fewer films released, the distributors required longer play dates, but after three or four days in Red Wing most films attracted small audiences. It was easier for Fraser to absorb the costs of emptier houses at the Chief.
[34] Notable films that were released without code approval included Otto Preminger's *The Moon Is Blue* (1953), *The Man with the Golden Arm* (1955), and *Anatomy of a Murder* (1959). Also significant was Alfred Hitchcock's *Psycho* (1960).
[35] See *U.S. Supreme Court Ginsberg v. New York*, 390 U.S.629 (1968) and *U.S. Supreme Court Interstate Circuit v. Dallas*, 390 U.S. 676 (1968).
[36] In the 1970s some X rated films, *Inserts* and others, contained full frontal nudity, near-explicit sexuality, and graphic drug abuse. In the past twenty years such films have

generally been edited to receive an R rating and thus wider commercial appeal.

[37] R.L. Healy, "R, X Flicks Pay the Bills," *Red Wing Republican Eagle*, November 8, 1976; "Difficult Times for Theater Owner," *Red Wing Republican Eagle*, November 13, 1980.

[38] Minutes, T.B. Sheldon Auditorium Board, March 11, 1974.

[39] Frederick Johnson, *Goodhue County, Minnesota: A Narrative History* (Red Wing: Goodhue County Historical Society Press, 2000), 313.

[40] Minutes, T.B. Sheldon Auditorium Board, October 21, 1974; July 14, 1975.

[41] Minutes, T.B. Sheldon Auditorium Board, January 10, 1972; February 7, 1972.

[42] Minutes, T.B. Sheldon Auditorium Board, July 10, 1972; February 23, 1976.

[43] Minutes, T.B. Sheldon Auditorium Board, September 8, 1975.

[44] Minutes, T.B. Sheldon Auditorium Board, September 8, 1975; April 18, 1977; July 18, 1977; October 7, 1977; June 19, 1979.

[45] Minutes, T.B. Sheldon Auditorium Board, April 18, 1977; February 22, 1977; October 16, 1978; July 18, 1977.

[46] Minutes, T.B. Sheldon Auditorium Board, July 18, 1977.

[47] Minutes, T.B. Sheldon Auditorium Board, November 20, 1978.

[48] Minutes, T.B. Sheldon Auditorium Board March 24, 1980; January 21, 1980; August 17, 1981; May 17, 1982.

[49] "Original Production to Premiere Here November 9," *Red Wing Republican Eagle*, October 30, 1980; "Eighty Thousand Is 70 Who Want to Entertain Hundreds," *Red Wing Republican Eagle*, November 8, 1980; "Sheldon Musical a Unique Gift," *Red Wing Republican Eagle*, November 10, 1980.

[50] Minutes, T.B. Sheldon Auditorium Board, January 18, 1982. Also see www.grandoperahouse.org/aboutus/history.

[51] Minutes, T.B. Sheldon Auditorium Board, April 19, 1982; May 17, 1982; June 9, 1982.

[52] Minutes, T.B. Sheldon Auditorium Board, April 19, 1982; June 9, 1982; December 20, 1982.

[53] Since demolished. See "Art Deco Auditorium Falls to Changing Times," *Minneapolis Star Tribune*, February 6, 2006.

[54] Minutes, T.B. Sheldon Auditorium Board, January 17, 1983; February 22, 1983; July 25, 1983.

[55] Minutes, T.B. Sheldon Auditorium Board, October 17, 1983; November 21, 1983.

[56] Minutes, T.B. Sheldon Auditorium Board, March 19, 1984; April 16, 1984; August 20, 1984.

[57] Minutes, T.B. Sheldon Auditorium Board January 7, 1985; August 20, 1984; April 15, 1985; "Theater Restoration Gets Aud Board Endorsement," *Red Wing Republican Eagle*, April 16, 1985.

[58] Minutes, T.B. Sheldon Auditorium Board, June 21, 1985.

[59] Minutes, T.B. Sheldon Auditorium Board, July 22, 1985.

[60] "Idea Rooted 5 Years Ago," *Red Wing Republican Eagle*, August 30, 1988.

[61] Minutes, T.B. Sheldon Auditorium Board, February 18, 1986.

[62] Ruth Nerhaugen, "Affection Goes Beyond Auditorium," *Red Wing Republican Eagle*, May 12, 1986.
[63] Ruth Nerhaugen, "New Aud Manager Views Restoration as Very Significant," *Red Wing Republican Eagle*, October 20, 1986.
[64] Steven Schmidt, interview with the author, July 14, 2009.
[65] Quoted in Ruth Nerhaugen, "New Manager Views Restoration as Very Significant," *Red Wing Republican Eagle*, October 20, 1986.
[66] Steven Schmidt, interview with the author, July 14, 2009. Also see Greg Breining, "New Old Red Wing," *Minnesota Monthly* (Vol. 22, No. 7, July 1988), 39; and Minutes, T.B. Sheldon Auditorium Board (February 2, 1987).
[67] Despite the Sheldon trust deed requirement for five members, the board recommended and the City Council approved, without question, an increase in board size from five to seven.
[68] Ferrin, who had been chairwoman of the Red Wing Downtown Development Association was a steadfast advocate for theater renovation and live performance. See "New DDA Officer: Red Wing Still Beautiful," *Red Wing Republican Eagle*, May 19, 1980.
[69] Quoted in Ruth Nerhaugen, "New Aud Manager Views Restoration As Very Significant," *Red Wing Republican Eagle*, October 20, 1986.
[70] Minutes, T.B. Sheldon Auditorium Board, July 20, 1987; January 21, 1988; April 4, 1988; May 2, 1988; May 16, 1988.
[71] Ruth Nerhaugen, "Sheldon to Serve Three Functions," *Red Wing Republican Eagle*, August 10, 1988.
[72] Quoted in Greg Breining, "New Old Red Wing," *Minnesota Monthly* (July 1988), 40.
[73] Ruth Nerhaugen, "It's Crunch Time at Sheldon," *Red Wing Republican Eagle*, September 8, 1988; Ruth Nerhaugen, "T.B. Sheldon Charms Its Visitors," *Red Wing Republican Eagle*, September 11, 1988.
[74] Minutes, T.B. Sheldon Auditorium Board, June 20, 1988; July 8, 1988; "What the Future Holds," *Red Wing Republican Eagle*, September 9, 1988.
[75] Quoted in Ruth Nerhaugen, "New Manager Views Restoration as Very Significant," *Red Wing Republican Eagle*, October 20, 1986.
[76] Ruth Nerhaugen, "Sheldon to Serve Three Functions," *Red Wing Republican Eagle*, August 10, 1988; "What the Future Holds," *Red Wing Republican Eagle*, September 9, 1988; "City Allots $100,000 to Sheldon," *Red Wing Republican Eagle*, October 7, 1988.
[77] Steven Schmidt, Interview with the Author, July 14, 2009.
[78] Minutes, T.B. Sheldon Auditorium Board, January 17, 1989
[79] Minutes, T.B. Sheldon Auditorium Board, December 12, 1988; January 17, 1989.
[80] Minutes, T.B. Sheldon Auditorium Board, April 17, 1989; June 19, 1989.
[81] Minutes, T.B. Sheldon Auditorium Board, February 7, 1989; November 20, 1989.

Epilogue

"We got a feel for Red Wing." ~Paul Rogers, Rogers Cinema Inc. (April 1985)

"If the artsy fartsy types are for it, I'm agin it." ~Letter to the Editor (2009)

When Red Wing's movie houses were visited last, James Fraser owned the Chief and Red Wing Drive-In and leased the Auditorium. Three theaters. Three screens. One operator. An exhibition industry in trouble. United States weekly film attendance peaked at nearly ninety million in 1947 and then skidded downward to a low, in the early 1970s, of about sixteen million. The number of movie houses plunged as well. Four wall theaters fell in half. Drive-ins peaked at 6,000 in 1961 but were halved by the early 1980s. As theaters and drive-ins bottomed, however, the number of theater screens began to increase due to multiplexing. Weekly attendance rebounded but only to twenty million.[1]

Multiplexing transformed exhibition. By combining two, three or more screens costs fell appreciably. What's more, popular films could now be "held over" almost indefinitely. As audiences diminished, films moved to smaller screening rooms. Humorist Bill Bryson explained the new theaters perfectly. The old theaters, where the audience faced a "vast screen in a cubic acre of darkness," were "entrancing." But in multiplexes, he wrote, from the poor sound to the high priced popcorn, "every feature . . . seemed carefully designed to make a visit a deeply regretted experience."[2]

Red Wing mirrored these trends. In 1985 Fraser sold his Chief to Rogers Cinema of Marshfield, Wisconsin, which divided it into a three screen triplex of 100 seats each. It was a formula, owner Paul Rogers said, that worked in four of his other theaters and would work in Red Wing. "We got a feel for Red Wing," he declared.[3]

Within two years, however, Rogers sold his renamed Chief 123 to the Chicago-based Essaness chain. A year later, Excellence bought it. In 1994 Carmike Cinemas, a chain of three hundred suburban and small city multiplexes bought Excellence. It was a nationwide trend. Independent theaters dropped like flies to multiplex chains that in turn fell to larger companies. Carmike, which filed for bankruptcy reorganization, wasn't immune. In Red Wing, a new five-screen multiplex opened in a small shopping mall on the city's outskirts in 1995. Its appearance marked the end of the Chief as a motion picture house. In the decade since, the Chief, under other names, has operated as an off-again/on-again nightclub. It stands, forlorn and deteriorating, with a "for sale or lease" sign on its door.

On the May 1986 evening when the Auditorium showed *Top Hat* as its last picture show, Jim Fraser's fifteen- and seventeen-year-old children couldn't attend because they were busy operating the family's drive-in. Unfortunately, their summer employment was cut short. In July the drive-in closed for the season, which meant it had closed. Fraser speculated that, "It probably could be used for sunrise church services."[4] He was either prescient or in negotiations, for when the big screen and cinderblock concession stand/projection booth were demolished, a Baptist church rose on the site.

Few single screens remain. Some, in urban areas, specialize in "sleepers," classics, foreign language, art, independent and other "sure seaters," that have always been a hard sell in towns like Red Wing. A handful of "first run" single screens survive in small cities. In Wells, Minnesota, a town of just 2,500, the city purchased the 304-seat art-deco Flame and operates it on weekends. Its offerings include recent releases and on occasion challenging and controversial films.[5]

Wherever single screens are alive in small cities, whether as a public, non-profit, or private venture, the reasons are the same. A primary impulse is to keep alive downtowns devastated by big boxes and strip malls at the edges. That commercial impulse was in part responsible for the Sheldon's restoration. A second impulse is to preserve architectural heritage. Although many cheer those efforts, lacking a viable-use plan, good intentions frequently come to naught. A third reason is to preserve shared experience. Jeff Frank, owner of the sleek, single screen

Epilogue

art deco Drexel in Bexley, Ohio, has said that these are places where "for a short time, you take people someplace they've never been before."[6] Just as importantly, patrons are transported communally. The Minnesota Supreme Court missed that point when it likened movie houses to dress shops. Wright was justified in demanding fair competition. Still, the court's analogy failed to grasp the importance of shared experiences that Red Wingites, although they articulated it inaptly, feared was lost. Urban planners, who long failed to recognize the importance of movie theaters to downtown vibrancy, missed the same point.[7]

In Red Wing, communality was heightened. While all movie houses are public space, at the Auditorium it was literally true. That fact elevated a belief that "all the people" owned Sheldon's gift even though democratic participation was marginal at best. Moreover, movies are a one-way communication and our nostalgic shared experiences were, with rare breathtaking and unforgettable exceptions, pure Hollywood fluff.

In some places, theater owners, developers, and municipalities have collaborated to build multiplexes in the heart of old downtowns. In Hopkins, Minnesota, a nonprofit performing and visual arts center and private multiplex cinema are directly across from one another on the town's historic Main Street.[8] Such developments strive to create a "theme-park" quality that draws people together in the core city where they can, as James Forsher wrote, "take advantage of a wide range of cultural arts, whether classical music, bluegrass, jazz, country, plays, or films." Downtown multiplexes aren't palatial, but their glitzy neon exteriors recreate an illusion of spectacle.[9] And what, after all, are the movies if not illusion? Such developments suggest that Red Wing might have benefited by inviting its multiplex, even had it meant public subsidy, into downtown. With its multiplex at the mall, entertainment as a linchpin to sustaining downtown cohesiveness rests on the Sheldon exclusively—a monopoly that city leaders thought for a century was its proper role.

~§~

Despite seventy-five years of missteps, shortcomings, misperceptions, and obsessions, when the Auditorium was flat busted it began to find its way and then got it very right. In the 1980s, thanks to leadership, public financing, philanthropy, and the examples of others, Red Wing found itself on the front side of a new trend to reinvigorate the arts in small cities. Activists looked outside of themselves and the community. Lessons were learned. Gift horses should be looked in the mouth. Support flows from involvement. When the board walled itself off it suffered. When it was honest and asked for help it succeeded. Most importantly, Red Wing's civic leaders accepted the lesson that Laurence Schmeckebier taught in 1946—the arts demand subsidy and philanthropic responsibility rests upon each generation.

As a result, Red Wing is justifiably proud of its Sheldon. It is, to be sure, an outstanding example of a grand Midwest opera house. More, it is one of a handful that function as built—as a community center for live entertainment. The restored Sheldon brings Red Wing lively, engaging, and occasionally provocative programming. It's especially to be commended for excellence in family and children's theater and for showcasing and providing a home for local talent including, since 1993, the Phoenix community theater,[10] singing groups, and the Sheldon Brass Band. It has built strong relationships with the public schools that allow them to use the Sheldon for some productions, cooperate on others, and provide meaningful children's and youth programming for students.

In the first years after restoration, the Sheldon ran the program gamut. In its first full season, for example, it presented Puccini's *Madame Butterfly* and a concert by the positivist Up With People singers. *Madame Butterfly* drew a puny crowd of 215 while Up With People drew an impressive 430. Worse, Puccini was twice the expense of the happy singers. In the next few years, as the Sheldon continued to present a wide program range, finances faltered. In 1992 there was a $54,000 deficit.[11]

The following year, however, the board reported a modest $2,800 surplus. The change, board president Doug Ritter said, resulted from more accurate projections of profit or loss on each event. "We now have a better understanding of music and theater that appeals to our patrons and are able to conduct healthy debates on the extent to which we will fund artistically important but money-losing events . . . ." Ritter said. Not surprisingly, of the eighty-six events attended by 22,000 ticket buyers that year, the profitable shows were country music, brass band concerts, and the Kingston Trio. Leading the list of money losers were the

Epilogue

Leipzig Chamber Orchestra and the Merce Cunningham Dance Company.[12] By 1995 attendance rose to 37,000 for ninety-six Sheldon and community-sponsored ticketed events. The year end surplus increased to $19,000.[13] The lesson was clear. Careful attention to market forces mattered.

"Highbrow" events—concert pianists, dance companies, and serious drama—have suffered because of financial exigencies and close attention to market demand and now account for just two or three performances annually. In 2007-2008 there were two—concert pianist Tadeusz Majewski and a performance of *Julius Caesar* by the Aquilla Theatre Company. Thanks to sponsorships, ticket prices for both were affordable.[14] Nevertheless, Sheldon Director Sean Dowse says that a mezzo soprano can fill only fifty seats, and that Ibsen's *Hedda Gabler* and the regional Cannon Valley Orchestra are each fortunate to draw 200.[15] This is not surprising. The audience for serious music especially declined because of hierarchical separation at the hands of people who claimed an inaccessible superiority for it and whose attitudes insured it was not viable financially without considerable subsidy.

In Red Wing, from the Auditorium's opening onward, no "highbrow" forms drew particularly well. Whether the Minneapolis Symphony or the dramatic works of Shaw or Ibsen,[16] turnouts were modest. Classical and neoclassical works[17] revived in a decade of post World War II enthusiasm and because of a large and hard-working volunteer ticket-selling corps. But as a generation aged and died, "middlebrow" classical and neoclassical performance of works that were the backbone of the Community Concert Series passed with it.

The confluence of market reality and the lowly state of high and middlebrow culture, especially in small cities, raises the question of whether community performing arts organizations have a responsibility to present challenging, controversial, and limited audience programs. Suggesting that some responsibility exists isn't arguing that the late Allan Bloom and others who seemed to claim that western civilization stopped dead in its tracks about 1900 were correct.[18] On the contrary, As sociologist Herbert Gans asserts, one "taste culture" is as good as another.[19] It is rather a brief for diversity. Programming exclusively to a known market not only disregards

SHELDON'S GIFT

those who prefer Beethoven, it diminishes those who might come to know him, or Britten, or Bartok, or thousands of new, creative artists.

Accepting responsibility for fully diverse programming requires regular presentation of "highbrow" music and drama at affordable prices. It also means embracing the truth that arts consultant Daniel Perotti told the Auditorium in 1993. "Live audiences do not just happen; they must be reached, cultivated and nurtured." Most importantly, an "audience must be educated as well as entertained."[20] Marketing and audience development go hand in hand.

"Today," Jeremy McCarter wrote recently, ". . . high and low culture sneer at each other across a gulf of incomprehension and politically useful ill will."[21] Although that's mostly true there are signs of a thaw. Opera, in part due to popularizing by the Three Tenors and others, and dance, have made modest comebacks with young people. It would be shameful to miss any opportunity to return in some measure to what Lawrence Levine called "a shared public culture." That earlier and entirely American culture was, as McCarter noted, "less hierarchically organized and split into fewer little categories than the scene we know today."[22] If a community performance center defines its "mission" in part as "enlightenment of the community and its visitors," as the Sheldon does currently, then audience development is key.[23] For the most part that means patiently building long-term relationships that result in education and committed philanthropy.[24]

Twenty years after restoration the Sheldon is reasonably sound financially. Since foundering early on it has kept its financial head above water. City subsidies are crucial. Of those, the city has accepted responsibility for capital expenditures in its own budget—costs that in the past caused the Auditorium financial disaster. It also provides an annual subsidy. This assistance and the fact that the Auditorium was once again "new" allowed it to get off on the right foot and to charge accessible ticket prices. At this writing the best shows, of whatever type, typically carry an adult ticket price of no more than twenty-five dollars and many are lower.[25]

Learning from past errors, a growing endowment has always been front and center in the restored Sheldon's financial plans. In the 1990s the Sheldon

Epilogue

aligned with other Red Wing institutions in a smart program to build awareness of the need for endowment and the possibilities for legacy giving. Those efforts, combined with a $500,000 matching gift from the City of Red Wing, enabled the endowment to grow to three million dollars by the end of 2008. The operating budget, according to Director Sean Dowse is about $700,000 per year. Of that amount, half is derived from ticket sales. The remainder is provided by endowment income ($135,000), Friends of the Sheldon gala ($30,000), city subsidy ($50,000), and the remainder from grants, sponsorship, rentals, and other philanthropy.[26]

These are meaningful accomplishments. The Sheldon does, however, face serious challenges. Competition is one. Within fifty miles is a profusion of major entertainments—highbrow and low—that are geographically, if not financially, accessible to all. Close by is Treasure Island Casino with a 1,000-seat auditorium that often presents nationally known talent—county musicians and comedians especially. Nearby small cities have created arts centers that sponsor plays, readings, and other arts events. To Executive Director Dowse, however, the Sheldon, because of its intimacy and quality remains an effective competitor. To him, the most formidable challenges are luring residents away from their home theaters and presenting programs that appeal to twenty- to forty-year-olds.[27]

The recent recession demonstrates that government support, especially grant monies, are unreliable and that in any crisis support for the arts, at the local, state, or national levels falters first. In this crisis the value of the Sheldon's endowment fell by a third, a decrease that, if not offset by rising markets or new contributions, will translate into an annual operating fund reduction of $40,000. There are other financial challenges. The city's contribution of $500,000 to the Sheldon's endowment came at the cost of gradual annual support reduction from over $140,000 per year to just $50,000.[28] The city's regard for its support, that it is a contribution or donation, has caused Director Dowse to ask that the city affirm its obligations.[29]

Dowse is justified to question commitment. Elected officials are always sensitive to public criticism, broad based or not. In the case of the arts, suspicion and criticism is omnipresent. In 2008, for example, when the Auditorium board supported a state arts and environment dedicated sales tax increase, it drew criticism as well as support. One citizen, identified as ed. w. expressed a view held likely by many when he wrote that, "If the artsy fartsy types are fer it, I'm agin it."[30] Americans have never been reliable arts supporters. Further, sustaining gifts and gala income have stagnated and recession can have double and triple effects—loss of government money, loss of audience, and loss of endowment principal.

To shore up finances, the Sheldon has shrunk its offerings. Currently, its "season," from September through May, presents approximately forty-five events, far fewer than the eighty to 150 hoped for at the time of the theater's restoration or the eighty or more of the mid-1990s. Of these, local talent and family and children's theater account for over half. The remainder are largely big bands, folk, blue grass and multi-repeat performers. Program shrinkage has prompted such comments as that from a letter writer who asked, reasonably, what public funds were going for when he noted that the Auditorium had presented only one event in a given month.[31] The same question will be asked, not always directly, by sustaining donors and those considering meaningful endowment gifts. For the Sheldon it is a "Catch-22." Reduce programming to be financially responsible and in so doing jeopardize public and private money.

Sustainability depends upon adequate and committed public and private support for both building maintenance and for program development and underwriting. This is a formidable challenge. For one thing, charitable and city support has fallen short of keeping pace with inflation let alone sustaining the kind of "growing" arts organization articulated by Director Steve Schmidt in 1988. For one thing, Red Wing, as have hundreds of other small cities, has changed notably. The manufacturing that provided good paying jobs and local profit is largely gone. Thankfully, the shoe and leather companies remain, but jobs have been sacrificed. Retailing is now in big box hands. Auto dealerships and banks are no longer owned locally. Profits flow from the community. Service industries, medicine and education especially, are important but don't provide direct tax revenues.

Wealthy individuals might plausibly conclude that the Sheldon hasn't adequately met its "middle" and "highbrow" expectations. Those citizens might also conclude that because of programming cutbacks and stagnant contributions that neither is it meeting the needs of the wider citizenry. The combination could be lethal. Dried up philanthropy might lead to cutbacks in local government sup-

Epilogue

port which looks to private giving as a bellwether for its own appropriations. Such cutbacks, which probably could not be offset through ticket-price increases, might be expected to lead to further program reductions.

One thing seems clear. Answers to challenges ahead are not external. Theater attendance from outside the city and foundation grants are marginally helpful. But true health depends upon Red Wing itself—a broadly representative and generous board, affordable prices, local philanthropy underwriting both operations and endowment, and taxpayers willing to commit to support the arts whether for intrinsic reasons, because they believe the arts are good for business, or because the arts foster community. Sustainability also depends, critically, on diverse, sharp-witted programming that distinguishes itself from the purely commercial while balancing what is popular and saleable with that which is challenging and culturally significant.

There's no question that arts and entertainment breathe life and excitement into communities. Though Theodore Sheldon never knew of it, that belief, we must assume, motivated his trustees over a hundred years ago. Although Sheldon's gift has now survived for over a century, it is never a good idea in America to take anything connected to the arts, or to historic preservation, for granted.[32] Red Wing no longer touts itself as "The Desirable City." It's current motto, "The Best Small City in America," however, is equally bumptious. Whether citizens and local government can justify that self-assurance depends in significant measure on how well the city and its residents foster and sustain the arts and whether each taste culture finds satisfaction with its share.

Notes

[1] Cobbett S. Steinberg, *Film Facts* (New York, Facts On File Inc., 1980), 41, 48.
[2] Bill Bryson, *I'm a Stranger Here Myself* (New York, Broadway Books, 1999), 115-116.
[3] Flora Burfeind, "Three for One Soon at Chief," *Red Wing Republican Eagle,* April 18, 1985.
[4] James Fraser (column), "Corn Price Is Chicken Feed," *Red Wing Republican Eagle*, July 24, 1986.
[5] Amanda Dyslin, "All Fired Up," *The* [Mankato, Minnesota] *Free Press*, August 10, 2006.
[6] Dan Barry, "Bringing Hollywood Boulevard to Main Street," *The New York Times*,

September 23, 2007.

[7] James Forsher, *The Community of Cinema: How Cinema and Spectacle Transformed the American Downtown* (Westport, Connecticut: Praeger, 2003), 137.

[8] "Hopkins Center Marks a Decade of Arts, Performance," *Minneapolis Star Tribune*, October 17, 2007.

[9] James Forsher, *The Community of Cinema: How Cinema and Spectacle Transformed the American Downtown* (Westport, Connecticut, Praeger, 2003), 105.

[10] The Phoenix Community Theater formed in 1993. See http://www.friendsofthesheldon.com.

[11] "Sheldon Theater Shows a Profit," *Red Wing Republican Eagle*, February 2, 1994.

[12] Ibid.

[13] Ruth Nerhaugen, "Sheldon's Dowse Reports 'Good Year Financially,'" *Red Wing Republican Eagle*, January 25, 1996.

[14] See Programs, 2006-2007 and 2007-2008 seasons, the Sheldon. See also www.sheldontheatre.org)

[15] Author interview with Sean Dowse, August 6, 2008.

[16] In fairness, neither Shaw nor Ibsen drew well in St. Paul either.

[17] Although twentieth century atonal music composers have believed that an audience for their music would develop, few have tried to understand it and it has consequently never developed more than a very small audience.

[18] See Alan Bloom, *The Closing of the American Mind* (New York: Simon and Schuster, 1987).

[19] Herbert J. Gans, *Popular Culture and High Culture: An Analysis and Evaluation of Taste* (New York, Basic Books, 1999), passim. It is impossible to imagine that most mid-19th century Americans would not agree.

[20] Daniel L. Perotti, *Program Management Study: Report and Recommendations* (unpublished, T.B. Sheldon Memorial Auditorium, June, 1993), 7.

[21] Jeremy McCarter, "The Original Culture Warrior," *Newsweek* (October 27, 2008). See www.newsweek.com/id/16499.

[22] Ibid.

[23] "Sheldon Strategic Plan," *Red Wing's Current*, January, 2009.

[24] To hear what is possible by fusing relationship building, philanthropy, audience development, and cultural types, listen to VocalEssence, Philip Brunelle, conductor, *The World Beloved: A Bluegrass Mass* (Clarion CLR931CD) (VocalEssence, 2007).

[25] On the question of properly establishing the city matching fund see Letter, Kenneth E. Raschke, Jr., Minnesota Assistant Attorney General to Peter Schaub, Red Wing City Attorney, August 9, 1996; Red Wing City Council, Resolution No. 3801, "A Joint Resolution Establishing a City Matching funds Program for the T.B. Sheldon Auditorium and Fund Therefor, February 10, 1997; City of Red Wing, Charter Amendment, August 25, 1998.

[26] Sean Dowse, interview with the author, August, 6, 2008; Ruth Nerhaugen, "Times are Tough, But Show Must go On," *Red Wing Republican Eagle*, February 14, 2009.

Epilogue

[27] Sean Dowse, interview with the author, August 6, 2008.

[28] Ruth Nerhaugen, "Times Are Tough, But Show Must go On," *Red Wing Republican Eagle*, February 14, 2009.

[29] "Sheldon Wants to Redefine Relationship with City," *Red Wing Republican Eagle*, February 19, 2009. 1911. In 1911 the city council granted the Auditorium $500 per year, not for janitorial services, as called for in the trust agreement, but for general purposes so as not to establish a precedent.

[30] "Sheldon Board Endorses Legacy Amendment," *Red Wing Republican Eagle*, October 24, 2008; ed w. comment, October 25, 2008, at www.Republican-eagle.com.

[31] People's Platform, *Red Wing Republican Eagle*, June 24, 2000.

[32] "Arts Supporters will Seek Equity in Cuts from State," *Red Wing Republican Eagle*, December 9, 2008; In 2006 the magnificent 2000 seat art deco Capp Emmons Auditorium, a theater that the Preservation Alliance of Minnesota called "a classic example of art deco architecture" was demolished. See Robert Franklin, "Art Deco Auditorium Falls to Changing Times," *Minneapolis Star Tribune*, February 6, 2006.

BIBLIOGRAPHY

NEWSPAPERS

Local newspapers have been a key source for this study. Fortunately, Red Wing had a significant number of them, many rather good, which went into and out of business and merged with one another until 1940. Since then one daily (except Sundays), has served the community. Red Wing's newspapers and their colorful editors and publishers await a serious historical study. For the nineteenth century, (The) *Red Wing Argus* (weekly) from 1864 to 1900 and *The Advance* (1877-1884) (weekly) as well as the *Red Wing Republican* proved especially helpful. After 1900 the *Red Wing Daily Republican* and its weekly edition (to 1941) regarded itself as the city's most important paper. It was challenged between 1911 and 1940 by N.P. Olson's *Red Wing Daily Eagle*, a newspaper created by Olson, who previously published *The Red Wing Free Press* (weekly). In 1940 Albert Marshall purchased the *Red Wing Daily Eagle* and the *Red Wing Daily Republican* and merged them as the *Red Wing Daily Republican Eagle*. Since 1970 that newspaper has been known as the *Republican Eagle*. No Red Wing newspapers are indexed but all are available on microfilm at the Minnesota Historical Society in St. Paul.

Other area newspapers consulted included the *Lake City Graphic*, *Cannon Falls Beacon*, the *Zumbrota News*, and the *New Prague Times* (all weeklies). The metropolitan dailies, The *St. Paul Pioneer Press* and the *St. Paul Dispatch* as well as the *Minneapolis Star Tribune* were also helpful. All are available on microfilm at the Minnesota Historical Society. Nationally, the trade newspaper *Variety*. New York: Variety, Inc., 1905-Present, proved useful, especially on blind and block booking and Minnesota exhibitor aspects of the Paramount case. *Variety* is available on microfilm at the Minneapolis Public Library.

Sheldon's Gift

PUBLIC DOCUMENTS

Primary public documents used extensively include Minutes of the T.B. Sheldon Auditorium Board (1919-Present) and Minutes of the Red Wing City Council (1907-Present). Both are available at Red Wing City Hall and online at http:www.red-wing.org. (Laserfiche server). Unfortunately, although T.B. Sheldon Auditorium records were said to have been rescued from the 1918 fire, no board minutes or other records survive prior to the city requiring (in 1919) that the Board meet in the presence of the City Clerk. Limited financial records of the T.B. Sheldon Memorial Auditorium are available in "Financial Reports Auditorium Board/Cash Receipts & Deposits 1918-1944" at the Minnesota Historical Society. Real estate transactions are available at the office of the County Recorder in the Goodhue County Government Center in Red Wing. Civil case files after 1951 are located at the Goodhue County Justice Center in Red Wing.

The Minnesota Historical Society in St. Paul is the repository for the civil case files of the Goodhue County District Court prior to 1951, the Minnesota Attorney General case files and records of the Minnesota Office of the Secretary of State, Minnesota Death Records, and printed and manuscript data of the Bureau of the Census. Although not official public records, microfilm copy of city directories for Red Wing (1907, 1909-1910, and 1911-1912 (All R.L. Polk Co. St. Paul) as well Minneapolis and St. Paul directories (various years) are on microfilm at the Minnesota Historical Society and have proved valuable in tracing the whereabouts of numerous subjects in this study. Session Laws of the State of Minnesota are located at the Minnesota Historical Society but are readily accessible online at http://www.revisor.leg.state.mn.us.

Case files and transcripts (two linear feet) of John Wright's federal case and appeal to the Eigth Circuit *(John Wright & Associates v. Harold R. Ullrich et. al.* (1962.) are now located at the National Archives, Central Plains Region, Kansas City, Missouri.

Minnesota Supreme Court opinions in *Longcor v. City of Red Wing, et. al.* (1940) *John Wright & Associates, Inc. v. Red Wing and others* (1958), *Anderson v. City of Montevideo* (1917) and federal trial court and appeals opinions in *John Wright & Associates v. Harold R. Ullrich et. al.* (1962) are available online from WESTLAW (Thomson Reuters Co). Hennepin County Libraries offer free use of WESTLAW.

INTERVIEWS AND ORAL HISTORIES

Bentson, Lawrence "Larry" (former CEO and Chairman, Midcontinent Media Inc. and son-in-law and partner of Edmond R. "Eddie" Ruben). Discussion with the Author, August 5, 2006.

Dowse, Sean (Manager, T.B. Sheldon Memorial Auditorium, 1989-Present). Discussion with the Author, August 6, 2008.

Schmidt, Steven, T.B. Sheldon Memorial Auditorium, 1988-1989). Discussion with the Author, July 14, 2009.

BIBLIOGRAPHY

Swanson, Mary Gwen Owen. Interview February 4, 1975. Oral history transcript I.5.34. Goodhue County Historical Society, Red Wing.

Vogel, Marjorie. Interview April 26, 1973. Oral history transcript I.5.16 . Goodhue County Historical Society. Red Wing.

Wintervold, Oscar. Interview November 15, 1977. Oral history transcript I.5.51. Goodhue County Historical Society, Red Wing.

BOOKS AND PERIODICALS

"Academy of Music Theatre (Northampton, Massachusetts)." http://academyofmusictheatre.com/history.

Angell, Madeline. *Red Wing, Minnesota: Saga of a River Town*, 2nd ed. Minneapolis: Dillon Press, 1978.

Arneson, Thomas. *And the Curtain Rises: The Story of the Fairmont Opera House*. Fairmont, Minnesota: Fairmont Photo Press, 1988.

Anon. "What's Playing at the Grove?" In *Moviegoing in America: A Sourcebook in the History of Film Exhibition*. Ed. by Gregory A. Waller. Malden, Massachusetts: Blackwell Publishers. 2002, Originally published in *Fortune*, August, 1948: 95-99.

Balio, Tino. *Grand Design: Hollywood as a Modern Business Enterprise 1930-1939*. Vol. 5. of *History of the American Cinema*, ed. by Charles Harpole. New York: Charles Scribner's Sons, 1993.

Balio, Tino, ed. *The American Film Industry*. Madison, Wisconsin: University of Wisconsin Press, 1976.

Baumol, William J., and William G. Bowen. *Performing Arts: The Economic Dilemma: A Study of Problems Common to Theater, Opera, Music, and Dance*. New York: Twentieth Century Fund, 1966.

Bee, Roger, Gary Browne, and John Luecke. *The Chicago Great Western in Minnesota*, 2nd ed. Anoka, Minnesota: Blue River Publications, 1984.

Bergman, Andrew. *We're in the Money: Depression America and Its Films*. New York: New York University Press, 1971.

Besse, Kirk J. *Show Houses: Twin Cities Style*. Minneapolis: Victoria Publications Ltd., 1997.

Bly, Carol. "Rural Feelings: Starting in the Mailroom and Having to Stay There." In Letters from the *Country* by Carol Bly, New York: Harper and Row, 1981, 64-68.

Bogle, Donald. *Toms, Coons, Mulattoes, Mammies, and Bucks: An Interpretive History of Blacks in American Films*. New York: The Viking Press, 1973.

Bordwell, David, and Kristin Thompson. "Technological Change and Classical Film Style." In *Grand Design: Hollywood As a Modern Business Enterprise 1930-1939*. Ed. by Tino Balio. Vol. 5 of *History of American Cinema*. Edited by Charles Harpole. New York: Charles Scribner's Sons, 1993.

Borneman, Ernest. "United States versus Hollywood: The Case Study of an Antitrust

Suit." In *The American Film Industry*. Edited by Tino Balio. Madison: University of Wisconsin Press, 1976. Originally published in *Sight and Sound*, 19 (February and March 1951): 448-450.

Bowers, Q. David. *Nickelodeon Theatres and Their Music*. Vestal, New York: Vestal Press, Ltd., 1986.

Bowser, Eileen. *The Transformation of Cinema, 1907-1915*. New York: Charles Scribner's and Sons, 1990.

Breining, Greg. "New Old Red Wing." *Minnesota Monthly* 22.7 (July 1988): 39-40.

Brown, Svend-Einar. Program Notes. Program. St. Paul Chamber Orchestra. March 23, 2007 to June 3, 2007, 2007.

Bryson, Bill. *I'm a Stranger Here Myself*. 1999. New York: Broadway Books, 1999.

──. *The Life and Times of the Thunderbolt Kid*. New York: Broadway Books, 2006.

Buhle, Paul, and Dave Wagner. *Radical Hollywood: The Untold Story Behind America's Favorite Movies*. New York: The New Press, 2002.

Burleigh, Louise. *The Community Theatre in Theory and Practice*. Boston: Little, Brown, 1917.

Chansky, Dorothy. *Composing Ourselves: The Little Theatre Movement and the American Audience*. Carbondale: Southern Illinois University Press, 2004.

Cheney, Sheldon. *The Art Theater: Its Character as Differentiated from the Commercial Theater; Its Ideals and Organization; and a Record of Certain European and American Examples*. New York: Knopf, 1925.

Chrislock, Carl H. *The Progressive Era in Minnesota 1899-1918*. St. Paul: Minnesota Historical Society Press, 1971.

Community Concert Series [folder]. Goodhue County Historical Society, Red Wing.

Conant, Michael. *Antitrust in the Motion Picture Industry*. Berkeley: University of California Press, 1960.

──. "The Impact of the Paramount Decrees." In *The American Film Industry*. Ed. by Tino Balio. Madison: University of Wisconsin Press, 1976, 346-370.

Cripps, Thomas. *Hollywood's High Noon: Moviemaking and Society Before Television*. Baltimore: The Johns Hopkins University Press, 1997.

Curtiss-Wedge, Franklyn. *History of Goodhue County Minnesota*. Chicago: H.C. Cooper Jr. & Company, 1909.

Davis, Ronald. *The Glamour Factory: Inside Hollywood's Big Studio System*. Dallas: Southern Methodist University Press, 1993.

DiMaggio, Paul. "Cultural Boundaries and Structural Change: The Extension of the High Culture Model to Theater, Opera, and the Dance, 1900-1940." In *Cultivating Differences: Symbolic Boundaries and the Making of Inequality*. Edited by Michelle Lamont and Marcel Fournier. Chicago: University of Chicago Press, 1992.

"Early Color Motion Picture Processes: A Nostalgic History of the Development of Color Cinematography." American Museum of Film Technology Center. American Widescreen Museum and Film Technology Center, 1995-2008. Martin B. Hart,

BIBLIOGRAPHY

Curator. http://www.widescreenmuseum.com.

"Early Sound Films of the Silent Era." Silent Era. http://www.silentera.com.

Eccles, Mrs. Edward. *Plum City Centennial 1857-1957*. NP: Helmer Printing Company, n.d. [1957].

Engelhardt, Tom. *The End of Victory Culture: Cold War America and the Disillusioning of a Generation*. New York: Basic Books, 1995.

Erlandson, James. "On Stage in the 19th Century." *Mpls-St.Paul* 9.9 (September 1981).

Forsher, James. *The Community of Cinema: How Cinema and Spectacle Transformed the American Downtown*. Westport, Connecticut: Praeger, 2003.

Frank, Stanley. "Sure Seaters Discover an Audience." Excerpted in *Moviegoing in America: A Sourcebook in the History of Film Exhibition*. Ed. by Gregory A. Waller. Malden, Massachusetts: Blackwell Publishers. 2002. Originally published in *Nation's Business 40*, (January 1952), 34-36.

Franklin, Harold B. *Motion Picture Theater Management*. Garden City NY: Doubleday, Doran, and Company, 1928.

Fuller, Kathryn H. "You Can Have the Strand in Your Own Town." In *Moviegoing in America: A Sourcebook in the History of Film Exhibition*. Ed. By Gregory A. Waller. Malden, Massachusetts: Blackwell Publishers. 2002. Originally published in *At the Picture Show: Small-Town Audiences and the Creation of Movie Fan Culture*. by Kathryn H. Fuller. Washington D.C.: Smithsonian Institution Press, 1996.

Gans, Herbert J. *Popular Culture & High Culture: An Analysis and Evaluation of Taste*. New York: Basic Books, 1999.

Gieske, Millard. *Minnesota Farmer Laborism*. Minneapolis: University of Minnesota Press, 1979.

Glenn, George D., and Richard L. Poole. *The Opera Houses of Iowa*. Ames. Iowa State University Press, 1993.

Gomery, Douglas. "The Coming of the Talkies: Invention, Innovation, and Diffusion." In *The American Film Industry*, Ed. by Tino Balio. Madison: University of Wisconsin Press, 1976, 193-211.

Hall, Ben M. "The Best Remaining Seats." In *Exhibition, The Film Reader*. Ed. by Ina-Rae Hark. New York: Routledge, 2002.

Hanson, Cynthia. "Catheryne Cooke Gilman and the Minneapolis Better Movie Movement." *Minnesota History* 51.6 (Summer 1989): 203-216.

Hark, Ina-Rae, Ed. *Exhibition, The Film Reader*. New York: Routledge, 2002.

Harrison, P.S. "Give the Movie Exhibitor a Chance." In *Moviegoing in America: A Sourcebook in the History of Film Exhibition*. Ed. by Gregory A. Waller. Malden, Massachusetts: Blackwell Publishers. 2002. Originally published in *Christian Century* 52 (19 June 1935), 819-821.

Hinsdell, Oliver. *Making the Little Theatre Pay: A Practical Handbook*. New York: Samuel French, 1925.

A History of the Red Wing Civic Male Chorus. Typescript. Red Wing: NP [1976?]. In the possession of the author.

Hodgson, Harriet. *Rochester: City of the Prairie*. Northridge, California: Windsor Publications, Inc., 1989.

Hornblow, Arthur. *A History of Theatre in America from its Beginnings to the Present Time*. Vol. 2. Philadelphia: J.B. Lippincott, 1919.

Huettig, Mae D. "Economic Control of the Motion Picture Industry." Excerpted in *Moviegoing in America: A Sourcebook in the History of Film Exhibition*, Ed. by Gregory A. Waller, Malden, Massachusetts: Blackwell Publishers, 2002: 214-218.

Hulfish, David. "Motion-Picture Work: A General Treatise on Picture Taking, Picture Making, Photoplays, and Theater Management and Operation," [1915]. In *Moviegoing in America: A Sourcebook in the History of Film Exhibition*. Ed. by Gregory A. Waller. Malden, Massachusetts: Blackwell Publishers, 2002.

(The) Internet Movie Database. IMDb.com.Inc, 1990-2009. http://www.imdb.com.

Jacoby, Susan. *The Age of American Unreason*. New York: Pantheon Books, 2008.

Johnson, Frederick L. *Goodhue County, Minnesota: A Narrative History*. Red Wing: Goodhue County Historical Society Press, 2000.

Kane, Lucile M., and John A. Dougherty. "Movie Debut: Films in the Twin Cities, 1894-1908." *Minnesota History* 54.8 (Winter 1995): 342-358.

Keller, Morton. *Regulating a New Economy: Public Policy and Economic Change in America, 1900-1953*. Cambridge: Harvard University Press, 1990.

Kolko, Gabriel. *The Triumph of Conservatism: A Reinterpretation of American History, 1900-1916*. New York: The Free Press of Glencoe, 1963.

Koppes, Clayton R., and Gregory D. Black. *Hollywood Goes to War: How Politics, Profits, and Propaganda Shaped World War II Movies*. New York: The Free Press, 1987.

Kusell, H.O. "Bank Night," In *Moviegoing in America: A Sourcebook in the History of Film Exhibition*. Ed. by Gregory A. Waller. Malden, Massachuestts: Blackwell Publishers, 2002: 189-191. Originally published in the *New Republic* 86 (May 1936), 363-365.

Lass, William E. *Minnesota: A History*, 2nd ed. New York: W.W. Norton, 1998.

Levine, Lawrence W. *Highbrow/Lowbrow: The Emergence of Cultural Hierarchy in America*. Cambridge: Harvard University Press, 1988.

Lincoln, Freeman. "The Comeback of the Movies." *Fortune* 51 (February 1955): 127-31.

[Jack] *Liebenberg's Movie Theaters, 1928-1941*. University Gallery Exhibition Catalog. Minneapolis: University of Minnesota, 1982.

Macgowan, Kenneth. *Footlights Across America: Towards a National Theatre*. New York: Harcourt Brace, 1929.

Marquis, Alice Goldfarb. *Art Lessons: Learning from the Rise and Fall of Public Arts Funding*. New York: Basic Books, 1995.

May, Lary. *The Big Tomorrow: Hollywood and the Politics of the American Way*. Chicago: University of Chicago Press, 2000.

Bibliography

———. *Screening Out the Past: The Birth of Mass Culture and the Motion Picture Industry*. New York: Oxford University Press, 1980.
McCusker, John J. "What Was the Inflation Rate Then?" *Economic History Services*. http://www.eh.net/hmit/inflationr.php.
Michael, McGerr. *A Fierce Discontent: The Rise and Fall of the Progressive Movement in America, 1870-1920*. New York: Free Press, 2003.
Mickel, Jere C. *Footlights on the Prairie*. St. Cloud, Minnesota: Northstar Press, 1974.
Mitau, G. Theodore. *Politics in Minnesota*. Minneapolis: University of Minnesota Press, 1960.
Musser, Charles, with Nelson Carol. *High Class Moving Pictures: Lyman H. Howe and the Forgotten Era of Traveling Exhibition, 1880-1920*. Princeton: Princeton University Press, 1991.
Nafziger, Ralph, and Thomas Barnhart. *Red Wing and Its Daily Newspaper*. Vol. 9. The Community Basis for Postwar Planning. Minneapolis: University of Minnesota, 1946.
Nelson, Lowry, and George Donohue. *Social Change in Goodhue County 1940-1965*. Minneapolis: University of Minnesota, Agricultural Experiment Station, 1966.
Newman, Paul S. "Theodore L. Hays: Theatrical Good Neighbor at the Turn of the Century." *Minnesota History* 53.6 (Summer 1993): 238-323.
Field, Cyrus A. "Proceedings in Memory of . . . Associate Justice Clifford L. Hilton. . . ." *Minnesota Reports* Vol. 246. http://www.lawlibrary.state.mn.us/judges/memorials.
Putnam, Michael. *Silent Screens: The Decline and Transformation of the American Movie Theater*. Baltimore: Johns Hopkins University Press, 2000.
Pygmalion. Souvenir Program. T.B. Sheldon Memorial Auditorium, April 1971.
Rasmussen, Christian A. *A History of the City of Red Wing Minnesota*, 5th ed. N.P., Red Wing, Minnesota, 1934.
Roney, Carlie Beach. "Show Lady." In *Moviegoing in America: A Sourcebook in the History of Film Exhibition*. Ed. By Gregory A. Waller. Malden, Massachusetts: Blackwell Publishers. 2002. Originally appeared in *Saturday Evening Post* 211 (18 February 1939): 38-40.
Sayre, Nora. *Running Time: Films of the Cold War*. New York: Dial, 1982.
Schatz, Thomas. *Boom and Bust: American Cinema in the 1940's*. Vol. 6, *History of American Cinema*. Ed by Charles Harpole. New York: Charles Scribner's Sons, 1997.
Schiller, Suzanne I. "The Relationship Between Motion Picture Distribution and Exhibition: An Analysis of the Effects of Anti-blind-bidding Legislation." In *Exhibition, The Film Reader*. Ed. by Ina-Rae Hark. New York: Routledge, 2002: 107-114.
Schlanger, Ben. "Motion Picture Theaters." Excerpted in *Moviegoing in America: A Sourcebook in the History of Film Exhibition*. Ed by Gregory A. Waller. Malden, Massachusetts: Blackwell Publishers. 2002, 221-223. Originally published in

Architectural Record 81 (February 1937), 17-20.

Schmeckebier, Laurence Eli. *Art in Red Wing*. Vol. 6. The Community Basis for Postwar Planning. Minneapolis: University of Minnesota Press, 1946.

Sherman, John K. *Music and Theater in Minnesota History*. Minneapolis: University of Minnesota Press, 1958.

Sklar, Robert. *Movie-Made America: A Social History of American Movies*. New York: Random House, 1975.

Steinberg, Cobbett. *Film Facts*. New York: Facts on File, 1980.

"Talking Pictures: Milestones in Sound." *American Widescreen Museum and Film Technology Center*. 1995-2008. Martin B. Hart, Curator. http://www.widescreenmuseum.com.

Taubman, Howard. *The American Theatre*. New York N.Y.: Coward McCann, 1965.

Taves, Brian. "The B Film: Hollywood's Other Half." In *Grand Design: Hollywood as a Modern Business Enterprise 1930-1939*. Ed. by Tino Balio. Vol. 5 of *History of American Cinema*. Ed. by Charles Harpole. New York: Charles Scribner's Sons, 1993: 313-350.

Tey, Josephine [Elizabeth MacKintosh]. *The Daughter of Time*. New York: MacMillan Publishing, 1951.

Thompson, Joel. "Four Movie Theatres Made Red Wing Unique." *Goodhue County Historical Society* 35.2 (Summer 2001): 11.

Tittle, Barbara, Fred Johnson, Elaine Robinson, and Eva Million. "The T.B. Sheldon Memorial Auditorium." *Goodhue County Historical Society News* 19.1 (March 1985).

Trimble, Steve. "Curtain Up in 1933: The Legacy of the St. Paul Opera Association." *Ramsey County History* 39.4 (Winter 2005): 4-18.

Twain, Mark. *Life on the Mississippi*. 1883. Boston, Massachusetts: James R. Osgood and Company, 1883.

Ulano, Mark, C.A.S. "Moving Pictures That Talk-The Early History of Film Sound." *Filmsound*. http://www.filmsound.org.

Wahlin, Mary Lee. "T.B. Sheldon Auditorium: County Treasure Still Providing Quality Entertainment as it Nears 100." *Goodhue County Historical Society News* 35.2 (Summer 2001): 2-4.

Waller, Gregory A. *Main Street Amusements: Movies and Commercial Entertainment in a Southern City, 1896-1930*. Washington, DC: Smithsonian Institution, 1995.

_____, ed. *Moviegoing in America: A Sourcebook in the History of Film Exhibition*. Malden, Massachusetts: Blackwell Publishers. 2002.

Weinstein, James. *The Corporate Ideal in the Liberal State: 1900-1918*. Boston: Beacon Press, 1968.

West Publishing Co. *Biographical Sketches of Justices of the Minnesota Supreme Court and Judges of the Minnesota Court of Appeals from Territorial Days to 1990*. St.Paul: West Publishing Company, 1990.

Whiting, Frank M. *Minnesota Theatre: From Old Fort Snelling to the Guthrie.*

Bibliography

Minneapolis: Pogo Press, 1988.
Wiebe, Robert H. *The Search for Order: 1877-1920*. New York: Hill and Wang, 1967.
Williamson, Samuel H. "What Is the Relative Value?" *Economic History Services*. http://www.eh.net/hmit/compare/.
Wood, Alley & Co. *History of Goodhue County*. Red Wing: Wood, Alley & Co.1878.
[Wright, John]. *The Chief News*. Broadside. Red Wing: NP, February 24, 1959. In the possession of the author.

INDEX

3-D, 169-171, 173.
A films, 103, 104, 111, 119, 152, 167, 180.
Abott, Bessie, 40.
Academy of Music Theater, The, 21.
"Aimless Amblings by Ambrose," 100, 128, 133, 190, 203.
Allied Theater Owners of the Northwest, 146.
American Association of University Women (AAUW), 152, 153.
American Mutoscope & Biograph Company, 39.
Anderson v. City of Montevideo, 193, 194.
Apollo Club, 32, 52, 53.
Arnold, Jack, 222.
Arntson, Arthur E., 116, 124, 125.
Art Association, Red Wing, 186.
Artists Series, 154-156.
Associated Film Distributors of America, 146.
Athletic field, 86, 80.
Attic Players, 84.
Auditorium fire (1918), 68-72.
Auditorium fire (1987), 226.

B films, 98, 103, 104, 119, 124, 146, 167, 172, 179.
Balls, 10, 29.
Bank Night, 107, 149, 150, 151.
Beattie, C. Robert "Bob," 148-150, 174, 192, 204.
Becker Building, 116, 120, 123.
Beckwith Memorial Theater, 21.
Beckwith, Philo D., 21.
Bennett, Harold "Hoot," 152.
Berger, Benjamin, 205, 206.
Berry, H.C, *Also* Berry, Harry, Berry, J.C., and Barry, John C., 119-122, 124, 131.
Best Years of Our Lives, The, 160.
Betcher, Charles A., 12, 19, 20, 28, 40, 48.
Billboards, 50, 51, 52, 85.
Blind booking, 65, 74.
Block booking, 65, 74, 79, 88, 89, 103, 104, 119, 145-147, 167, 168.
Blodgett, E.H., 18.
Bloom, Alan, 237.
Bombach, C.J., 97, 98, 108, 111, 116, 119.
Boxrud, George, 153.
Bracher, C.C., 122, 136, 138, 144, 150, 158.
Broadway, xi, xii, 82, 83, 144.
Broughton, Spence, 225, 228.
Buena Vista, 180, 181.
Burnquist, J.A.A., 135, 136, 138-140.
Burton, Marion L., 16, 26, 27.
Busch, Frederick, 18.

255

Business and Professional Women's Club, 186.

Cahill, Judge John C., 179, 193, 194.
Cameraphone, 42, 43.
Carmike Cinemas, 234.
Casino, The, 8-12, 20.
Charitable Trust Statute (1927), 135.
Chicago, Milwaukee, and St. Paul Railway Co., 3, 46.
Chief News, The, 189, 190.
Chief Theater, 108, 116-118, 122, 125, 132, 137, 138, 144-147, 150, 152, 166, 169-172, 175, 179-182, 187, 189, 190, 194, 202-210, 215-217, 219-221, 232-234.
Chief-Metro Theater Corporation, 152, 168.
Christianson, William C., 112, 119, 121, 122, 124, 134, 138, 139, 148, 149.
Cinemascope, 169-173.
Citizens Postwar Advisory Committee, 153.
City hall, viii, 18.
Civic Music League, 83.
Columbia Pictures, 22, 103, 145, 146, 170, 188, 219.
Community Concert Association, 157, 219.
Community Concerts, 157, 158, 217, 219, 224, 236.
Community theater, xii, 25, 26, 84, 152, 153, 159, 160, 218, 228, 236.
Community Theater Guild, 159.
Concessions (candy counter), 87, 182, 173, 205.
Conklin, Carrie, 223, 224.
Consent Decree, 145, 146.
Cornell, Ruben, 140, 156.
Curran, R.S. "Staff," 86, 107, 132, 134, 138, 145.

Davenport, Robert, 41, 45, 48, 55, 56, 66, 72.
Davenport, the, 45-48, 55, 56, 63.

Davenport, William, 43.
DeLambert, R.H., 131, 134, 135.
Demurrer, 134.
Dengler, John, 86, 88-90, 98, 106, 120, 132, 138, 145, 150.
Donovan, Judge Dennis, 202, 206-209.
Dowse, Sean, vii, 228, 237, 239.
Duff, Philip, 201-204.

Edison Films, 38, 64.
Edquist, Edward, 147.
Electric theater, 39-41, 45.
Endowment, 18, 31, 32, 158, 225, 227, 228, 238-241.
Erb, E.C., 107-109.
Essaness Theaters, 234.
Ewing, Duane, 203, 204, 206.

Family, the, 29, 45-47, 49, 55, 56, 63-67, 152.
Federal Theater Project, 152.
Ferrin, Frank, 129, 138, 147.
Ferrin, Mary Ann, 222, 223, 227.
Film Row, Currie Avenue, vii, 103.
Finkelstein and Ruben, 95.
Foot, S.B., 174, 205, 217, 220.
Fort Snelling, 1.
Fraser, James, 170-172, 179-182, 186-189, 193, 200-206, 208-210, 214-218, 220-222, 224, 225, 228, 233, 234.
Fraser, Jan, 224.
Friends of the Auditorium, 191, 225, 227.
Frohman, Charles, 24.
Frosch Theater Supply Company, 170.

Gallagher, Justice Frank, 192-194.
Gem, the, 38, 40-46, 48.
General Film Corporation, 64.
Gentleman's agreement, 95, 103, 119, 137, 152, 169, 171, 179, 180, 189, 190, 215.
Gerlach, Ben, 19, 73, 138.
Giffin, Walter A., 29.

Goodhue County National Bank, 129, 139.
Gopher Amusement Company, 120-124, 145.
Grainger, Percy, 154.
Granada Theater (New Prague), 137.
Grand Electric Theater, 40, 45.
Grand Opera House (Oshkosh, Wisconsin), 223.
Green, F.O., 85, 99, 100, 106, 129.
Grondahl, Jens K., 48, 51, 53, 54, 64, 191.
Gruhl, Curtis, 223-225.

Hall, Charles P., 18, 21, 52, 66, 67, 71, 74, 75, 134, 148.
Hall, Ossee Matson, 18, 19, 22, 28, 30.
Hand, Judge Learned, 209, 210.
Haustein, J.A., 95, 97, 98, 107, 108, 110, 111, 120, 122, 133.
Hawes, J.C., 9.
Hawley, Dr. George, 217.
Hedin, Dr. Raymond, 153, 156, 158, 219.
Hernlem, Arthur, 129, 138, 143, 150.
Hilton, Judge Clifford L., 129, 134, 135.
Hodgman, J.M., 3.
Holst, Milton, 203.
Holst, Mrs. Milton, 221.
Hosp, Joseph A., 120, 121.
Howe, Hiram, 21, 52, 66, 67, 72, 84.
Howe, Lyman, 38, 46.
Hughes, Howard, 180, 208.

Ibsen, Henrik, 25, 237.
In Old Kentucky, 54.
Interstate Amusement Company, 119, 120, 122, 123.

Johnson, Enoch "Nickie," 122, 131, 143, 145, 148.
Johnson, Eva, 158.
Johnson, George W., 46, 63, 65, 66, 73-75, 79, 80, 84, 85, 87-90, 95-99, 102-104, 106, 107, 110, 111, 118, 119, 131, 152.
Johnson, Jack, 46.
Johnson, Etta, 65.
Jones, Ora Jr., 174, 204, 216, 217, 225.
Jones, Scott, 224, 228.
Justice Department, U.S., 145.

KAAA, 160, 169.
Kaehler, Mrs. Arnold, 185.
Kaliher, Leon, 148-150.
Kappel, John, 88, 95, 98, 107-112, 116, 120, 121, 144.
Kilgen organ, 81, 222, 224.
Koehler, Walter E., 79, 86, 88, 89, 98, 107-109, 111, 112, 123, 124, 131, 132, 138, 145, 150, 152.
Kosec, Arnold, 122, 137, 138, 145, 150.
Krise, William, 88, 107.
Kroeger, Fred, 72, 73.

LaGrange Shoe Company, 204.
Lamoreau, Lowell A., 20, 71.
Langley, Clarence, 153.
Lawther, James, 12, 16.
Legion of Decency, 180.
Leslie, John and Jennifer, 30.
Levine, Lawrence, 9, 238.
Library (Carnege - Lawther), 12, 128.
Lilyblad, Harry, 120.
Lion's Club, Red Wing, 187.
Little Theater, 84.
Longcor, William J., 12, 42, 99, 128, 130-140, 144, `55, `82, 184, 193, 194.

Majestic Family Theater, 29.
Majestic Theater (Rochester). 42.
Majesticscope, 38.
Male Civic Chorus, 158.
Marshall, Albert, 169.
Martha, 7, 29.
Maud Powell Trio, 27, 28.
May, Lary, 96, 166.
Mayo Civic Auditorium, 153, 224.
Mehaffy, Justice Pat, 209.
Menge, Mr. And Mrs. Willis, 216.

Metro Goldwyn Mayer, 103, 146, 170, 180, 189.
Metro, the Theater, 66, 72, 74, 75, 79-82, 8489, 95-98, 100, 103-106, 118, 119, 123, 132, 137, 138, 144, 146, 151, 152, 167-169, 179.
Meyer, Merle and Roy, 227.
Minneapolis Symphony Orchestra, 27, 48, 237.
Minnesota Attorney General, 246.
Minnesota Legislature, 146.
Minnesota Stock Company, 152, 153.
Minnesota Supreme Court, xi, 107, 129, 134, 138, 183, 188, 192, 194, 202, 214, 235.
Mohn, Thomas, 86-89, 97, 98, 107-110, 112, 119, 123, 130-133, 139, 140.
Molitor, Leo, 123.
Monogram Films, 146.
Moore, Ed, 159.
Mossberg, William, 109, 111, 145.
Multiplex, 79, 234, 235.
Munson, Leroy "Muntz," 186, 191.
Murphy, Justice William P., 21, 183, 184, 190-194.
Music Hall, 3, 4, 16.

Neighborhood theaters (nabs), 93, 97, 167.
Nelson, Julia B., 18.
Nickelodeon, 39.
Nielsen, Axel, 63, 66-74.
Northern States Power Company (Xcel Energy), 145, 221.

Olson, Elmer W., 63, 74, 75, 90, 99, 133, 200.
Olson, H.L., 42, 48.
Olson, Nels P., 53, 54, 66, 73, 74.
Olson, Ole, 11.
On-screen advertising, 174, 204.
Opera, viii, xii, 1, 5, 6, 8, 10, 22, 25, 26, 29, 224, 228, 238.
Opera house, xii, 4-7, 9-12, 14, 16, 18, 22, 26, 29, 38, 80, 192, 223, 236.

Panic of 1907, 31.
Paramount Case, 167, 168, 245.
Paramount Pictures, 65, 80, 94, 103, 145, 146, 188, 200, 202, 206, 245.
Parquet and ramp, 117.
Pastime, The, 63, 64, 66.
Pearce, Helen, 156, 158.
Penthouse Club, 218.
Percentage films, 65, 74, 88, 138, 147, 168.
Peterson, Judge Albin, 9, 146.
Philanthropy, xii, 32, 52, 53, 155, 225, 227, 235, 238-241.
Philleo Hall, 2.
Pierce, A.P., 21, 31, 51-53, 56.
Plum City, 118, 216.
Poverty Row, 119, 121, 208.
Powderly, Mayor Ed, 221.
Prairie Island, 221.
Prizefight films, 41, 44.
Problem films, 167.
Progressivism, 75, 85.
Prohibition, 80, 118.
Pygmalion, 218.

Raglan, J.K. and Company, 112, 124.
Rardin, Harry, 179, 181-184, 190, 202.
Red Wing Advance, 6.
Red Wing Argus, 1, 8.
Red Wing College Women's Club (AAUW), 152.
Red Wing Drive-In Theater, 173, 180, 189, 205, 210, 215, 216, 233.
Red Wing Historic Sites Committee, 221.
Red Wing Opera Company, 25.
Red Wing Summer Playhouse, 218, 224.
Red Wing Theater, The, 123, 125, 152, 216.
Reich, Orville, 117, 125, 150.
Republic Pictures, 146, 180.
Rethschlag, Fire Chief, 68-70.
Rich, Horace, 18.
Rich, John, 50.
Richardson, Charles, 183, 188, 205, 206, 217.

Ritter, Doug, 236.
RKO (Radio Keith Orpheum), 83, 89, 103, 169, 180, 208, 225.
Robe, The, 171, 172, 180.
Roberg, Sam, 41, 45, 48.
Rogers Cinema, 233.
Royal Chef, The, 22.
Ruben, E.R. "Eddie," vii, 95-97, 99, 103, 104, 106, 119, 137, 140, 152, 170, 179, 185.

San Carlo Opera Company, 67.
Schilling, Bernard, 112, 123, 143-146.
Schmidt, Steven, 214, 225-228, 240.
Schultz, Judge W.A., 134, 182-184, 188.
Scott, Wilbur, 44, 45, 48, 50-55, 66, 67, 72.
Seebach, Fred, 51, 86.
Shakespeare, 4, 6, 20, 24.
Shaw, George Bernard, 25, 218, 236.
Sheldon Players, The, 153.
Sheldon, Annie, 15, 22.
Sheldon, Charles E., 17, 38, 49, 50, 51, 53.
Sheldon, T.B., Xii, 3, 4, 12, 16, 18-20, 22, 31, 51, 72, 86, 106, 131, 134, 135, 182, 184, 188, 189, 200, 241.
Sherman Antitrust Act, 200, 202.
Simplex projection and sound, 117.
Solid Gold Cadillac, The, 219.
Sousa, John Phillip, 9, 26.
Sovick, Mathre, Sathrum, and Quanbeck, 225.
Speiss, Lowell and Gordon, 173, 180, 216.
Spot, The, 200, 203.
Stolberg, Judge Alfred, 134, 135.
Sunday motion pictures, 56, 154.
Sunden, C.W., 116.
Sutherland, Carl, 158.
Swanson, "Eddie," 106, 150, 151, 153, 154, 159, 168, 189, 171, 174, 175, 180, 208.
Swanson, Mary Gwen Owen, 157, 159, 165, 174, 185, 218, 219.

Sweasy, William "Bill," 222, 224, 226.
Swimming pool, 85, 86, 130.

Taber, Arthur, 99.
Taber, Ralph Graham, 21, 24, 25, 30, 32, 42, 44, 50, 51, 99.
Talkies/sound films, 83.
Technicolor, 82, 83, 118, 142, 144.
Teele, James, 224.
Television, 154, 165, 166, 171, 174, 205, 207, 209, 215, 216.
Tennessee Valley Authority cases, 198.
Theater organs, 81.
Three Twins, The, 24, 25, 54.
Thurston, Adelaide, 24.
Tiedeman, Henry, 89, 109-111, 120, 121, 124, 147, 148.
Todd, Stone, and DeLambert, 131.
Torrison, Mandt, 202.
Townsend, G.W., 179, 188, 196.
Trades and Labor Council, 110, 124, 130, 144.
Treasure Island, 239.
Tripp, C.E., 147.
Turner Opera Hall, 4, 7, 12.
Turnerverein, 4, 5, 7, 12.
Twain, Mark, 1.
Twentieth Century Fox, 103, 146, 170-172, 189, 201, 202.

Ullrich, Harold, 156-158, 168, 180, 186, 204, 219.
Uncle Tom's Cabin, 29.
United Artists, 84, 102, 118, 144, 188, 201, 202.
United States v. Aluminum Company of America (ALCOA), 209.
United States v. Griffith, 207. 209.
Universal Pictures, 167, 168.
University of Minnesota, 26, 28, 152, 153, 156.

Van Liew, Henry, 2.
Vaudeville, 55.
Vitagraph, 66.

Vitaphone, 82.
Vogel, Marjorie, 157.
Volstead Act, 80.

Wacouta, Hazen, 117.
Wahlin, Mary Lee, 214, 215.
Walsh, John, 45, 49, 56.
Walt Disney, 152, 169, 180, 214, 220.
Warner Bros., 82, 103, 116, 146, 170, 180, 188.
Warren, Milt, 79, 88, 89, 95, 97, 108-110, 120.
Wells, Minnesota, 234.
Welworth Theaters, 29, 96, 97, 118, 152, 171, 179.
Wendler, Charles, 88, 89, 97, 98, 110, 124.
Western Electric, 100, 104.
Westerns, oaters, 146.
White Vaudette, 39-41.
Wilkinson, Anna, 30.
Wilkinson, George A., 7-9, 12, 16.
Wilson, F.M., 21, 29, 31, 71.
Wintervold, Oscar, 23, 217, 218, 222.
Women's Glee Club, 158.
Works Progress, Administration (WPA), 118.
Wright, F. Gordon, 121, 189.
Wright, John, vii, xi, xii, 95, 102, 103, 106, 116, 119, 121, 123-125, 129, 131, 136-138, 144-152, 170, 171, 175, 179-194, 200-209, 215-218, 220, 234.
Wright, Myra, 102, 123.
Writ of Mandamus, 188, 189.
Wronski, Todd, 224.

Yanisch, Jerry, 152, 168, 169.